Funk
on
Parables

"Professor Funk,
spell out for me
what you appear trans-
parently to see: the mind
set
free of tyranny."

"Were I to *tell* you
thus-and-such . . . " (his
enigmatic, quick-
silver grimace spells chagrin)
". . . I'd say too much."

Ed Beutner

Funk
on
Parables

COLLECTED ESSAYS

Robert W. Funk

Edited with an Introduction by
Bernard Brandon Scott

POLEBRIDGE PRESS

Cover and interior design by Robaire Ream
Cover illustration by Robaire Ream

Library of Congress Cataloging-in-Publication Data

Funk, Robert Walter, 1926-2005.
  Funk on parables / Robert W. Funk ; edited with an introduction
by Bernard Brandon Scott.
      p. cm.
  "Bibliography of Robert W. Funk on parables"--P.
  Includes bibliographical references (p.   ) and index.
  ISBN 978-0-944344-99-6 (alk. paper)
  1. Bible--Parables. 2. Jesus Christ--Parables. 3. Parables. I. Scott,
Bernard Brandon, 1941- II. Title. III. Title: On parables.
  BS680.P3F86 2006
  226.8'06--dc22
                                                    2006036625

to Alyson, Katie, and Jake
heirs to the fabulous yonder

Contents

Acknowledgments ix

Introduction   by Bernard Brandon Scott

Movements: Robert W. Funk's Contribution to the
Study of Parables   1

Robert W. Funk: Parables Publications 25

Part One   On Parables

1 The Parable as Metaphor 29

2 Crossing Over 53

3 Parable as Trope 61

Part Two   Lurking behind the Samaritan

4 The Old Testament in Parable: The Good Samaritan 67

5 The Good Samaritan as Metaphor 85

Part Three   Sauntering through the Parables

6 The Leaven: Away-from-here as Destination 93

7 The Looking-glass Tree Is for the Birds 113

8 The Narrative Parables: The Birth of a Language Tradition 121

9 Parable, Paradox, and Power: The Prodigal Samaritan ... 131

Part Four   Dismantling and Recovering

10 From Parable to Gospel: Domesticating the Tradition 143

11 Jesus: The Silent Sage 165

12 Jesus: A Voice Print 171

13 The Mythical Matrix and God as Metaphor 177

Notes 195

Works Consulted 209

Indices 216

Acknowledgments

When I first suggested to Char Matejovsky over dinner at a Lebanese restaurant that Robert Funk's essays on the parables should be collected, she immediately turned my suggestion into a proposal and has supported it ever since. I am grateful to her for this opportunity both to acknowledge my debt to her late husband but also bring to the public a synoptic view of Funk's pioneering work on the parables.

A number of folks have made major contributions to this project. Mary Guy helped me with early editing tasks and has put the indexes together. Tom Hall clarified the "English" of my Introduction. Jon Andreas went through the manuscript carefully searching for mistakes. John Dosier checked the editing of the footnotes which Char Matejovsky had gathered together. Ed Beutner not only gave the proofs one final reading, he also graciously provided a poem for the frontispiece. Robaire Ream designed the cover and the interior of the book. Even with all these people to thank, all mistakes are my responsibility.

I have employed a light hand in the editing of these essays. Funk himself had edited three of the essays for the second edition of *Jesus as Precursor* (1994). He made his language inclusionary and used the Scholars Version translation from *The Complete Gospels*. I followed his example. Otherwise, these essays are as originally published.

Movements

Robert W. Funk's Contribution
to the Study of Parables

by Bernard Brandon Scott

Robert W. Funk was one of the most insightful and influential parable interpreters of the twentieth century, yet he never wrote a book on that subject alone. Quite appropriately, the essay was his preferred form for dealing with parables, and his work on them has therefore been scattered throughout a number of publications. Although one of his books was entitled *Parables and Presence* (1982), it also dealt with issues other than parables. This present collection brings together his most important essays on Jesus' parables. These seminal contributions not only inaugurated a new age in parable criticism and interpretation, but also set an agenda that still remains to be further investigated. Only by bringing together under one cover the broad sweep of Funk's work on parables can we begin to recognize its far-reaching implications.

Funk's career as a parable interpreter can be divided into four movements. As with a symphony, a strong continuity marks the shift from movement to movement, and yet each has distinctive accents, themes, and rhythms of its own.

- The initial and revolutionary movement begins with Funk's effort to understand parable as metaphor. *Language, Hermeneutic, and Word of God* (1966) is the major work of this period.
- Then comes Kafka as Precursor, which heralds one of his most creative periods. *Jesus as Precursor* (1975) gathers together the major essays of this period.
- In the next movement, Funk employs more formal linguistic methods, culminating in the publication of his *Poetics of Biblical Narrative* (1988).
- In the final movement—away from academia and on to the formation of Westar—Funk shifted his audience and with it his style and way of thinking. *Honest to Jesus* (1996) and *A Credible Jesus: Fragments of a Vision* (2002) typify this movement.

I shall use these four movements to organize this introductory essay and thus help the reader understand the development of Funk's thinking about parables as well as its significance. In the book, however, the essays are organized topically. At the head of each of the four sections dealing with the four movements in Funk's career, I have listed the essays in this volume that come from and illustrate that movement. A reader can therefore choose to read the essays either chronologically or topically. Funk would have supported this implicit rejection of a canonical way of reading his texts.

While this book concentrates on Funk's work on parable, the full range of his scholarship was much wider. He was an important Greek grammarian, a scholar of Paul and hermeneutics, a transforming executive secretary of the Society of Biblical Literature (SBL), and his teaching career left its mark on a number of campuses. Still, despite the wide diversity of his interests and competencies, his writings on parable run like a rich vein throughout his life's work.

My task is not to summarize Funk's work, for his analyses always require careful reading and grant rich rewards. Rather, my purpose is to indicate the ongoing development of his thought and its significance. I have tried to evaluate his work in light of the history of scholarship, but have said little on contemporary parable criticism. After all, it took more than forty years for Adolf Jülicher's work to take hold; and if I am right in my assessment that Funk initiated a revolution at least as momentous as Jülicher's, then it is too soon to evaluate the response. Indeed, in the course of rereading Funk's oeuvre, I was constantly surprised at how much I had missed or misread. He once told me, "I taught you. You just forgot!" Perhaps I could argue in defense that the episodic essay form makes it difficult to arrive at a synoptic view of Funk's accomplishment, and that this book is a way of saying, "I should have paid better attention."

Movement One: Metaphor (1962–1966)

Chapter 1: "Parable as Metaphor" (*Language, Hermeneutic, and Word of God*)

Chapter 4: "The Old Testament in Parable: The Good Samaritan" (*Language, Hermeneutic, and Word of God*)

Language, Hermeneutic, and Word of God, published in 1966, contained essays investigating hermeneutics, Paul, and parables. This book was part of a broad front called the New Hermeneutics,[1] which in the aftermath of WWII involved scholars in both Germany and the United States who were influenced by Rudolf Bultmann, the most important New Testament scholar of the first half of the twentieth century. It put language at the heart of scholarly concern. In Funk's case this focus on language underlines two ingredients that remained central throughout his long career. First was the formal study of language itself, a pursuit that had its origin in his doctoral dissertation on Greek grammar. As Daryl Schmidt said, "It all began with grammar."[2] The second element derives directly from Bultmann's program of Form Criticism, and can be seen in Funk's major essays on the form of the Pauline letters and that of Jesus' parables.

In "Parable as Metaphor" and "The Old Testament in Parable: The Good Samaritan," two of the essays in *Language, Hermeneutic, and Word of God*, Funk initiated a seismic shift in parable scholarship, one that has reverberated throughout the study of the historical Jesus and with which scholarship is still coming to terms. Yet while earthshaking in its effects, the move was deceptively simple: Funk asked how a parable was a metaphor, and then applied his answer to the Good Samaritan.

Parable as metaphor

Funk understood himself as standing in and moving forward a tradition of parable interpretation that began with Adolf Jülicher's *Die Gleichnisreden Jesu* (1889, 1899). Jülicher had challenged the pervasive allegorical hermeneutic that had been in place at least since the Gospel of Mark allegorized the parable of the Sower. The tree of allegory had grown so wildly since that modest effort that in Augustine's interpretation the man who fell among thieves stands for Adam, Jericho represents the moon, the thieves portray Satan and his angels, the Samaritan denotes Jesus, and so on and on for each element of the parable.[3]

Jülicher did not simply trim this tree of its luxuriant growth, he attempted to cut it down. His strategy was to reduce the parable to a single moral point. In Jülicher's rejection of allegory Funk recognized a permanent gain for scholarship—one that he strove to advance. Along the same line, Funk gratefully recognized the work of C. H. Dodd and Joachim Jeremias, both of whom launched their sharpest critique of Jülicher on the issue of a single *moral* point. They agreed on a single point, but made it a single *historical* point. While acknowledging the importance of Jeremias, whose work had dominated the post WWII study of the parables, Funk was much more in sympathy with Dodd. Nonetheless, he attacked both for their insistence on using a single interpretive point.

Funk opens his essay not with this attack, however, but by turning to the issue of "parable as metaphor." His approach appears simple. After all, a parable is a *mashal*, the Hebrew word for a comparison. He begins, then, by quoting with approval Dodd's definition of parable, which had begun, "At its simplest the parable is a metaphor or simile" (29);* but then he starts to dismantle the definition as a way to gain leverage on parable itself. Dismantling a received tradition, a key strategy in Funk's methodology, is a move he appropriated from Heidegger. He applies this dismantling operation not only to the history of scholarship but also to the historical tradition of each parable. One must "dismantle the tradition in order to reach its source" (38). Neither hostile nor even essentially destructive, this analysis is an effort to make careful note of where the tradition cannot account for the evidence or the text. Yet dismantling is not a peeling away, a separation of the kernel from the husk (as Harnack saw history's task),[4] but rather involves a careful observation of where the tradition betrays itself, where it masks or covers over its own fissures or fault lines.

Following Owen Barfield, Funk distinguishes metaphoric discourse from the logical or dictionary language in which the meanings of words are presumed to be fixed. The "logic" of metaphor is quite different. It is about the discovery and creation of new meaning. "[M]etaphor shatters the conventions of predication in the interests of a new vision, one which grasps the 'thing' in relation to a new 'field,' and thus in relation to a fresh experience of reality" (33). Thus metaphor is the ultimate dismantling of language itself. Indeed, it dismantles the everyday world, the world of dictionary meanings, in an effort to discover a new horizon of meaning, a new source of envisioning. Funk quotes Barfield with approval: "It is not surprising . . . that philologists should have had such a vivid hallucination of metaphor bending over the cradle of meaning" (33).

The traditional definition of metaphor argues that *A is B*, in which *A* is the unknown term and *B* is the known term. But Funk goes deeper. "[T]he maker of a metaphor, like the maker of a parable, utilizes *B* [the known term] in such a way as to (*a*) break the grip of tradition on the language, and (*b*) discover new meaning"

(35). In this twofold move we see Funk's key methodological insight stripped to its bare essentials.

- Since he identifies metaphor and parable, Jesus the maker of parables becomes a poet.
- Since metaphor must operate within language, it must dismantle its language tradition. This implies that in his parables Jesus was stripping away his language tradition. Thus Funk will always see the priority of the criterion of dissimilarity as the proper way to understand Jesus. It is as though Jesus himself used this criterion.
- To get at a parable's root metaphor, its ultimate source, the interpreter must likewise dismantle the interpretive tradition in which the parable has been encased or ossified. The latter metaphor is one Funk often uses to describe the effect of traditions—those of scholarship, the church, and especially of the written gospels. We will see more of this below.
- Because *A* and *B* are bound together in metaphor:
  - Their relationship creates meaning. There is no single point, as Jülicher argued, but a multiplicity of points as each person makes that relationship for herself. Funk here explicitly anticipates the use of literary criticism in parable analysis.
  - The relationship is historically determined. It always demands historical reconstruction because all language is historically conditioned.
  - Finally, the metaphor/parable cannot be dispensed with. It is the only way to uncover mystery. Without the parable, mystery is lost and meaning is at the mercy of lexicographers.

The "meaning" of a parable is not some new discursive point, the creation of which dictionary language would be equally capable. The metaphor discloses new meaning—and more than that, a new reality. "It is not too much to say that true metaphor reveals a mystery: the mystery of kaleidoscopic reality directly apprehended" (34). In this view of language, metaphor has an almost sacramental reality in making the mystery directly apprehendable. This view of metaphor has at times been critiqued as romantic.[5] In later years, Funk himself backed away from an overly romantic formulation, but insisted on the essential point: "The parables open onto an alternative reality . . . to which we have customarily given term Kingdom of God. They constitute an invitation to enter that world and live in it" (62). Of course, the alternative world Funk envisions is the result of a conceptual shift; it is not spatially 'elsewhere' than this world. "The parable does not direct attention . . . *away from* mundane existence, but *toward* it" (46).

Funk uses this understanding of metaphor/parable to take on some of the important issues in parable criticism. Not only had Dodd and Jeremias understood the parables as argumentative, but to confute Jülicher's notion of a single moral point Jeremias had emphasized the argumentative context, seeing in Jesus' recurring debates with his opponents—notably the Pharisees—what amounted to a single historical point. Funk argues that Jeremias is reducing the parable to ideas and thus to its dictionary meaning, and insists that what the parable means can never replace the parable. "The emphasis on one point over against the allegorization of the parables was a necessary corrective, but one point understood as an idea valid for all times is as erroneous as Jülicher's moral maxims, even if that idea is eschatological" (43). The parable remains primary: it is never mere ornament; it does not stand for something else; it provides a necessary vehicle for the reality it opens onto.

Against Jeremias, Funk points out that since the original context is lost, so must likely be the original meaning. And if that is the case, how can the parable be understood—and in what sense is it "historical"? When understood as metaphor, the parable creates its own meaning and can convey "as many points as there are situations into which it is spoken" (42). The historical context—and hence any historical understanding of the parable—has as its referent not a specific historical incident in the ministry of Jesus, but the parable's everydayness, a quality rooted in the realism of first-century Galilean village life. This everydayness is a key issue for Funk, because it means that one must pay attention to the parable's details. Here he faces two traditional opponents. At one hand stands allegory, which pays such close attention to the specifics of the story that "every detail or most details are conceptual ciphers" (43). The result is that the parable's details disappear, overwhelmed by their supposed or imported meanings. At the other hand stands Jeremias, whose excessive historicization of the parable limits its reference to a single historical moment and thus causes it to disappear into a predication of eternal meaning extracted from that moment. For Funk the parable as metaphor always remains primary, ever ready to create new meaning. He approvingly paraphrases Ernst Fuchs: "[T]he parable is not meant to *be* interpre*ted*, but to interpret" (43). An historical understanding of the parable comes about from setting the details of its everydayness within the context of first-century Galilean village life. These historically understood elements of secularity then become the vehicle that enables the parable as image to project the new vision of reality that the parable as metaphor discloses and invites.

The everydayness of the parable "tempts the hearer to substitute another meaning, that is, to disregard the literal and thus to allegorize" (48). This temptation arises because "the hearer or reader assumes that the literal subject matter could not possibly be the real subject matter." Allegory is then a temptation to go against the parable's literal image, and thus towards a reduction of the parable's real intention. "In the parable of the Sower, for example, the equations seed = word and soils = people can be made and the literal meaning quietly abandoned" (48). Funk sees the temptation to allegorize a parable built into the very everydayness of its imagery, and also the very nature of allegory poses a further temptation because it allows us to ignore a parable's image that serves as the vehicle of the metaphor. Still more, much of the parable's communicative potential is created by a hearer's response to its assault or effrontery; interpretation is not a matter of searching for some "meaning" hidden behind the parable.

Yet the everyday is not just everyday. Carefully dismantling the tradition of the parable, paying close historical attention to its everydayness and its secularity, prompts a hearer to ask, "What's wrong with this picture?" Under the influence of Amos Wilder, Funk is now moving beyond those interpreters who had accented the parable's everydayness as a perfect picture of ancient life. He sees that everydayness is somehow eschewed. "Distortions of everydayness, exaggerated realism, distended concreteness, incompatible elements—often subtly drawn—are what prohibit the parable from coming to rest in the literal sense" (48). Ignoring the off-centeredness of the literal prompts allegorization and all the other strategies of interpretation that substitute meaning for the parable's image; paying careful attention to the parable's literal content raises the question of the interplay between its literal and metaphorical levels. "The literal and the metaphorical meanings of the parable have to be grasped concomitantly" (48). Forfeit either one, and the interpretation devolves into allegory.

The Good Samaritan as parable
In his essay "Parable as Metaphor" Funk called attention to the mistaken interpretation of the category of parables often referred to

as "exemplary-stories" or "example stories." These parables offer the opposite enticement to that of allegory: "The reader is tempted to find the meaning in the literal sense" (48).

In "The Old Testament in Parable: The Good Samaritan" he takes up the challenge of explaining how this is a parable and not an example story.

Jülicher had proposed three forms for parables: similitude (the Leaven), parable proper (the Sower) and example story (Good Samaritan). An example story (*Beispielerzählung*) "has no figurative element at all. . . . The Samaritan is just an example of a true neighbor, . . . nothing more" (76). But Funk's careful dismantling of the interpretive history that began with Luke's moralizing contextualization ("Then go and do the same youself") demonstrates that the tradition fails to account for the details: it does not even address the basic question of why the protagonist is a Samaritan!

Since a hearer completes the parable's meaning by weighing its literal and metaphorical elements concomitantly, Funk begins his analysis by asking, "From what perspective is the parable told?" Clearly perspective makes all the difference in hearing a narrative. He argues that this story presupposes the point of view of a traveler going down the road from Jerusalem to Jericho. Its picture of life is violent but neither shocking nor even unusual. Funk underlines the Jewish sensibilities of the parable's audience: the traveler who was mugged and left in the ditch is a Jew, and the priest and Levite are Jewish characters. He even suggests the listeners' uniquely Jewish anticlerical response to the unfolding scenario.

As the narrative develops, hearers observe its everydayness: yes, this is the way things are. But then, "to the utter amazement and chagrin of every listener as Jew, . . . a hated enemy, a half-breed, a perverter of true religion comes into view and ministers to the helpless victim when he is powerless to prevent him" (76). The Samaritan's actions shatter everyday expectation.

Funk continues to pursue the question, Why the Samaritan? If one responds that the Samaritan is an example of neighborliness, "in that case the parable is reduced to a commonplace and its bite completely vitiated." He drives home the point that the Samaritan is "he whom the victim does not, could not expect would help, indeed does not want help from" (77). It is "the literal, that is, the historical, significance" of the Samaritan that smashes the everydayness and shocks the original listeners.

A narrative begun with all the traits of an experience about which everyone knows, or thinks he knows, is ruptured at the crucial juncture by a factor which does not square with everyday experience. The "logic" of everydayness is broken upon the "logic" of the parable. It is the juxtaposition of the two logics that turns the Samaritan, and hence the parable, into a metaphor. (77)

Here we have in a nutshell Funk's seismic shift. To be sure, Jülicher had initiated the tectonic movement with his decisive rejection of allegory, but Funk's move here represents much more than just an interpretive or methodological advance beyond Jülicher—something that Dodd, Jeremias, and others had already accomplished. Rather Funk makes the case that all parables are metaphors and operate by means of the same dynamic: "The literal and the metaphorical meanings of the parable have to be grasped concomitantly" (48). By demonstrating that the Good Samaritan operates this way, he shows that it is a true parable and that "example story" is not a separate form, as Jülicher and the subsequent tradition in his wake had maintained; it is simply an interpretive method, just like allegory. Actually, the example story is shown to be only an extension of allegory, and all of Jülicher's terms are now turned on their heads.

- Parables do not have a single point, but multiple points.
- Parables do not have a single *moral,* or in Dodd's and Jeremias' case eschatological point. Parables are metaphors that disclose a new way of construing or envisioning reality.
- The parable does not present some lesson or idea, because its literal and metaphorical aspects must be held in a creative tension.
- The parable is not to be interpreted; rather it interprets the hearer.
- The parable is not just the everyday on display, a remarkably "complete picture of *petit-bourgeois* and peasant life,"[6] but the everyday torn asunder by the unexpected.

All of this becomes obvious in an essay from later in Funk's career, "The Good Samaritan as Metaphor." This essay, which first appeared in *Semeia* 2 and later in *Parables and Presence,* is not simply a restatement of the points made in the critique we have been discussing, but responds to Dan Via's discussion that originally appeared in *Semeia* 1. Via's book *The Parables* had been published the year after Funk's *Language, Hermeneutic, and Word of God,* and the two works are often seen as inaugurating a new period in parable criticism.[7] Both employ literary criticism to understand the parable, although they use different types: Funk is more influenced by

Wilder and Barfield, while Via employs the new literary criticism. Both are concerned with hermeneutics, with Funk more dependent upon Heidegger, while Via moves in a more existentialist vein. But the decisive difference centers on the understanding of the Good Samaritan and thus the nature of parable itself. Via still considers it an example story, while Funk argues it is a parable, a metaphor proper. Thus while Via retains Jülicher's template—though certainly expanding it—Funk has broken out of that paradigm, dismantling it in order to discover the tradition's true source.

Movement Two: Precursors (1971–1975)

Chapter 2: "Crossing Over" (*Jesus as Precursor*)

Chapter 6: "The Leaven. Away-from-here as Destination" (*Jesus as Precursor*)

Chapter 7: "The Looking-glass Tree Is for the Birds" (*Jesus as Precursor*)

This second movement follows shortly after the publication of *Language, Hermeneutic, and Word of God* in 1966. "Beyond Criticism in Quest of Literacy: The Parable of the Leaven" first appeared in 1971 in *Interpretation*, in 1972 "Jesus and Kafka" came out in *CAS Faculty Journal* and, in 1973, "The Looking-Glass Tree is for the Birds" was published in *Interpretation*. These three essays were retitled and collected with other essays in *Jesus as Precursor* in 1975. During this period, Funk had left teaching in divinity schools and had moved to the University of Montana. This move signaled his increasing disenchantment with the churches and his conviction that any real future for the study of religion lay in the secular arena. Also during this period he became the executive secretary of the Society of Biblical Literature and launched an ambitious publications project called Scholars Press. And by the time *Jesus as Precursor* appeared in 1975, the third movement was well under way.

Funk's discovery of Franz Kafka seems to have tapped a creative wellspring and initiated a freedom of expression that characterizes this second movement. The essays in *Jesus as Precursor* pick up on themes or projects announced in *Language, Hermeneutic, and Word of God*, but they also introduce a new tone or motif. In the first volume he demonstrated that the Good Samaritan was not an example story but a parable proper. In these new essays he turns his attention to the first of Jülicher's three categories, the similitude, with essays on the Leaven and the Mustard Seed. But before we turn our attention to these parables, we should pause to consider Funk's precursor, Kafka.

Crossing over

In his initial essay, "Crossing Over," Funk begins by acknowledging that it may seem odd to list Franz Kafka among the authorities on Jesus' parables. A late nineteenth- and early twentieth-century Jewish Czech writer, Kafka nowhere mentions Jesus; but it is not really strange, Funk notes, when one considers that both Kafka and Jesus are noted for their rare skill as makers of parables.

Just as Funk had begun "Parable as Metaphor" with Dodd's classic definition, in this essay he begins with Kafka's allusive definition, "On Parables." Kafka offers Funk the possibility of talking about parables *in* parables—about Jesus' parables in terms of Kafka's parables. Kafka's parable "On Parables" becomes in Funk's hands a parable on Jesus' parables. This is a delightful essay and I have no wish to rob the reader of enjoying the playfulness it offers by a series of wooden comments and interpretations. Let me simply indicate, therefore, how I think Kafka provided Funk with a significant insight into Jesus' parables.

Kafka distinguishes between the everyday and the "fabulous yonder" to which the true sage points. This is very much like Funk's earlier distinction between the dictionary or literal meaning of a word and metaphorical construal that opens new vistas. The command to "Go over" and the invocation of a "fabulous yonder" point to the unutterable quality of new discovery. In "Parable as Metaphor" and the "Good Samaritan as Parable," Funk had been searching for a way to talk about the meaning of a parable. In arguing against a one-point interpretation of the parable, he was rejecting the tradition of reducing a parable to a single meaning, to discursive language, to an idea; he was repudiating the idea of parable as mere ornament that can be done away with once its meaning is discovered. In a later essay he calls the meaning created by metaphor "pre-conceptual knowledge" that both the speaker and hearer discover in parable (86). Kafka offers a way to talk about that in simple, yet metaphoric language. His "Go over" presupposes not an actual place, but a somewhere "away-from-here," a breathtaking beyond.

Even more, this way of designating what the parable is speaking about allows Funk to introduce a theme absent from *Language, Hermeneutic, and Word of God*, namely, the Kingdom of God or

God's domain. Now he can ask, ". . . is it too much to suggest that the implicit subject of his parables, 'God's domain,' qualifies as the 'fabulous yonder' of Kafka's parable on parables?" (54) This sets Funk on a path that enables him to understand the Kingdom of God not as an apocalyptic cipher (as most of the scholarly tradition had done), but as itself metaphorical.[8] Kingdom of God as metaphor becomes part of the metaphoric/parabolic process.

Kafka's influence endured. In an essay written towards the end of his life, "Jesus: A Voice Print" (2002), Funk speaks of Jesus' parables in words that directly echo Kafka's parable "On Parables." He refers to parable as fantasy, a theme first developed under Kafka's influence. The parable, he insists, speaks "about an order of reality that lies beyond, but just barely beyond, the everyday" (172). And finally it is "an invitation to cross over." Is Funk consciously rehearsing Kafka, or has Kafka become so completely Funk's precursor as to be Funk's way of hearing Jesus?

The Leaven as parable

Earlier we noted Jülicher's three parable forms: similitude, parable proper, and example story as well as Funk's demonstration that the second and third categories were the same. Now he turns his attention to the similitude, a form characterized by the preposition "like": "The Kingdom of God is like . . ." As such it seems to present an illustration; but Funk sets out to show that similitude is likewise a parabolic metaphor.

In this essay his rejection of Jülicher, Dodd, and Jeremias is more forthright and bold. He argues that for Jülicher and all his successors "the parables score a didactic point that can readily be reduced to discursive language" (97). Despite their efforts to reject and escape allegory, Jülicher's single-point strategy has trapped them. They have made parable interpretation "a form of reduced allegory" (98).

Funk returns to his tried and true method—he dismantles by paying attention to details that the tradition cannot interpret. He begins by noticing that the parable of the Leaven presents a common enough scene, the baking of bread, a piece of everydayness. But then, if one looks closely at the details within Jesus' own tradition, the everydayness suddenly comes unglued. One example of this disturbance of the everyday will suffice, although this briefest of parables provides at least five or six such dissonances with the everyday expectations of its listeners.

Funk notes "the curious choice of the central figure of the parable," namely, leaven. Just as formerly he had asked, "Why a Samaritan?", now he asks, "Why leaven?" He quotes Hebrew Bible and New Testament texts to show that leaven "was apparently universally regarded as a symbol of corruption." Only a few scholars had noted this negative implication of leaven, but even those who did had set it aside because it did not comport with the positive meaning of the kingdom of God. Funk issues a sharp challenge to their blithe disregard: ". . . did Jesus allow his understanding of God's rule to be determined by the received tradition regarding that rule?" (103) Thus the parable of the Leaven forces open a new window on God's rule and thereby undermines and indeed overturns the sedimented understanding of the kingdom. The parable is ". . . a wrecking bar . . . designed to precipitate the loss of the received world of traditional religion in favor of the gain of the world of God's imperial rule" (107).

But as the parable was handed on, it became re-sedimented and its metaphorical meaning lost. By being paired with the parable of the Mustard Seed (see "The Looking-glass Tree Is for the birds"), it became an illustration of the "infectiousness of God's imperial rule" (108). This loss of metaphor by re-sedimentation seems to be an inevitable trajectory. The new construal of the world revealed by the parable is always at risk of being overwhelmed by the everyday. As Kafka had noted, "many complain that the words of the wise are . . . of no use in our everyday lives." When the parable is yoked to the everyday, the ordinary, the secular, it is at risk of trivialization and thus the forfeiture of the kingdom's fabulous yonder that is available only in metaphor.

For Funk the parable of the Leaven "parsimoniously encapsulates the horizons of the message of Jesus" (107). As such the clues to its foundational meaning lie strewn about, awaiting to be discovered.

> It is for this reason the secondary analysis, like that undertaken in biblical interpretation, may rediscover the wave length of foundational language, as it were, by "listening in" on that language and its sedimentations, as though from a great distance. In stumbling around for clues in the texts of the Jesus tradition and the history of interpretation, the interpreter is endeavoring to locate the trajectory of the original language by attending to the ways in which that language has "fallen out" in its subsequent history. Once on the right wave length, the alert interpreter may hope to recover something of its original horizon. (109)

No more succinct summary of Funk's method is available. Parsi-mony has distilled method to its penetrating essentials.

Movement Three: Formalism (1974–1988)

Chapter 5: "The Good Samaritan as Metaphor" (*Parables and Presence*)

Chapter 9: "Parable, Paradox, and Power: The Prodigal Samaritan" (*Parables and Presence*)

Chapter 8: "The Narrative Parables: The Birth of a Language Tradition" (*Parables and Presence*)

Chapter 10: "From Parable to Gospel" (*Forum* 1,3)

Funk had begun his career as a New Testament scholar in the field of Greek grammar with a doctoral dissertation on the defi-nite article in the Pauline letters. He translated and edited Blass and Debrunner's *A Greek Grammar of the New Testament* (1961), the standard scholarly reference. But he went well beyond a simple translation of the German original; he substantially revised it. He also developed his own three volume counterpart, *A Beginning-Intermediate Grammar of Hellenistic Greek* (1973). This interest led naturally to studies in linguistics, especially with descriptive linguists like H. A. Gleason, with whom he studied while on sab-batical in Toronto during 1973–1974. Under the sponsorship of the Society of Biblical Literature (SBL), he had inaugurated the experimental Journal *Semeia*, which published new methodologi-cal studies, especially those from linguistics and structuralism. Funk's *Jesus as Precursor* was published as the second volume in *Semeia* Supplements, the Journal's monograph series. Prominent among the initial publications in *Semeia* were submissions from SBL's newly initiated Seminar on Parables. All of this activity produced a notable ferment in both American biblical studies and Funk's own methodology. Many of his essays from this period were collected in *Parables and Presence* (1982). The culmination of these efforts and deliberations was his *The Poetics of Biblical Narrative* (1988).

Characteristic of Funk's parable studies during this movement is what might be called formalism, an approach that sometimes makes these essays difficult reading for the non-specialist. The tone is neither theological nor exegetical, for ecclesiastical concerns have disappeared from his consideration of parables, but the text is parsed into functions and participants, often with symbols and diagrams representing the results. One easily sees the influence of Gleason's descriptive linguistics, and to a certain extent French structuralism. Funk seeks to analyze and describe how the parables were shaped and formed, and how they in turn initiate and unfold into a language tradition. The model he had developed for understanding parable in the previous two movements now becomes a "mega-model" for the development of the whole Jesus tradition, which he now sees as having taken place almost exclusively in language.

Birth of language tradition

While this movement often appears very different from the first two, and to my ear is at times almost dissonant with the Kafkaesque lyricism of the second movement, the themes remain the same, but are played in a different key. One pivotal essay, "The Narrative Parables: The Birth of a Language Tradition," illustrates both the difference and the continuity. Funk begins by defining a common plot pattern underlying the narrative parables: opening, development and crisis-denouement (122). Then he derives formal rules for how each of these parts is structured: the development and crisis-denouement, for example, begin with temporal phrases (123). Then he turns to rhyme, rhythm, and assonance. Such a complex analysis naturally requires a very careful hearing/reading of the Greek text. His earlier exegeses of the Good Samaritan and Leaven were characterized by precise attention to the relation between parable and the sedimented language tradition of which it was a part; now his analyses penetrate even deeper by taking cognizance of intricate details of narrative structure and the very sounds of the language itself.

All this leads to a startling conclusion, one as radical as the interpretations of the Good Samaritan and the Leaven. On the basis of this in-depth analysis of the language of the parables, Funk argues that they were originally *composed* in Greek! Not only does the text lack the normal characteristics of a translation, but it also exhibits the type of rhetorical usage one would expect of someone using simple Greek. Even here Kafka is a precursor. The Greek of Jesus' parables, Funk asserts, "is as clean of resonances as the German of Franz Kafka" (129). Perhaps, he suggests, this is because both Jesus and Kafka were working in a second language. In other words, the parables work better in Greek than they do in any of their translations—even better than in a hypothetical translation "back" into

Jesus' mother tongue of Aramaic. While this proposal that the parables were originally told in Greek has not found widespread support, neither has it been refuted. It remains a compelling argument.

Prodigal Samaritan

In "Parable, Paradox, and Power: The Prodigal Samaritan" Funk
engages in a formal plot-structure analysis of the narrative parables
in order to show how they work and why some are more sophisticated and therefore more compelling than others. He arrives at a
hierarchy of the parables. To my knowledge this is a unique argument in the history of parable criticism. He examines six parables:
the Ten Maidens, the Money in Trust, the Vineyard Laborers, the
Great Supper, the Prodigal Son, and Good Samaritan. In each of
these parables the plot involves a "determiner," a character who
determines the plot line, and two sets of responders, who respond
to a crisis around which the plot revolves.

In Funk's analysis the first group of parables, the Ten Maidens
and the Money in Trust, are rather unimpressive performances;
since they contain no unforeseen occurrences and because events
turn out as expected, they fail to draw the hearer into their web.
This is clearly the case in the Ten Maidens—their very characterization as wise and foolish betrays the plot and obviates any
involvement that might arise from challenge or surprise. To be sure,
Richard Rohrbaugh has proposed a reading of the Money in Trust
that challenges its everydayness,[9] but in the traditional reading that
Funk follows, this lack of novelty is again clearly the case. While
Funk does not say so, it seems that if these parables came from
Jesus, they show him having an off day.*

Just as in the two previous parables, the Vineyard Laborers, the
Great Supper, and the Prodigal Son each incorporate a determiner
and two respondents or groups thereof. But here the plots do not
turn out as expected. The last hired get the same wage as the first
hired; those invited reject the feast and the uninvited become the
guests; and the elder son, the legal heir, is rejected while the father
kills the fatted calf for the younger son. These parables are more
sophisticated than the first group because they draw an audience
in by requiring the hearer to take sides. Therefore, they "may be
taken to be more compelling, more provocative, more carefully

---

*As reported in *The Five Gospels*, the Jesus Seminar voted the Ten Maidens
gray and the Money in Trust pink.

constructed, and closer to the heart of the message of Jesus" (135). Now the method not only determines a hierarchy of sophistication, but also becomes a criterion of authenticity. These parables are clearly from Jesus, Funk argues, because they exhibit the dismantling of the everyday world.

He points out that the plot of the Prodigal Son can be seen in several ways. In the traditional view, the father determines the plot by being the one who rewards and punishes the sons; but one could consider the younger son as the determiner of the plot and the father and elder son as the two respondents. Against reading the parable this way is the consideration that the determiner in the previous parables was an authority figure. In favor of understanding the younger son as the determiner is the example of the Good Samaritan, because there the determiner is the Jewish man in the ditch. Funk notes that this way of reading these two parables entails a very sophisticated rearrangement of the participants and their functions in the plot. Not only is the end unexpected in this second group of parables, but the roles the characters play are unexpected, topsy-turvy, and perhaps even reversible.

In the essay's final section, Funk turns to the Good Samaritan; for him it represents the apex of Jesus' artistry as a fashioner of parables. "As a parable, the Samaritan is a very powerful instrument. It sets the message of Jesus in unequivocal terms for its audience. . . . No other parable in the Jesus tradition carries a comparable punch. The Christian community moralizes it in order to be able to live with it, and that is inverted testimony to its power" (139).

Although this essay demands a close and attentive reading, its precise formal analysis of the parable's plot structure frees us from the traditional Christian moralizing. The reader will find much to argue with here, but also much to learn. Most important of all, we begin to see just why and how the parables achieve their effect, and why Funk considers the Good Samaritan—as parable, not example-story—to be the height of Jesus' artistry and the core of his message. For Funk, the Good Samaritan is *the* parable and it contains the quintessential Jesus.

From parable to gospel

The essay "From Parable to Gospel," comes from the end of Funk's Formal Movement. It is very different from the other essays we have examined, and brings this movement to an end while also anticipating the dominant concerns of the final movement. More important, it combines previous insights about metaphor and parable into a new configuration to shed light on the development of the Jesus tradition. The essay reveals the hand of a virtuoso who has so mastered the material and honed it down to the essential points so that now it appears as something new.

The title, "From Parable to Gospel" gives away the essay's trajectory. He starts with *the* parable, the Good Samaritan, and rehearses all the arguments we have followed to this point. But now he expands the exegesis with his new reading of the Prodigal Son and then brings in an interpretation of the Markan saying on True Relations (Mark 3:31–35),[10] which he argues is "a parabolic act—a parable acted out, or an act turned into a parable" (151). These two parables and the saying-parable now serve as the archetypes of the Jesus material. From this analysis he draws a startling but astute conclusion: "In his parables and in his other sayings, Jesus has the received-world under attack; it is not easy to hear a challenge that subverts one's habituated reality sense, one's unstudied relation to things" (154). This sets up a double dynamic:

- Jesus is attacking the "received-world."
- The community that preserves the parables will frequently not have ears to hear and so will smother the radical challenge of the parables with moralizing interpretations.

Funk had begun in the tradition of Dodd and Jeremias by accenting the everydayness of the world described by the parable. But even in his very first essays he had seen something was amiss in this facile ascription of normality—so amiss that it obscured Jesus' attack on the received world. Later, he began to see that the Good Samaritan was a flight of fancy, its action far removed from the expectations of the everyday world; and finally he argued that what the parable pointed to, the kingdom of God, was itself the vision. "Parable, aphorism, and parabolic act are the threshold opening onto the new reality, the fantasy, called the kingdom [of God]" (160).

This leads him to part company with Bultmann, who had powerfully influenced *Language, Hermeneutic, and Word of God*. Bultmann had argued that Easter or the Christian kerygma (preaching) was the origin of Christian faith, but Funk now sees that the resurrection is the product of Jesus' language. "The imaginative discourse of Jesus is therefore the house of faith: in it faith lives and moves and has its being" (164). This creative use of language offers a new reality, the vision of the kingdom.

Movement Four: To the West (1986–2005)

Chapter 3: "Parable as Trope" (Unpublished)
Chapter 11: "Jesus the Silent Sage" (*Jesus as Precursor*, rev. ed.)
Chapter 12: "Jesus: a Voice Print" (*Profiles of Jesus*)
Chapter 13: "The Mythical Matrix and God as Metaphor"
(*Forum* NS, 3,2)

In 1986 Funk began the final movement of his symphony when he left the University of Montana to found Westar Institute and the Jesus Seminar. He has finished his great work on parables, but the fruit of that work is now directed towards studies on the historical Jesus. This is especially evident in his founding of the Jesus Seminar project and its attendant publications. He had moved out of the divinity school context and then away from the academy because he was concerned that scholarship no longer had a viable audience and recognized that religious illiteracy in the United States had become a dangerous reactionary force. At Westar Funk began to consider a new audience—the Institute's associate members, mostly lay people who have confronted the issues of modernity and are seeking a new way to be religious. Hence the programs of the Westar Institute, and hence his books on Jesus that sought to reach that new audience aborning. The themes of *Honest to Jesus* and *A Credible Jesus: Fragments of a Vision* were clearly anticipated in "From Parable to Gospel," but now the audience is different.

Of the four essays from this final period reprinted in the present volume, three are relatively short, and "Parable as Trope" has never been published before. All four are important summary pieces. "Parable as Trope" is especially important as a compendium of his work on parable methodology, while the other pieces indicate how parables inform his understanding of Jesus and the contemporary theological task.

Jesus

"Jesus: The Silent Sage" was written in 1994 for a revised edition of *Jesus as Precursor*. A year earlier the publication of *The Five Gospels* had marked the completion of the first stage of the Jesus Seminar's work—its assessment of the sayings material. This essay is Funk's reflections on the results of that monumental seven-year task, yet it is noteworthy that while he was founder of the Jesus Seminar, he was but one member. His erudition often won the point at issue, but he lost votes, too!

He begins by noting the twenty-two parables that the Seminar deemed authentic. The Leaven and the Samaritan, two critical parables for Funk, top the list. The Mustard Seed made the top five, while the Prodigal Son is further down the list (number 9). All in all, his list of primary parables fared well.

Funk has always been noted for his precise, even stethoscopic reading of a text; he focuses unerringly on what is really there, rather than what people sometimes imagine to be there. This is what dismantling enables him to do. He begins this essay with a list of things that one might expect to be parable subjects, but are not. At the head of this list are God and Jesus: they simply do not appear as topics of the parables. Indeed, Funk notes, "On the basis of his parables, we might conclude that Jesus rarely spoke about religion at all" (166). When he *does* speak about God (mainly in such aphorisms as those concerning the sparrows and lilies of the field, Luke 12:6–7, 22–24, 27–28), "Jesus is not adopting a metaphysical creed—or preparing the way for one—but observing the world as he sees it—as though it were in an intensive care unit run by his Father" (167).

As Funk had earlier argued, traditional exegetes had always overlooked what ties the parables and aphorisms together: their use of everyday images. They missed the obvious point that "in spite of ambiguities, in spite of parody, hyperbole, paradox, and injunctions impossible to heed, the invitation to cross over is clear." Again we hear Kafka as precursor in the invocation of "crossing over." The essay had begun with a list of those things Jesus was silent on—although they were of great concern to the tradition (and often are to us). He concludes with the pithy observation that "Adam and Eve were ejected from the Garden because divine silence was not good enough for them" (169); and we likewise demand answers. So where are we to cross over?

"Jesus: A Voice Print" appeared in *Profiles of Jesus*, a collection of sketches by Fellows of the Jesus Seminar. The Seminar as a group never attempted to determine how the historically verifiable material fit together, or to reconstruct Jesus' inner self or his life goals. Their task was to isolate what came from Jesus. "Voice Print" was Funk's profile, his effort to arrange the material attributed to Jesus into a coherent picture.

Funk comes up with a new image for Jesus, describing him as "comic savant" and "the first standup Jewish comic" (174). He is searching for rhetorical strategies that will express to his new audience of non-scholars the scholarly conclusion that Jesus was a sage, that he properly belonged in the wisdom tradition rather than the apocalyptic camp. Funk had rejected this latter location for Jesus as early as "Parable as Metaphor." In parable, he insisted, the sage "constructs a new fiction that becomes the basis for his or her own action and the action of others" (174). And fortuitously, the comic side of his teaching—all those tropes that create the oddness of Jesus' language—blocks the effort to moralize the fiction. "[T]hey are also open to multiple and deeper interpretations as a way of keeping them open to reinterpretation in ever new contexts" (174). Having from the very beginning rejected Jülicher's single point strategy, Funk continued to favor the multiple interpretations that he now re-invoked in the service of ever new insights into ever new contexts. For those who have ears, the comic sage's voiceprint comes alive yet again.

The mythical matrix

The last two essays of this period are very different, but both are important summaries of Funk's parable work. "Parable as Trope" is his final statement on parable methodology—and even at this late date he is still innovating. "The Mythical Matrix" outlines his notion of "away-from-here as destination." Parts of this essay have a mournful tone, for Funk gazes back and sees a fast-dying tradition before he looks forward to see where we might be going. It should come as no surprise that he turns to the Jesus of the parables as his prophet for whatever new world lies ahead.

Funk looks back on his own precursors and those of his readers, beginning with David Friedrich Strauss and concluding with such contemporary figures as Lloyd Geering, Don Cupitt, and John S. Spong. The trajectory of these thinkers is a clear indication of where he is going. Ironically he does not include Kafka in this list. I take heart in this because Funk had earlier argued that Jorge Luis Borges had omitted Jesus from Kafka's list of precursors because "he felt that a direct reference to Jesus would thwart not only his [Borges'] interest in Jesus but his concern to locate Kafka also" (59). It appears that Funk may not be telling us all—the teacher in him letting his silence wink across the room rather than spell out the entire lesson on the chalkboard.

Funk's survey of his precursors indicates that both the Christ myth and the God myth have died. He succinctly summarizes our dilemma:

> What we need is a faith to bridge our need to know scientifically and historically and our need to form symbols and create

myths. . . . [for] symbols and myths provide us with an integrated vision of the world and our places within the world. We cannot do without them. (190)

Funk makes two moves to respond to this dilemma. He proposes that God is a metaphor—the God myth has died but God as metaphor is alive—and he points to Jesus' language as a way to vivify these necessary metaphors. For Funk the divine domain lies just over the hill, a divide that is worth crossing over in order to discover some fabulous yonder. Jesus' "vision offers some hope for our collective future on planet earth, especially if taken in concert with the wisdom of other sages and visionaries from our own and other cultures" (194).

Parable as trope

This note, never before published, was written by Funk in late 2004 to sum up his views on *Many Things in Parables*, a book by Charles Hedrick, who is an expert in Coptic, especially Nag Hammadi studies, and a long time member of the Jesus Seminar. In a series of exchanges posted on a website used by Seminar Fellows to share matters of mutual interest, Funk had sharply differed with portions of the book, and this was a concise summary of his disagreements addressed to his fellow scholars.

When Funk wrote this piece, his technical work on the parables was, as he acknowledges, in the past, but as we have seen it had undergirded his recent research and reflection on the historical Jesus. In this short piece he revisits his former conclusions about how the parables of Jesus operate.

We find two surprises:

- No mention is made of the Samaritan; instead his example parable is the Prodigal. (Who is prodigal—father or sons?)
- He has abandoned the argument from metaphor.

Since he had long understood the Prodigal through the lens of the Good Samaritan, perhaps this substitution is not altogether surprising. But metaphor had laid the foundation of his parable study. Inasmuch as his house had been built on metaphor, its omission demands explanation.

One sees in the way this note proceeds the continuing influence of formalism. He employs the well known distinction between story and discourse (Chatman). The narrative text is what is written, while the story is the "continuous sequence of events" that is implied in what the narrative says.

Funk sees much more implied than stated in a narrative text. He distinguishes between a *frame* of reference and a *field* of reference. The Galilean village life implied in a parable narrative is a frame of reference, the reconstruction of which has often occupied historical criticism. It includes all those items implied in a text that the parable teller and his audience shared as common knowledge, and over which non-native readers often stumble. Examples would include farming practices and people's attitudes toward leaven and Samaritans.

The concept of a field of reference is a questionable innovation on Funk's part. A basic problem is that it has several overlapping meanings:

- It initially refers to the "the larger frame of Galilee, the whole region, the Roman empire" (61).
- It can refer to the "world" in the sense of the phenomenal world. This has been a primary concern of Funk's since the very beginning of his work. The phenomenal world is all those values that inform a text—"what passes for the acceptable in thought, expression, and behavior, for the plausible in a given time and place."[11]
- Finally, it can mean "the kingdom of God" or "the divine domain," which constitutes the "alternative reality," or "altered frame of reference" (62).

This *altered* field of reference is what Funk formerly termed "the parable as metaphor." The "metaphorical" effect now takes place precisely in the alteration (not replacement) of the everyday world (that is, the common assumptions of the hearer). Parables "exaggerate, poke fun at, employ irony, and other devices in order to reshape the lived world of his listeners." The move to "altered" rather than alternative reality is a real gain in precision, although he is inconsistent with his new gain. As a result, the so-called realism of the parables becomes surreal, "owing to the proclivity to deform or subvert the everyday world of Galilee" (62). Thus the parables are on the "fringe of fantasy" and he can call the divine domain a "fantasy." At this point Funk rejects sociological, social world, or even historical readings of the text precisely because they lack this surreal dimension. For Funk such analysis can never be the end point of parable exegesis, but it is helpful in reconstructing the implied frame of reference. He probably has in mind William Herzog's *Parables as Subversive Speech*.

Funk notes that the presence of all these surreal characteristics of the parable's language—"a wink to audience" as he calls it—"undermines or subverts the 'they say' mentality of his Galilean neighbors in order to get them to see that he is talking about an alternative world into which he is inviting them." The upsetting of the everyday world, the tropes, the figures, "provide hints but do not spell out that world" (63).

Funk ends the essay in what seems to be a summary, but is really a pregnant beginning. The conclusion of his argument is that parables "contain clues that prompt us to read them in this imaginative way" (63). So the reading of parables is always at the beginning, always open to new possibilities, never emptied of nor reduced to its frame of reference. A parable provokes the imagination to create an altered everyday, and thus to participate in it. "Jesus is describing life in Galilee as it may be seen through God's eyes" (64)—and by imaginative extension, everywhere the story is retold.

In his early foundational essay "Parable as Metaphor" Funk had remarked, "The secularity of the parables may give expression to the only way of legitimately speaking of the incursion of the divine into history: metaphorical or symbolic language is proper to the subject matter because God remains hidden" (44). In "The Mythical Matrix" he argued that God was metaphor and in his concluding note on parable methodology he had been so bold as to say in the parables "Jesus is describing life in Galilee as it may be seen through God's eyes" (64). Funk's work on parables has come full circle. He has laid a foundation for the followers of Jesus to cross over to a new, imaginative, altered everyday world. And with creation imperiled[12] by our destructive activity, crossing over to the altered, imaginative new world of the parables may be the only option left to us.

Robert W. Funk

Parables Publications

1964 "`How Do You Read?' (Luke 10:25–37)." *Interpretation* 18, pp. 56–61.

1965 "The Old Testament in Parable: A Study of Luke 10:25–37." *Encounter* 26.2, pp. 251–67.

"Parable." *Children's Religion* 26, pp. 14–16.

1966 *Language, Hermeneutic, and Word of God: The Problem of Language in the New Testament and in Contemporary Theology.* New York: Harper & Row.

1968 "Myth and the Literal Non-Literal." Pp. 57–65 in *Parable, Myth, and Language.* Edited by Tony Stoneburner. Cambridge, MA: The Church Society for College Work.

1971 "Beyond Criticism in Quest of Literacy: The Parable of the Leaven." *Interpretation* 25, pp. 149–70.

"The Parables: A Fragmentary Agenda." Pp. 287–303 in *Jesus and Man's Hope,* vol. II. Pittsburgh Theological Seminary: A Perspective Book.

1972 "Jesus and Kafka." *CAS Faculty Journal* 1. Missoula, MT: University of Montana, pp. 25–32.

1973 "The Looking-Glass Tree Is for the Birds." *Interpretation* 27, pp. 3–9.

1974 "Critical Note." *Semeia* 1, pp. 191–94.

"The Good Samaritan as Metaphor." *Semeia* 2, pp. 74–81.

"The Narrative Parables." *St. Andrews Review*, pp. 299–323.

"Structure in the Narrative Parables of Jesus." *Semeia* 2, pp. 51–73.

Editor: *A Structuralist Approach to the Parables. Semeia* 1. Missoula, MT: Scholars Press.

1975 *Jesus as Precursor. Semeia* Supplements 2. Philadelphia: Fortress Press and Missoula, MT: Scholars Press.

"The Significance of Discourse Structure for the Study of the New Testament." Pp. 209–21 in *No Famine in the Land: Studies in Honor of John L. McKenzie.* Edited by James Flanagan and Anita Weisbrod Robinson. Missoula, MT: Scholars Press.

1977 "The Narrative Parables: The Birth of a Language Tradition."
Pp. 43–58 in *God's Christ and His People: Studies in Honour
of Nils A. Dahl*. J. Jervell and W. A. Meeks, eds. Oslo:
Universitetsforlaget.

1981 "Parable, Paradox, Power: The Prodigal Samaritan," *Journal of
the American Academy of Religion Thematic Studies* 48,1, pp. 83–97.

1982 *Parables and Presence: Forms of the New Testament Tradition.*
Philadelphia: Fortress Press.

1985 "From Parable to Gospel: Domesticating the Tradition." *Forum*
1,3, pp. 3–24.

1986 "Poll on the Parables." *Forum* 2,1, pp. 54–80.

1988 *The Parables of Jesus: Red Letter Edition*. A Report of the Jesus
Seminar (with Bernard B. Scott and James R. Butts). Santa Rosa,
CA: Polebridge Press.

  The Poetics of Biblical Narrative. Santa Rosa, CA: Polebridge Press.

  "Gospel of Mark: Parables and Aphorisms." *Forum* 4,3,
  pp. 124–43.

1993 "The Gospel of Jesus and the Jesus of the Gospels," *The Fourth
R* 6,6, pp. 3–10.

1994 *Jesus as Precursor*. Revised edition. Santa Rosa, CA: Polebridge
Press.

1996 *Honest to Jesus: Jesus for a New Millennium*. San Francisco:
HarperSanFrancisco, 1996.

2002 *A Credible Jesus: Fragments of a Vision*. Santa Rosa, CA:
Polebridge Press.

  "Jesus: A Voice Print." Pp. 9–13 in *Profiles of Jesus*, edited by
  Roy W. Hoover. Santa Rosa, CA: Polebridge Press.

2003 "The Mythical Matrix and God as Metaphor," *Forum* NS 3,2,
pp. 381–99.

Part One

ON PARABLES

CHAPTER

The Parable as Metaphor

C.H. Dodd has provided a classic definition of the parable.

> At its simplest the parable is a metaphor or simile drawn from nature or common life, arresting the hearer by its vividness or strangeness, and leaving the mind in sufficient doubt about its precise application to tease it into active thought.[1]

This definition provides four essential clues to the nature of the parable: (1) the parable is a metaphor or simile which may *(a)* remain simple, *(b)* be elaborated into a picture, or (c) be expanded into a story;[2] (2) the metaphor or simile is drawn from nature or common life; (3) the metaphor arrests the hearer by its vividness or strangeness; and (4) the application is left imprecise in order to tease hearers into making their own applications.

It will be profitable to pursue these clues, which Dodd has not always followed up, as a means of broaching the phenomenon. We may begin with the last (4).

I

The parable, according to Dodd, leaves the mind "in sufficient doubt about its precise application to tease it into active thought." This may be taken to mean that the parable is not closed, so to speak, until the listener is drawn into it as a participant. The application is not specified until the hearer, led by the "logic" of the parable, specifies it. This goes together with Dodd's further observation that the parable is argumentative, inducing the listener to make a judgment upon the situation set out in the parable and to apply that judgment, either explicitly or implicitly, to the matter at hand.[3] The parable thus involves what Bultmann calls a transference of judgment.[4] This would not seem to be the case with the so-called "exemplary-stories," where the application is evident in the example.[5]

From *Language, Hermeneutic, and Word of God,* 1966.

Few, if any, of the parables were originally given *applications* by Jesus.[6] This is not to say that Jesus did not sometimes call attention to the *point* of the parable by means of a question or some other device.[7] In any case, if Dodd is correct, a parable with an application affixed would be a contradiction in terms.[8] There is a strong tendency in the Synoptic tradition, however, to provide the parables with applications. In the process of handing the tradition around and on, the horizon of meaning tends to become fixed and is transmitted along with the parable. It may become fixed in relation to a particular situation in the life of the primitive church, or it may be crystallized in the form of a generalizing conclusion.[9] The parable may be given one or more conclusions to stabilize interpretation, or the application may be made apparent by a modification of the parable itself; in some instances both forms of stabilization are employed.[10] The hardening and crystallization of the tradition in this way produces what may be called the loss of hermeneutical potential; i.e., the open end of the parable, which invites the listener to make an application, is closed off.

What can be said of the disposition on the part of the primitive church to give applications to the parables? Scholars sometimes assume that, in identifying interpretive accretions as secondary, they are purging the dregs of early Christian interpretation from the pure nectar of the original utterance. In a sense they are justified in this attitude. It is always necessary to dismantle the tradition in order to reach its source, and reach its source we must if the parables are to be reinterpreted for another time and place. For this reason alone the critical historical work of Dodd and Jeremias is indispensable. For this reason, too, the fact that the church canonized its interpretations along with the parables is regrettable. At the same time, the parable invites application. In fact, it compels it. The proper question, therefore, is not whether the church was justified in interpreting the parables, but *how* in fact it did so, i.e., what specific application did it make of particular parables? A second legitimate question is whether this application was in harmony with the intent of the parable.[11] The resolution of the second question is more difficult than that of the first, for the reason that it requires reinterpretation of the parable in order to win its intent. In the end it may be possible to say only that the church interpreted the parables in such and such a way, while one application, in view of the contemporary situation, is . . . Nevertheless, it is both possible and necessary to risk normative judgments based on a critical grasp of the intent of each parable.

Taking Dodd's fourth clue in the strict sense, however, means that it is not possible to specify once and for all what the parables mean. For to do so would mean that the parable, once the application has been made and reduced to didactic language, is expendable. That Dodd's clue points to an essential characteristic of the parable is supported by the fact that the church preserved the parable along with the interpretation, in some cases even preserving the parable without appended interpretation. The parable, then, is not expendable. Why this is so, and why the application cannot be finally specified, impels a consideration of the nature of the parable as metaphor or simile.

II

Referring to point (1), above: the parable is a metaphor or simile.[12] Whether there is involved a simple metaphor, an elaborated or picture metaphor (similitude), or a metaphor expanded into a story (parable proper) is not immediately differentiating. The lines between the first and second and the second and third are, at all events, by no means easy to draw.[13] What is more significant is the nature of the metaphor or simile itself.

To say A is *like* B is a simile. The less known is clarified by the better known.[14] To say A *is* B is a metaphor, which, because of the juxtaposition of two discrete and not entirely comparable entities, produces an impact upon the imagination and induces a vision of that which cannot be conveyed by prosaic or discursive speech.[15] To go one step further, Owen Barfield suggests that in symbolic speech one speaks of B without referring to A, although it is supposed that A, or an A, is intended.[16] An element of comparison or analogy is thus common to all three, but the role which the comparison plays varies decisively. In simile it is illustrative; in metaphorical language it is creative of meaning. In simile as illustration the point to be clarified or illuminated has already been made and can be assumed; in metaphor the point is discovered.[17] The critical line comes between simile and metaphor; symbolism is metaphor with the primary term suppressed.

The proposed distinction between simile as illustration and metaphor as the means by which meaning is discovered is comparable to C. S. Lewis' demarcation between a master's metaphor and a pupil's metaphor.[18] The "magistral" metaphor is one invented by the master to explain a point for which the pupil's thought is not yet adequate; it is therefore optional insofar as the teacher is able to entertain the same idea without the support of the image. On the other hand, understanding itself emerges with the "pupillary" metaphor, with which it is consequently bound up; the "pupillary" metaphor is indispensable to the extent that understanding could not and cannot be reached in any other way. This distinction is also paralleled by Ian Ramsey's differentiation between a picture model and a disclosure model.[19] Ramsey draws the parallel himself, in fact, by likening similes to picture models (similes have "a descriptive use in respect of some important and relevant feature of the object they model"[20]), and metaphors to disclosure models (metaphors "generate a disclosure," yield "many possibilities of articulation," are not descriptive, and do not invite explanation or paraphrase[21]).

Illuminating as it would be to follow up what has been written on simile, metaphor, and symbol, especially in literary criticism, it is more germane, in view of the dominant understanding of parable, to concentrate on the difference between metaphorical and discursive language, or between the "logic" of the metaphor and the logic of predication.

"The logical use of language," writes Barfield, "presupposes the meanings of the words it employs and presupposes them constant."[22] Logic is not normally employed in the creation of meaning, but in making it explicit. The propositions of logic are therefore tautologies.[23] The ideal of the logician is to evolve a language which is drained of recalcitrant elements, i.e., which perfectly obeys the laws of thought. Such a language would, of course, be captive to the knowledge already implicit in its terms.[24] This is what Philip Wheelwright calls steno-language by prescription.[25]

This understanding of logic is akin to what Heidegger analyzes as the logic of predication.[26] Predication focuses the seeing sharply,[27] narrows it by calling attention to this or that. The predicate allows that to be seen to which it directs attention. The attention thus restricted, the predicate can be abstracted from the primordial referential totality to which it belonged and handled in isolation. Logical language—to indicate now the extremity toward which this process gravitates—is a tissue of abstracted predicates which are manipulated by formal rules. For both Barfield and Heidegger the logic of prediction necessarily fragments the circumspective referential totality upon which language is founded.[28]

Metaphor, on the other hand, raises the potential for new meaning. Metaphor redirects attention, not to this or that attribute but, by means of imaginative shock, to a circumspective whole that presents itself as focalized in this or that thing or event. Metaphor involves a "soft," as opposed to a sharp, focus.[29] If imagination may be substituted for metaphor in this context (the justification is that imagination traffics in symbols[30]), then Ray Hart's delineation of the active imagination is apropos: "What active imagination sunders is the 'givenness' of the delineated object with respect to the focalized limits of its allegedly self-presentation. It wrests the 'thing' out of its customary context, taken for granted by the perceiver or reasoner, and puts it into an alien (to the everyday mentality) context that is however its natural habitat, viz., the context of interaction-event."[31] That is to say, metaphor shatters the conventions of predication in the interests of a new vision, one which grasps the "thing" in relation to a new "field," and thus in relation to a fresh experience of reality.[32] Metaphor does not illustrate this or that idea; it abuses ideas with their propensity for censoring sight. To be sure, once a metaphor has passed into the language, it may become ossified and subsequently adapted to lexicons and logic, with the consequent loss of its hermeneutical potential—until rediscovered by some would-be poet.

"It is not surprising," Barfield muses, "that philologists should have had such a vivid hallucination of metaphor bending over the cradle of meaning."[33] The poetic predilection for metaphor and symbol is not at all arbitrary.[34] If *A* stands for the fresh insight that beckons the poet mutely, and *B* stands for the available language fund, a fund that has acquired conventions and is presided over by tradition, the poet must allow *A* to come to expression *through* and *out of B. A* is not "there" except as it enters language, but it cannot, because it is a fresh insight, be merely accommodated in conventional language. *A* is raised to cognitive status in language only as the linguistic tradition undergoes some modification. The metaphor is a means of modifying the tradition—it is talking "what is nonsense on the face of it"[35]—and as such is not expendable in the apprehension of *A*.

The latent cognitive outreach of *A*, on the other hand, is by no means exhausted in metaphor. Metaphor is only one of the modalities of cognition. A fresh apprehension of reality can, of course, be articulated in discursive speech—with some gain as well as some loss. But metaphor is the cognitive threshold of poetic intuition. As such it concentrates a circumspective whole, it embodies a "world" in a "soft" focus. For this reason the metaphor resists literal interpretation (the poetic metaphor is often a pretty tall story, taken literally[36]); it constitutes a gesture which points to but does not spell

out the background and foreground, the penumbral field, of an
entity or event. The poet summons and is summoned by metaphor
in the travail of the birth of meaning.

Many a poet has summoned metaphor when it was on holiday.
Fabricated figures are not up to the work of the genuine image.
Yet the difference between true and false metaphor is not easy to
specify. In general it may be said that "a true metaphor or symbol is
more than a sign; it is a bearer of the reality to which it refers. The
hearer not only learns about that reality, he participates in it. He is
invaded by it."[37] The word gives presence to the referent in such a
way that the listener is confronted by it; the auditor does not make
a distinction between the vocables and the reality to which the
vocables give presence. Word and reality are encountered in their
inner unity. Language becomes event.

Going together with the eventfulness of metaphor is its trans-
lucency. As a rule of thumb, if it is transparent that when the poet
says B she is really talking about A, if she is riding a figure as a
literary means of transport, the metaphor is contrived. On the other
hand, if the image is opaque, if the writer is giving vent to a fancy, it
is equally contrived. True metaphor comes into being in that misty
strait between transparent and opaque figurative speech, at the
point where metaphor and reality are irrevocably wedded, so that
one illuminates and gives life to the other. It is not too much to say
that true metaphor reveals a mystery: the mystery of kaleidoscopic
reality directly apprehended.

These considerations of the nature of metaphor have attempted
to keep the previous questions regarding the parable in view. If the
parable is metaphor, as Dodd maintains, the nature of metaphor
will have some bearing on how the parable is to be understood.
That bearing may now be pursued.

If B may now be allowed to stand for the parable and A for its
putative meaning (we might say, application), it may be asked (1)
why is B indispensable as the means of access to A? And (2) why
cannot the "meaning" of B, i.e. A, be finally specified?

1. A must be heard in language. The common, everyday understanding which inheres in language is the result of the process of
the crystallization, of the stabilization, of tradition. Dictionary language is steno-language by habit.[38] Language acquires conventions
which are further refined by means of logic. This shared understanding embodied in language is the stuff of which B is made.[39]
Since the maker of metaphor must employ language, A must come
to expression in B. But the maker of metaphor, like the maker of the

parable, utilizes *B* in such a way as to *(a)* break the grip of tradition on the language, and *(b)* discover new meaning. The two are recipical: rupturing the tradition permits a glimpse of another world through the cracks; the discovery of new meaning fosters the penetration of the tradition. Unlike Athena, who sprang from the head of Zeus full grown, new meaning does not emerge in full bloom. The fact that language is historical thus imposes the link between *A* and *B* upon the maker of the metaphor, and hence the parable.

This way of putting the matter is one-sided owing to the fact that *A* and *B* have been represented as two discrete things. As the "meaning" the parable intends, *A* cannot be accommodated, to be sure, in language crystallized in its everydayness. There is thus a theoretical discrepancy between *A* and *B*. The metaphor or parable, however, in drawing upon the common language reservoir, delivers language from the tyranny of fossilized tradition, so that *B* undergoes a coherent deformation. *B* is thus accommodated to *A* in the process of discovery. But the matter can and must be put the other way around: the deformation of *B* is what leads to the discovery of *A; A* is not "there" prior to the language which "speaks" it, and in this sense, it is *B*, the language tradition, in evoking an unpredisposed view of itself, that leads the poet and parable-maker to descry *A* in the first place. The linguistic tradition delivers itself over to historicness in spite of the efforts of the makers of dictionaries and grammars to hold it at bay. *A* is thus not superimposed on *B*, but *B*, language as it is known and used, invites its own deformation by refusing its total complicity to the manipulator of words. In order not to let the point fall prey to yet another form of one-sidedness, it should be added that it is the interplay between the effort to create a fund of rational discourse with stable terms, and the deformation of that fund, that makes human knowledge move—i.e., gives it a history.

2. There is a second reason why *B* is indispensable to *A*, and with it we come to the reason why the "meaning" of the parable cannot be finally articulated. The crux of the matter lies in the temporal and existential horizons of metaphorical language.

The logic of predication, as noted earlier, is narrowing, restricting. It identifies an "attribute" of the phenomenon, isolates it, and then handles it as an abstraction. The metaphor, by contrast, inheres in a vibrant nexus which resists reduction by predication. It resists specificity. It intends more, much more, than it says. What it says is minimal; what it intends is maximal. Discursive speech reduces the intentionality of language as near to explicit reference as possible; metaphorical language conserves the implicit tentacles of its vision, inasmuch as it concentrates a "world" in its figure or narrative.

If predication disengages the attribute from the phenomenon and thus from the primordial referential totality to which it belonged, it also arrests the phenomenon. It lifts the thing or event out of the flux of time in order to have a fixed term with which to deal. It is rather like clipping a single frame out of a motion picture film and then, on the basis of the still picture, conceptualizing the various elements which appear in that frame in a way that is intended to do service for the whole show. Precisely because the predicate has a static picture as its object, it is taken to be "timeless"; it appears not to depend on any particular disposition to entities.[40] However little in fact this may be the case, the logical use of language, or steno-language by prescription, as a matter of course has to resist the toll of time in order to preserve the constancy of its terms. Pure logic is purely abstract.

The metaphor, on the other hand, is open-ended temporally. It opens onto a vibrant nexus, whose movement it seeks to reflect in its "tensive" language.[41] That is, metaphor does not clip a single frame from the film, but seeks to concentrate the movement, the flow, in an image or constellation of images which gives presence to the movement. It must perforce resist rational fragmentation and refuse ideational crystallization. It endeavors to let the next one see what the previous one saw but to see it *in that one's own way*. As a result, it opens onto a plurality of situations, a diversity of audiences, and the future. It does not foreclose but discloses the future; it invites but does not come to rest in eventful actualization. Metaphors may live on indefinitely, since the constellation of meaning which they conjure up depends both on their revelatory power *and* the perceptive power of the mind which encounters them. They are constantly being refracted in the changing light of the historical situation.[42]

Closely connected with the temporal horizon of the metaphor is its existential tenor; it may be said to have the one because of the other. In contrast to rational abstraction, which evidences the greatest cognitive distance from event, the metaphor belongs to that mode of cognition, the imagination, which stands closest to event. "Since non-discursive forms of articulation (to take an example other than poetry, the sacrament of the Eucharist) intend to embody an event 'on its own terms,' they sustain a more intimate connection with the imaginative perpetuation of it than do the discursive

modes. . . ."[43] Imagination and its metaphorical vehicle give themselves to being in process, to unfinished reality, so to speak, which
they do not merely report but actually participate in. "Imagination
is both a cognitive and an ontic power, participating in the very
being of the realities it opens upon."[44] The metaphor, like the parable, is incomplete until the hearer is drawn into it as participant;
this is the reason the parables are said to be argumentative, calling
for a transference of judgment. Metaphor and parable sustain their
existential tenor because they participate in immediacy, and immediacy pertaining to the future as well as to the present and past.

Tentative consent was given, in the discussion of Dodd's fourth
clue above, to the affirmation that the parables are "argumentative." It is important to understand precisely in what sense this
is meant. A. T. Cadoux has argued that "almost all the parables,
of whose occasion we are fairly sure, were spoken in attack or
defense."[45] He therefore concludes that the parable is characteristically a "weapon of controversy."[46] Jeremias clearly draws on
Cadoux at this point, for the similarity of formulation is unmis-
takable.[47] Yet when Cadoux invokes Bultmann in support of his
view that the parables always seek to persuade (opponents),[48] he is
not entirely correct. Bultmann nowhere limits the audience of the
parable to critics, but assumes that diverse segments of the public
constituted Jesus' listeners.[49] Nor does Dodd support Cadoux in
this restriction. It would appear, then, that Cadoux and Jeremias
have correlated the "argumentative" character of the parable with
an alleged context of debate and controversy.

This correlation goes together with their view of the function of
the parable: Cadoux holds that the parable persuades.

> It will be noted that here too the parable is never merely illustra-
> tive: it is always something of an argument, with one or more of
> the characteristics already noted—emotional persuasion, argu-
> ment from analogy, allurement of the hearer to self-conviction,
> the clothing of new or difficult thought in form more easy of
> assimilation than direct statement, expression of what is incapable
> of definition.[50]

Jeremias argues that it is always a defense of the gospel.[51] Cadoux
and Jeremias thus link character ("argumentative"), function, and
context together. The question is whether a particular understanding of the "argumentative" character of the parable has not in fact
been determinative for the other two points.[52]

"Argumentative," on the other hand, may mean simply that the
hearer's judgment is precipitated,[53] without the qualification that

the hearer is hostile to or actively engaged in debate with Jesus. The auditor may, of course, be a critic or opponent, in which case he may well take the view of the parable that Cadoux and Jeremias hold. But he may also be friendly to Jesus, in which event he is likely to have a rather different disposition to the parable. The temporal and existential tenors of the parable as metaphor suggest that the hearer may be drawn into the parable, i.e., judgment precipitated, now in this way, now in that. This I take to be the intention also of Dodd's fourth clue. On this view, the parable is not an argument in the strict sense, but rather a "revelation" which calls for response. Amos Wilder has it that the basic character of the gospel as a whole is revelation, not persuasion.[54]

The true metaphor, it was said, reveals a mystery. The parable, too, betokens a mystery, which it adumbrates in something very like a riddle or a picture puzzle.[55] Both function like Alice's looking glass, through which one peers upon a strangely familiar world, where strangeness is suggested by the dislocation or rearrangement of the familiar. If the logic of predication looks *at* the phenomenon, the logic of the metaphor looks *through* it. The one looks *toward* the phenomenon, the other looks *away from* or *around* it (circumspectively: Heidegger). The poet directs attention to *B* in order to allow *A* to come into view, for *A* is not there to be looked at directly. Again, the mystery is the mystery of being, in transit from the past to the future. Being presents itself in the moment of transition, permitting only a glimpse: out of the fissures wrought by metaphorical impact upon surface reality into a future that has not yet fallen out. The glimpse, as it were, is bodied forth in metaphor, which seeks to preserve its character as glimpse (mystery), while conjuring up the background and foreground, the past and future, concentrated in that glimpse.

Returning to Dodd's definition of the parable as simile or metaphor, I have distinguished somewhat arbitrarily between the two terms he uses interchangeably.[56] This appears to coincide with Dodd's meaning, for he, too, inveighs against the understanding of the parables as "forcible illustrations of eminently sound moral and religious principles. . . ."[57] If simile is understood as illustration, it is metaphor that characterizes the parable.

The preceding reflections on the parable as metaphor require further elucidation in relation to the history of the modern interpretation of the parables. In a limited but pointed way, we now propose to probe the dominant line of parable-interpretation, as represented by the Jülicher-Dodd-Jeremias axis, in an effort to

expose the critical nerve of the prevailing view, with reference to
the parable understood as metaphor.

The parables in the Synoptic tradition are of two formal types:
those introduced with a comparative formula, and those begun
simply with a noun.[58] It is possible that this difference indicates a
difference also in the nature of the parable. Since, however, there
is a tendency to prefix the comparative formula in the process
of transmission,[59] it would be premature to rest a substantive
distinction on the introductory phrase. On the other hand, the
introduction may have no bearing at all on the nature of the parable. Amos Wilder is of the opinion that even the parables of the
kingdom introduced by such a phrase as "The Kingdom of Heaven
is like . . ." are not true similes.[60] According to Jeremias, the introductory phrase, in its simplest form the bare dative,[61] should not be
translated "It is like . . ." but "It is the case with . . . as with. . . ."[62]
These considerations support the view that the parables are metaphorical and should not be taken as similes.

The translation "It is like . . ." is often misleading, says Jeremias,
for the point of comparison is not always the initial element in the
figure, e.g., the kingdom is not like a merchant, but like a pearl
(Mt. 13:45–46); it is not like a householder, but like the distribu-
tion of wages (Mt. 20:1–16).[63] Granted that the comparison does
not turn on the initial element in the parable, it remains a moot
question, it seems to me, whether it is possible, especially in
the narrative parables, to identify the point of comparison with
such precision as Jeremias thinks possible. The translation of the
introductory phrase, "It is the case with . . . as with. . . ." rightly
suggests that the parable has some, as yet unspecified, bearing on
the subject at hand. While the introductory formula sometimes
identifies the topic, e.g., the kingdom, it does not provide any
clues to the way in which the story relates to this subject matter.
If the parable is a genuine metaphor, it is more likely that the parable *as a whole* is to be brought into relation to the subject. To say
that the kingdom is like the pearl is not much better than to say
the kingdom is like the merchant. The kingdom is likened to the
merchant in quest of fine pearls, who, in finding one of unusual
quality, sells all he has and buys that one. Who can say which
item in the figure represents the kingdom? Jeremias' inclination to
pinpoint the comparison strikes one as the old allegorical method
of interpretation narrowed to a single point: instead of the figure
touching the subject matter at a number of points, it touches it at
only one.

Cadoux was certainly correct in his view that the restriction of contact between subject matter and parable to a single point has unfortunate consequences. In the first instance, it renders everything in the parable unnecessary ornamentation, save for the single element which serves as the point of comparison. Beyond that, it induces one to miss the organic unity of the parable.

> A parable is the work of a poor artist if the picture or story is a collection of items out of which we have to pick one and discard the rest. A good parable is an organic whole in which each part is vital to the rest; it is the story of a complex and sometimes unique situation or event, so told that the outstanding features of the story contribute to the indication and nature of its point.[64]

Cadoux, let it be said, also opposed the allegorical method of interpretation, but he did so in the interest of preserving the integrity of the parable.

In pursuing this point, it will be illuminating to go back to the beginning of modern research on the parable. The work of A. Jülicher[65] is usually identified as the turning point, for it was he who dispelled the centuries-long domination of allegorical interpretation.[66] Dodd and Jeremias, as well as other modern scholars, build directly on the conclusions of Jülicher. Nevertheless, Jülicher is regarded as having made one fundamental mistake: he took the parables to convey one point of the broadest possible application. Let Jeremias summarize.

> His struggle to free the parables from the fantastic and arbitrary allegorical interpretations of every detail caused Jülicher to fall into a fatal error. In his view the surest safeguard against such arbitrary treatment lay in regarding the parables as a piece of real life and in drawing from each of them a single idea of the widest possible generality (here lay the error).[67]

For Jeremias, as for Dodd,[68] the parables are a piece of real life from which a single point or idea is to be drawn, but this point or idea is *not a general principle;* it is rather a point made with reference to a particular situation within the ministry of Jesus.[69] Jülicher's "broadest possible application" has been replaced by the particular historical application circumscribed by the conditions of the ministry. In other respects Jülicher's position is unmodified.

The advances made with Jülicher's rejection of the allegorical method of interpretation and with the attention of Dodd and Jeremias to the historical context of the parable are scarcely to be rejected. If Jülicher laid to rest the view that the details of the parable may be assigned independent significance, Dodd and Jeremias have made it impossible to regard the parable as illustrating a generalized moral maxim. Nevertheless, Dodd and Jeremias are as much exercised with the *content* Jülicher assigned to the parabolic teaching as they are with the nature of the parable. On Jülicher's view, they feel, the parables "are stripped of their eschatological import. Imperceptibly Jesus is transformed into an 'apostle of progress,' a teacher of wisdom who inculcates moral precepts and a simplified theology by means of striking metaphors and stories. But nothing could be less like him."[70] Jülicher did not appreciate the eschatological orientation of Jesus' message, but Dodd and Jeremias do, and so can make the consequent correction in his reading of the parables.

Jülicher's moral *point* of broadest possible application has become the eschatological *point* of particular historical application. The terms which have undergone modification in these formulations mark the advance; the term which has remained constant constitutes the problem. The parables of Jesus, concludes Jeremias, can be summed up in "a few simple essential ideas."[71] Each parable represents a single idea, and the synthesis of ideas conveyed by the parables affords "a comprehensive conception of the message of Jesus."[72] Like Jülicher, Dodd and Jeremias derive a set of ideas from the parables, a set historically oriented, to be sure, and not a set of general moral maxims, but nevertheless *a set of ideas*. The ideational *point* of Jülicher remains ideational.[73]

Is the parable as metaphor amenable to ideational reduction? Interpreted historically, i.e., in relation to a particular context, what a given parable meant to its various hearers or readers can probably be reconstructed with lesser or greater success, provided the context can be recovered. But the original meaning of many of the parables is beyond recovery owing to the fact that the situation in which they were uttered has been lost.[74] Insofar as the original setting can be reconstructed out of the tradition, Dodd and Jeremias may be said to have met with a degree of success in particularizing the original intent of the parables. It has to be kept in mind, however, that Jesus' audience was diverse, so that the single audience/single idea correlation is fallacious. Furthermore, the parable as metaphor is many-faceted, with the consequence that a "historical" interpretation in terms of the leading "idea" truncates the parable, even for those who originally heard it.[75] And finally, if the parable lays a burden on the future, as was indicated by considerations relative to the metaphor, it would also have to be said that the parable itself gives warrant for broaching the question of what

the parable *means* (as well as what it meant), a warrant which the
church claimed for its part from the earliest days. Ernst Fuchs has
seen the significance of this point.[76] Since the nonideational nature
of the parable as metaphor has not been taken sufficiently into
account, a historical interpretation (what the parables meant) has
tended to crystallize the parable into a leading idea, to correlate this
with a delimited audience, and to foreclose the future. Jeremias in
particular appears to be content with the recovery of the "authentic
voice" of Jesus,[77] by which he means the idea Jesus had in mind in
speaking any particular parable to a specific group. But the "actual
living voice of Jesus" must be accorded the right to its own mode
of discourse if that voice is to be "actual" and "living."

It is to Dodd's credit that he has recognized the temporally
restrictive character of a purely historical interpretation of the
parables. In the preface to the third edition of his *Parables of the
Kingdom*, he has responded to criticism of just this order in the following way:

> By all means draw from the parables any "lesson" they may sug-
> gest, provided it is not incongruous with what we may learn of
> their original intention. We shall not easily exhaust their mean-
> ing.[78]

This remark refers to a passage in his original text that is very
instructive:

> The parables, however, have an imaginative and poetical quality.
> They are works of art, and any serious work of art has significance
> beyond its original occasion. No pedantry of exegesis could ever
> prevent those who have "ears to hear," as Jesus said, from finding
> that the parables "speak to their condition." Their teaching may
> be fruitfully applied and re-applied to all sorts of new situations
> which were never contemplated at the time when they were spo-
> ken. But a just understanding of their original import in relation to
> a particular situation in the past will put us on right lines in apply-
> ing them to our own new situations.[79]

Dodd correctly emphasizes two points: (*a*) the meaning of the
parables is not exhausted with their original import; (*b*) the original
import, i.e., the historical interpretation, is controlling with respect
to reinterpretation. The latter is not to be forgotten in pursuing the
former.[80]

It is thus possible—I say "possible" to indicate that prudence
is required—to affirm that the parable, as metaphor, has not one
but many "points," as many points as there are situations into
which it is spoken. And that applies to the original as well as sub-

sequent audiences. The emphasis on one point over against the allegorization of the parables was a necessary corrective, but one point understood as an idea valid for all times is as erroneous as Jülicher's moral maxims, even if that idea is eschatological!

It should here be reaffirmed, in the interest of avoiding misunderstanding, that the details of the parable do not have independent significance.[81] They are subordinated to the whole so as not to disturb its unity.[82] In the allegory every detail or most details are conceptual ciphers; the allegorization of the parables is therefore their rationalization.[83] The parable does not lend itself to allegorization because the parable as metaphor is designed to retain its own authority; the rationalization of its meaning tends to destroy its power as image. This is the reason Fuchs insists that the parable is not meant to *be* interpreted but to interpret. The parable keeps the initiative in its own hand. Therein lies its hermeneutical potential.

Reduction of the meaning of the parables to a single idea, be it eschatological or christological, is only a restricted form of rationalization. As is the case with the allegory, theological reduction seeks to control the metaphor. In the same way and for the same reason, correlating the kingdom with the pearl maims the image. The strict subordination of detail to the whole and the independent power of the figure warns against such solitary reductions and correlations. The metaphor must be left intact if it is to retain its interpretive power.

III

The consideration of the parable as metaphor has thus far skirted Dodd's second and third clues, although we occasionally caught sight of the realism of the parables and the element of vividness or strangeness. The parabolic metaphor, it will be recalled from above, (2) is drawn from nature or the common life, and (3) arrests the hearer by its vividness or strangeness.[84] It will be necessary to reflect upon these two clues together, as the following questions suggest. Why should a commonplace, even if fetchingly depicted or narrated, be vivid or strange? Suppose it be allowed that a catch of fish or a wedding feast can be vividly narrated. Why should that be arresting, if arresting is taken to imply more than a pause to note with aesthetic pleasure? And why should such a vivid vignette be argumentative, precipitating the hearer's judgment? Why should it call for, even compel, decision? If these questions pose problems difficult of solution, it might be well to inquire why the parables are realistic in the first place.

Dodd has observed, with the backing of numerous other scholars, that the parables provide a reliable index to petit-bourgeois
and peasant life in a provincial village in the Roman Levant.[85] The
realism of the parables is so acute that, in the judgment of Jeremias,
it is natural to suppose that some of them were suggested by actual
events.[86] Wilder, too, can scarcely overemphasize how human and
realistic the parables are.[87] They provide intimate and accurate
observations on nature and life. What was once thought to be
an inaccuracy, because it did not square with Western ways, has
proved to be commonplace in the East.[88]

Perhaps more important than accuracy in detail is what Wilder
calls the impact of their "immediate realistic authenticity."[89]
Authenticity consists in the absence of romance, idealization, false
mysticism, escapism, fantasy, miracles, sentimentality; in short, the
parables are rooted in things as they are.[90] Jeremias has put the
matter succinctly.

> The hearers find themselves in a familiar scene where everything is
> so simple and clear that a child can understand, so plain that those
> who hear can say, "Yes, that's how it is."[91]

Jeremias, I fear, has quite another point in mind than the one I wish
to make, but his characterization, so far as I can see, tallies with
Wilder's use of the term authenticity.

Wilder ventures to speak of the secularity of the parables.[92]
The parables rarely take up explicitly "religious" themes. Is this
because, in wishing to speak about *A* (religion), Jesus directs
attention to *B* (a secular image), as is the case with metaphorical
and symbolic language generally, in that they look away from the
subject-matter? Or can one say that the really authentic world, the
everyday world, is one in which God does not "appear"? In the
latter case, the secularity of the parables is correlative with their
realism. In the former, the secularity of the parables is bound up
with the nature of metaphorical language. A third possibility presents itself, viz., the union of the two. The secularity of the parables
may give expression to the only way of legitimately speaking of the
incursion of the divine into history: metaphorical or symbolic language is proper to the subject matter because God remains hidden.
In that case even "religious" themes may be presented in "secular"
dress, i.e., "religious" subject matter is viewed merely as a part of
the profane landscape. But this point, as others, must await further
consideration of the element of realism.

Dodd offers a typically lucid explanation for the realism of the
parables:

It [the realism] arises from a conviction that there is no mere analogy, but an inward affinity, between the natural order and the spiritual order; or as we might put it in the language of the parables themselves, the Kingdom of God is intrinsically like the processes of nature and of the daily life of men. . . . Since nature and supernature are one order, you can take any part of that order and find in it illumination for other parts. . . . This sense of the divineness of the natural order is the major premise of all the parables. . . .[93]

In this context Dodd denies any affinity between Jesus and the apocalyptists, who disparaged the present order. His accounting is the more surprising in view of the fact that, a few pages later, he describes the message of Jesus as related to a "tremendous crisis in which He is the principal figure and which indeed His appearance brought about."[94] To this he adds that the course of events, involving disasters upon the Jewish people, persecution of the disciples, and the suffering and death of Jesus himself, contains within itself the mystery of the kingdom, the *paradoxical* revelation of the glory of God. "Behind or within the paradoxical turn of events lies that timeless reality which is the kingdom, the power and the glory of the blessed God."[95]

In what sense can this "tremendous crisis," this paradoxical revelation, be illuminated out of the natural order? If we may assume a common-sense or everyday view of what the term "natural" denotes—which corresponds to the "immediate realistic authenticity" of the parables, to which everyone can say, "Yes, that's how it is"—then it may be said that this is precisely what the kingdom is *not* like. For the mystery or paradox of the kingdom upsets the conventions, the standards of the common judgment—in sum, the "natural" order. But then Dodd may have in mind "that timeless reality which is the kingdom" when he writes "natural"; in fact, it must be so if he can wed nature and supernature. In any case, by his own definition the coming of the kingdom is a paradox: it contradicts common-sense opinions. To its manifestation not everyone is willing to say, "Yes, that's how it is."

It is not the mystery of the kingdom to which one promptly says, "Yes"; it is rather the everydayness embodied in the imagery of the parable. Everyone knows what it means to have lost a sheep or a coin, to sow a field, to have weeds grow in that field, to have a wayward son, to suffer injustice, to stand idle in the market place, to see an unscrupulous steward feather his own nest: these are things everyone knows and can affirm, "That's how it is."

But there is more to it than identification with the coarse realities of existence. Amos Wilder is on the mark when he writes, "Jesus,

without saying so, by his very way of presenting man, shows that
for him man's destiny is at stake in his ordinary creaturely existence, domestic, economic and social."[96] That is to say, the everydayness of the parables is translucent to the ground of existence.
When Jesus speaks of a lost sheep, a mustard seed, a banquet, or
some other commonplace, the auditor senses without prompting
that more is involved than a pleasant or amusing anecdote, even
one which relieves the coarseness of life by jesting. The parabolic
imagery lays bare the structure of human existence that is masked
by convention, custom, consensus. It exposes the "world" in which
everyone is enmeshed and to which and for which everyone
must give account. It is this element of ultimate seriousness that
is implicit in the patent everydayness of the parable. The "field"
which the parable thus conjures up is not merely this or that isolated piece of earthiness, but the very tissue of reality, the nexus of
relations, which constitutes the arena of human existence where
life is won or lost.[97]

If the parable cracks the shell of mundane temporality, it does
so without an explicit call to ultimate seriousness. The listener is
not overtly prompted. The parable simply and artfully calls up
the "world" in such a way that "anyone who has ears" knows that
more is at issue than a piece of change or a doting old father.

Taking Wilder's statement, quoted above, as axiomatic, it is nevertheless the case that *everydayness* is not merely incidental to the
"field" intended by the parabolic image. One's destiny is at stake
in everyday creaturely existence. The parable does not direct attention
by its earthy imagery *away from* mundane existence, but *toward* it.
The realism of the parable is not merely a device. Everydayness is
ingredient in the parable because everydayness constitutes the locus
of the parable's intentionality. In that case, however, why speak of
metaphorical language at all? If the parable speaks directly about
what it intends, in what sense is it metaphorical? The observation
that everydayness is ingredient in the field intended by the parable
because it constitutes the locus of the parable's intentionality, and
the previous assertion that the parable conceals its call to ultimacy
by looking out upon the mundane, appear to be contradictory.

This dilemma may be resolved by referring once again to the
nature of metaphorical language. Barfield has observed that the literal and nonliteral meanings of a word or sentence can bear various
relations to each other.[98] There is, first of all, the substituted meaning: a young Englishman announces to various persons outside
an underground station, "There will be rain in Northumberland

tomorrow," by which he means "Are you the person who adver-
tised in the Personal Column . . . etc.?"[99] In the prearranged code
one meaning is substituted for another. This is also the case, in
a less categorical fashion, with the fossilized metaphor: there are
very few oats left in the sentence "He is sowing his wild oats." In
the second place, figures which convey a nonliteral meaning while
retaining something of the literal force may be said, to use Barfield's
designation, to have concomitant meanings.[100] Concomitant meanings are characteristic of the poetic metaphor, as, for example,

> She dwelt among the untrodden ways
>
> . . .
>
> A violet by a mossy stone . . .

where the metaphorical and literal meanings are obviously inter-
twined. One might expect, Barfield suggests, that the retention of
the literal sense in the poetic metaphor would be dependent on its
plausibility.

> "But that is not in practice the case. The literal meaning of
>
> > The moon is my eye,
> > Smiling only at night. . . .
>
> or
>
> > There is a garden in her face
> > is a pretty tall story."[101]

Literal plausibility, it would seem, often permits the metaphorical
meaning to be divorced from the image with flattening results.
With reference to Christina Rosetti's poem "Does the road wind
uphill all the way?" Barfield avers that the metaphorical sense (A)
detaches itself from B, like a soul leaving a body, and the road and
the inn and the beds are not a real road and inn and beds, they
look faintly heraldic—or as if portrayed in lacquer. They are not
even poetically real. We never get a fair chance to accord to their
existence that willing suspension of disbelief which we are told
constitutes "poetic faith."[102]

Such metaphorical language approaches the status of the prearranged code. But where the literal meaning is not simply credible,
attention is called to it all the more. This line of Coleridge,

> As if this earth in fast thick pants were breathing

does not commend itself empirically, but one is inclined, as a consequence, to take a second look at this particular piece of ground.

The parable in which everydayness is ingredient would appear
to be a special case of metaphorical language. Its initial plausibility,

in the case of the nature parables and certain others drawn from the sphere of human life, tempts the hearer to substitute another meaning, i.e. to disregard the literal and thus to allegorize. The temptation is in force because the hearer or reader assumes that the literal subject matter could not possibly be the real subject matter. In the parable of the Sower, for example, the equations seed = word and soils = people can be made and the literal meaning quietly abandoned. Similarly, Matthew's allegorical code for the parable of the Weeds (13:36–43) invites the reader to disregard the imagery (B) and attend only to the meaning (A), in which case "meaning" rises from image "like a soul leaving a body." In the parables characterized as "exemplary-stories," on the other hand, the opposite temptation is in force: the reader is tempted to find the meaning in the literal sense. Classical examples are the Good Samaritan and the Pharisee and the Publican.

But to accede to either temptation is to overlook another characteristic of the metaphor and particularly the parable, viz., that it is not merely credible. Like the cleverly distorted picture puzzles children used to work, the parable is a picture puzzle which prompts the question, What's wrong with this picture? Distortions of everydayness, exaggerated realism, distended concreteness, incompatible elements—often subtly drawn—are what prohibit the parable from coming to rest in the literal sense; yet these very factors call attention to the literal all the more. Just as the literal imagery is not simply credible, so the parable points to a world where things run backward or counter to the mundane world. Yet that other world, like the literal sense, has a certain plausibility, a strange familiarity. It is the interplay between, or the concomitance of, the literal and the metaphorical that makes the two reciprocally revelatory. The literal and the metaphorical meanings of the parable have to be grasped concomitantly.

Metaphorical language, it was suggested, does not look *at* the phenomenon, but *through* it. Metaphor seeks to rupture the grip of tradition on one's apprehension of the world in order to permit a glimpse of another world, which is not really a different but a strangely familiar world. Metaphor, moreover, remains temporally open-ended, thus permitting the hermeneutical potential of the vision conjured up to make its own claim upon the future. It is in these senses that parabolic imagery is genuinely metaphorical. It does not look *at* everydayness, but *through* it. It fractures everydayness in the interest of a referential totality of a peculiar order. It does not pre-empt the world it opens onto, but allows that world to emerge in encounter with the hearer. The realism of parabolic imagery, consequently, is not, without qualification, simply the locus of the parable's intentionality; although the latter is rooted in everydayness, secularity, it is of a different order altogether. The parable induces an imaginative grasp of the one by the way in which it presents the other. And only in this way can the "world" of the parable be grasped at all.

In saying that parabolic metaphor induces an imaginative grasp of the "world" of the parable by the way in which the everyday world is presented, we are brought, finally, to the explicit consideration of what has been described as vividness or strangeness.

To be sure, vividness can be accounted for in part by virtue of the fact that the parables catch everyone in the commonplace acts of daily living. More than that, they catch folks at those junctures which they think of as *characteristic* of existence. Not all sons are wayward, not every sheep or coin is lost, one is not awakened every night by a friend in need. Yet these sporadic, even rare, occurrences are taken to epitomize life. Concentration on a familiar thing, or a thing taken to be familiar, makes it stand out suddenly from its background. One notices the sower perhaps for the first time. But, as Owen Barfield says in observing the poetic use of this device, it is concentration on a familiar thing in making it stand out from an *unfamiliar* background.[103] That is to say, the familiar is brought into the context of the unfamiliar and so is vivified. The familiar couched in the familiar is boring; the familiar and unfamiliar in juxtaposition are stimulating.

Parabolic imagery is vivid in just this way. Everydayness is framed by the ultimate. The commonplace is penetrated so that it becomes uncommonly significant. That which is taken to characterize the humdrum, fatigue, and irritation of experience is set in a context from which, in the common opinion, it is estranged. The superimposition of the two is revealing.

Vividness of this order, as Barfield also notes, requires that the strangeness produced by the superimposition shall have *interior* significance. It cannot be artificial, contrived, or merely eccentric. Vividness must inhere in the different thing that is said, not solely in the way that it is said. "It must be felt as arising from a different plane or mode of consciousness. . . . It must be a strangeness of *meaning*."[104] The everyday imagery of the parable is vivid fundamentally, then, because it juxtaposes the common and the uncommon, the everyday and the ultimate, but only so that each has interior significance for the other. The world of the parable is like

Alice's looking-glass world: all is familiar, yet all is strange, and the one illuminates the other.

Closely related is what Dodd describes as the surprise element in many of the parables, i.e., an unusual action. If the development of the story is unnatural, Dodd apologizes, it is because the point of the parable is that such actions are surprising.[105] Jeremias, too, takes note of such unusual features, while adding that Jesus employs extravagant exaggerations which are characteristic of Oriental storytelling; both are intended either to call attention to the point or to impress it upon the hearers by means of "shock tactics."[106] The trait of hyperbole, according to Wilder, echoes Jesus' eschatological challenge, and is the only point at which the parables diverge from realism.[107]

The underlying assumption, it is worth noting, is that the surprising and hyperbolic aspects of the parables require justification over against the otherwise predominant realism. They are explained as indicating or emphasizing the point, or as an echo of the eschatological crisis. Bultmann, on the other hand, suggests that the "immense concreteness" of the language of Jesus can be *raised* to hyperbole, to which paradox is related.[108] I take this to mean that hyperbole is stepped-up realism, surrealism if you will. Paradox, as Bultmann illustrates it, is hyperbole raised to the level of the impossible (e.g., the Pharisees strain out gnats and swallow camels).[109] In that case, what may be conveniently embraced under the term hyperbole (i.e., all unrealistic elements) may not be the opposite of realism, but its intensification.

This line, however, promises to fall short of the goal, unless it is recalled once again that the realism—which I prefer to call everydayness—of the parable concentrates on the familiar in such a way that it is shattered: Every hearer can affirm the everydayness of the parables, but is rudely shocked at two points. The hearer is startled when the parabolic narrative unfolds in such a way as to turn everydayness inside out or upside down: it is simply not cricket for the employer to pay those who worked only one hour the same wage as those who worked the full day. One is shocked, too, at the so-called transference of judgment: a just God does not indiscriminately reward the children of God. Here, of course, it is necessary to distinguish among the hearers. If the auditor happens to have worked one hour, such a person may take a more congenial view of the proceedings. That person's everydayness is happily disrupted. For both, nevertheless, the everyday world is surprisingly and oddly disfigured.

Hyperbole and paradox, for this reason, are intrinsic to the parable.[110] They are one means, among others, of indicating the "gappiness" of conventional existence. If they do so more overtly, they may be regarded as helpful signs of what transpires in other parabolic metaphors more covertly.

In sum, the parables as pieces of everydayness have an unexpected "turn" in them which looks through the commonplace to a new view of reality. This "turn" may be overt in the form of a surprising development in the narrative, an extravagant exaggeration, a paradox; or it may lurk below the surface in the so-called transference of judgment for which the parable calls. In either case the listener is led through the parable into a strange world where everything is familiar yet radically different.

This characterization of the parable also explains their argumentative or provocative character, why they demand a decision. They present a world the listener recognizes, acknowledges. Then the hearer is caught up in the dilemma of the metaphor: it is not the familiar world after all! Should one proceed on this venture into strangeness or draw back? The listener must choose to unfold with the story, be illuminated by the metaphor, or reject the call and abide with the conventional. It is too little to call the parables as metaphors teaching devices; they are that, but much more. They are language events in which the hearer has to choose between worlds. Those who elect the parabolic world are invited to dispose themselves to concrete reality as it is ordered in the parable, and venture, without benefit of landmark but on the parable's authority, into the future.

CHAPTER

2

Crossing Over

It may seem strange to augment the list of authorities on the parables of Jesus with the name of Franz Kafka. On second thought, however, the linking of Kafka's name with that of Jesus may not seem so odd after all. Jesus is known for his parables, and Kafka is known for his parable "On Parables," which stands appropriately first in the collection entitled *Parables and Paradoxes*. The first paragraph runs as follows:

> Many complain that the words of the wise are always merely parables and of no use in daily life, which is the only life we have. When the sage says: "Go over," he does not mean that we should cross to some actual place, which we could do anyhow if the labor were worth it; he means some fabulous yonder, something unknown to us, something too that he cannot designate more precisely, and therefore cannot help us here in the very least. And these parables really set out to say merely that the incomprehensible is incomprehensible, and we know that already. But the cares we have to struggle with every day: that is a different matter.

This paragraph delights those who agree that parables are incomprehensible and therefore useless. Others are bemused and some even irritated because they think Kafka subverts the perfectly cogent and entirely lucid parable tradition they know and love. Still others—relatively few in number—are amused by the delight of the one group and the consternation of the other.

The second paragraph, to be considered momentarily, tends to sow confusion everywhere. But that is to anticipate.

"Many complain," we are told, "that the words of the wise are merely parables and of no use in daily life." The complaint itself represents a certain discernment. Those who find no reason to complain take the parables of the wise to have an ascertainable message translatable into non-parabolic language, usually in prosaic and moralistic terms. The translation makes the parable applicable to

From *Jesus as Precursor*, 1975, rev. 1994.

everyday life. The loss of parable as parable inevitably reminds one of the admonition of Jesus often attached to parables in the gospel tradition: "Anyone here with two good ears had better listen!" The hard of hearing are the swine before whom one should not cast pearls. The complainers, on the other hand, have some premonition that the parables have to do with the incomprehensible and so cannot be of any practical use.

Kafka obliges his readers to complain: he refuses any recognizable frame of reference for his work and thus compels his interpreters to speculate. He achieves this remarkable goal by narrating only in the most concrete and specific terms, yet nothing in his prose can be taken literally. He rejects every particular metaphor in order to turn the whole of his work into one grand figure of speech. The first hearers of Jesus apparently voiced a similar dissatisfaction, which is now "remembered" only obliquely in the tradition. Mark has Jesus accuse his closest disciples: "Though you have eyes, you still don't see, and though you have ears, you still don't hear!" Those habituated in the Christian tradition of interpretation (mis)take the parable to be a dispensable ornament for a prosaic point, long ago determined. That makes the tradition swinish. Kafka provides a gentle (because implicit) reminder that the parables of Jesus have been eclipsed by their interpretations. The makers of genuine parables should be known by the complaints they precipitate, not by the moralisms they propagate.

The initial complaint is linked to a second observation: when the sage says, "Go over," he does not refer to some actual place, but to a fabulous yonder. The prosaic mind is not interested in fabulous places unless they are real places, like Las Vegas or Disneyland. This fabulous place, moreover, is not here but "yonder": it lies in some strange and perhaps exotic land, "away-from-here." And when the sage speaks of a fabulous yonder in parables, she apparently does so because she cannot designate it more precisely. In sum, the parable speaks of a *nowhere,* located *somewhere else,* in language intrinsically inexact. The topography of the parable is not "unreal," but neither is it "actual": it is an away-from-here, a yonder, that can be reached only by perpetually departing.

Sooner or later the question of the topography will occur to the readers of Jesus' parables: is it too much to suggest that the implicit subject of his parables, "God's domain," qualifies as the "fabulous yonder" of Kafka's parable on parables?

The complaint of many is fully justified: parables are frustrating, if not maddening. Sages speak of fabulous yonders of which they cannot or will not be more precise. Why can they not be more precise? And why do they not address themselves to common cares? When frustration borders on resignation, it is time to consider Kafka's second paragraph:

> Concerning this a man once said: Why such reluctance? If you only followed the parables you yourselves would become parables and with that rid of all your daily cares.
> Another said: I bet that is also a parable.
> The first said: You have won.
> The second said: But unfortunately only in parable.
> The first said: No, in reality; in parable you have lost.

The first paragraph reflects a common frustration with parables where they have not been entirely domesticated. The second paragraph embodies this frustration. Students asked to write an interpretation of this paragraph often give up in utter perplexity; some drop the course in protest.

The second paragraph opens with an invitation, extended anonymously, to become a parable and with that be rid of daily cares. The response, also anonymous, is equivocal: rather than accepting or rejecting the invitation, this participant prefers to indulge in a game of definition. The invitation, he says, must itself be a parable!

This maneuver is designed to forestall the issue. It holds the question at arm's length while pretending to address it. The penultimate frustration of the rational mind is immanent: the definition or identification of the parable as parable is of no immediate or ultimate help; recognition is the homage the prosaic mind pays the sage from the safety of a habituated world. Even the slow learner will regularly come this far in the game: "I'll bet that is also a parable." It is crushing to discover that identification is a form of not-knowing, that recognition is the final refusal. The parable must be seized as parable or not at all. The parable cannot be reduced to other terms, not even when it is identified as parable.

The final frustration of rationality is to be wrong while being right, to lose while winning. The second man has won his bet, but unfortunately only in reality. And that is to suffer the loss of parable, of that fabulous yonder, of the opportunity to divest himself of daily cares.

The two final lines of dialogue make it clear that the parable, for Kafka, does indeed have to do with a dispute over the "real," but a dispute that transcends the literal. To have won in reality is to remain bound to the everyday world, to daily cares, to be unable

to heed the invitation to "go over"; it also means to be imprisoned
in the literal. All of this is contrasted with the parable, with that
fabulous yonder, with the ability to cross over. Kafka does not
claim the word "reality" for the parable; he is content to issue an
invitation to vacate the real—by which he means the everyday—in
favor of the parabolic. To win in parable means to have shifted the
locus of the real.

Kafka sensed a steady and unblinking resistance to the parable, to his work in general, which does not contain a literal word.
Although fascinated and even greatly amused by his stories,
friends and readers paused before whatever implications they felt
constrained to draw from them. This hesitation is expressed by the
opening sentence in paragraph two:

> "Concerning this a man once said: Why such reluctance?"

The reluctance to "cross over" is given characteristic Kafkan voice
in the parable entitled "The Watchman":

> I ran past the first watchman. Then I was horrified, ran back again
> and said to the watchman: "I ran through here while you were
> looking the other way." The watchman gazed ahead of him and
> said nothing. "I suppose I really oughtn't to have done it," I said.
> The watchman still said nothing. "Does your silence indicate per-
> mission to pass? . . .

It is not enough that the way is open, that an invitation has been
issued, that the watchman is unseeing. The literal mind insists on
explicit permission to pass.

The reluctance to become parables is linked to the lack of explic-
itness, to the imprecision with which the sage speaks of that fabulous yonder. The parable has none of the allegorical transparency
of *Pilgrim's Progress*; it is a poor road map for the traveler who has
lost his way, particularly when the hour is late. To those who wish
to place such demands on the parable, Kafka gives the recommen-
dation to "Give It Up!" in this paragraph discovered among his
papers upon his death:

> It was very early in the morning, the streets clean and deserted, I
> was on my way to the railroad station. As I compared the tower
> clock with my watch I realized it was already much later than I
> had thought, I had to hurry, the shock of this discovery made me
> feel uncertain of the way, I was not very well acquainted with the
> town as yet, fortunately there was a policeman nearby, I ran to him
> and breathlessly asked him the way. He smiled and said: "From
> me you want to learn the way?" "Yes," I said, "since I cannot
> find it myself." "Give it up, give it up," said he, and turned away

with a great sweep, like someone who wants to be alone with his laughter.[1]

There is a great, high humor in the refusal to give directions—a humor that goes with the riddle of the way already set before the traveler. In this riddle, the destination is clearly indicated, but maps, guides, advance reservations are useless; the journey is too immense.

> I gave orders for my horse to be brought round from the stable. The servant did not understand me. I myself went to the stable, saddled my horse and mounted. In the distance I heard a bugle call, I asked him what this meant. He knew nothing and had heard nothing. At the gate he stopped me, asking: "Where are you riding to, master?" "I don't know," I said, "only away from here, away from here. Always away from here, only by doing so can I reach my destination." "And so you know your destination?" he asked. "Yes," I answered, "didn't I say so? Away-From-Here, that is my destination." "You have no provisions with you," he said. "I need none," I said, "the journey is so long that I must die of hunger if I don't get anything on the way. No provisions can save me. For it is, fortunately, a truly immense journey."[2]

That fabulous yonder is away-from-here; those who would reach it must set out from where they are—without provisions, and without directions.

This talk about immense journeys, giving it up, unseeing and un-hearing watchmen—if we may pause for a backward glance—undoubtedly appears unrelated to and remote from the parables of Jesus. One might ask, in fact, whether Kafka has anything at all to say about Jesus. The answer to that question can only be, certainly not. To which I hasten to add: that is the best reason for invoking Kafka in contemplating Jesus.

Although Kafka has nothing to say about Jesus, the two men are nevertheless related. The curious will be struck by four remarkable affinities:

- both men were displaced Jews;
- both wrote or spoke in an alien tongue (if Jesus did not speak Greek, we must give the name Jesus to the composer of the parables and aphorisms in the gospel tradition);
- both anticipated a holocaust;
- both were makers of parables.

Blood brothers or sisters often have less to bind them together. However, I remark these affinities only in passing.

To return to the previous point: perhaps the only sound reason for considering Kafka in connection with Jesus is to divert attention from the clamor of traditional voices that drowns out the voice of Jesus. Jesus is relieved of the burden of his interpreters, so to speak, for the brief time he sojourns in the shadow of Kafka. This might transpire, for example, during a course of lectures ostensibly treating both men but in fact making reference only to one. The anticipation that the other man will be spoken of is constantly frustrated; this has an emptying effect, if persisted in, like the practice of zazen in Buddhism.

It may be argued that, for this purpose, any interesting writer will do. Unfortunately, that is not the case. For the one author to be effectively distractive with respect to the other, the one must be *proximally distractive.* The one must skirt, penetrate, or traverse the territory essentially occupied by the other. Distraction occasioned by the new or novel merely shifts attention and will not produce catharsis; proximal distraction, by contrast, is redemptive of what is eclipsed.

The question of Kafka and Jesus should therefore be put differently: is Jesus in any fundamental sense a *precursor* of Kafka?

The Argentine writer, Jorge Luis Borges, has declared, in an essay on Kafka, "the fact is that each writer *creates* his own precursors." Borges was at first inclined to the view that Kafka was as singular as the Phoenix; then he came to see that Kafka had many precursors. Kafka's precursors have little in common among themselves; it is only in Kafka that they are brought together, only in him that their affinities come to light. This is because Kafka modifies the way we read his precursors; had Kafka not taught us to read them, we would not know the real tradition to which they belong.

Borges does not include Jesus among the precursors of Kafka. Among others, he identifies Zeno, Han Yu, Kierkegaard, Robert Browning, but not the Nazarene. The omission is curious, especially when one notices that Jesus, Kafka, and Borges are among the few great tellers of parables in the West. It is just possible that the omission is deliberate.

I make this suggestion at the prompting of Borges himself. In his short story entitled, "The Garden of Forking Paths," two men are discussing a novel called "The Garden of Forking Paths." One is a descendant of the famous Chinese general who had written the novel, the other a renowned Sinologist. It is known that the general, a philosopher and mystic, was preoccupied all his life with the problem of time. Yet his novel, which contains much abstruse metaphysical speculation and on which he labored for thirteen years, never refers to the problem of time. Indeed, time is never mentioned. The two discussants are pondering this strange fact. The Sinologist asks the other:

> "In a riddle whose answer is chess, what is the only prohibited word?"
> I thought a moment and replied, "The word *chess*."
> "Precisely," said Albert. "'The Garden of Forking Paths' is an enormous riddle, whose theme is time; this hidden reason prohibits its mention."

For this reason, it is possible that Borges was also interested in Jesus as a precursor of Kafka, but felt that direct reference to Jesus would thwart not only his interest in Jesus but his concern to locate Kafka also.

This may also be the reason Kafka has nothing to say about Jesus, and the reason Jesus does not refer to Moses in *his* parables.

It is of course absurd to claim that books written about certain subjects are in fact books about other subjects, although that is sometimes the case. Owen Barfield reports the story of a perplexed author who lacked a title for his book. A friend asked him, "Do you make any reference to angels? Any reference to trumpets?" "No?" "Then, why not call it, 'No Angels, No Trumpets'?" But we are speaking here of parables and makers of parables. In a parable whose answer is "God's domain," that is the forbidden subject matter. In a parable whose answer is "the parables of Jesus," *that* is the forbidden topic.

We are left, consequently, with the question whether Kafka is proximally distractive in relation to Jesus. That question can only be answered concretely: does Kafka modify the way we read Jesus? Is Jesus a bona fide precursor of Kafka? Conversely, is Kafka one of the authentic successors to whom Jesus gives rise? If the answer is "yes," the discussion of the parables of Kafka with which this essay began is entirely appropriate, and Kafka's parables are materially related to the parables of Jesus. In that case, nothing further need be said. If Kafka does not "create" Jesus as a precursor, the discussion has been futile.

CHAPTER

3

Parable as Trope

Colleagues:

Forgive the length of this post. It has been a long time since I wrote specifically about parables, so I thought I should hone my responses.

A narrative text consists of two parts: the part that is written and the part that is unwritten. Let me explain.

The first sense in which the narrative is unwritten is the story. A story may be defined as a continuous sequence of events, into which descriptions (time, place, characters) are interspersed. The narrative text is merely a selection of items that suggests the story but does not spell it out.

The narrative text also implies a frame of reference. The frame of reference for the parables as poetic fictions is the Galilean village, plus other things not strictly belonging to the village. (I think we have read the frame of the parables too narrowly as Jewish defined by Rabbinic Judaism, and omitted the Hellenistic aspects of Jesus' social world.) The frame is also unwritten in the sense that we have to infer it from what is said in the narrative text and implied in the story.

There is also the field of reference , which in the case of the parables is the larger frame of Galilee, the whole of the region, the Roman empire, etc. The field can extend in all directions, depending on how rich the narrative text is.

Another name for the field of reference is the term 'world'. At least, that is how I use the term in my essays, including the *Poetics of Biblical Narrative*.[1]

This note was written in November of 2004 in response to Charles Hedrick's recent book, *Many Things in Parables,* and posted on the Jesus Seminar Fellows list serve.

Now to simplify, the narrative parables and the picture parables both have frames, which consist of scenes set in Galilee. But the parables also imply a story, part of which is unwritten and a field of reference, which is only implied in these brief accounts, which are extremely parsimonious in the use of language, but are rich in the use of provocative overtones.

The parables open onto an alternative reality, or altered frame of reference, or field of reference, to which we have customarily given the term Kingdom of God. They constitute an invitation to enter that world and live in it. (Even if the gospel frame is secondary, the real subject is implied in the body of the texts themselves, and appears elsewhere in the tradition, for instance, Thomas.)

The point about the parables being non-literal (I avoid the term metaphorical since it seems to confuse) is that they are not merely descriptive. They exaggerate, poke fun at, employ irony, and other devices in order to reshape the lived world of his listeners. That world is a social world and is socially constructed, so he employs the poetic fiction as a way of deforming the everyday world of Galileans.

I would and do describe them as realistic, but a more accurate term is surrealistic, owing to the proclivity to deform or subvert the everyday world of Galilee. On the other hand, the parables are not realistic in the sociological sense, or even in the historical sense. They are on the fringe of fantasy. They are just plausible enough to work as a way to undermine the received reality. Or, as Amos Wilder used to say, they are sufficiently plausible (read: realistic) to get initially under the guard of the listener.

Stories that are wholly plausible are realistic without remainder. It is very difficult to create a fiction that belongs wholly to this category. Think how difficult it is to describe a thing or event without deviating from a close description, without interpretation, and without adding or subtracting one's own sensibilities. Plausibility at the next level conforms to public opinion, what we may call the 'they say' mentality: this is what everybody takes to be the case (but of course not everybody does). The parables begin with that initial 'they say' plausibility. The third form of plausibility is the narrative frame of reference: it is the world that has already been storied, that is taken for granted by the culture, by the living myth, so that this narrative version is immediately plausible and convincing. The fourth kind of plausibility is the use of strategies and moves the author employs to convince us that the story is accurate, realistic, plausible, even though she is making it all up or most of it up. And finally, authors may interrupt their own narrative to make a comment, in case we are missing what is going on. When we say things that are ironic or exaggerated, in oral presentations, we can wink at the audience to let them know that we are kidding. Rhetorical strategies are the means by which writers wink at readers.

The parable movement attempted to show that, in the authentic parables, Jesus consistently undermines or subverts the 'they say' mentality of his Galilean neighbors in order to get them to see that he is talking about an alternative world into which he is inviting them. The parables and aphorisms are full of tropes that provide hints but do not spell out that world. So parables do not tell us what they 'mean', if by that is meant what to believe and how to act, beyond the intention to undermine the way we usually construe reality. It is only in that sense that the parables are 'apocalyptic', that is, that they have a temporal horizon: the parables are open to a different future. The gospel tradition, on the other hand, immediately set to work to moralize the parables and aphorisms to supply them with specific courses of action or thought. And scholars have trotted right along in the footsteps of the evangelists.

Nevertheless, some innocent readers and listeners got it right away and never let it go. Fortunately, the evangelists did not erase all the clues from the narrative and aphoristic texts, so we can also see through the interpretive overlay back toward the original horizon of the stories and tropes.

Dare I risk an example? The Prodigal is not just the story of a dysfunctional family. It has both syntagmatic and paradigmatic elements. The syntagmatic plot is the story of departure and return, leaving home and returning home. It is also the story of someone who forsook his patrimony and threw it away in a 'foreign' land. I say 'foreign' to indicate that passing through the alien is one way to discover who we are, to discover our own identify. Quite a number of the fairy tales collected by Grimm are of this type. The paradigmatic aspects of the parable have to do with the relationship between parent and two siblings, who take opposite sides of the family equation. Neither is right and neither wrong. But in the kingdom of God, or the divine domain, as I now prefer to term it, generosity is the rule, because God is generous. But I have not drawn any rules about behavior from the story, other than to indicate the horizon of the world as Jesus imagined it.

If this analysis is not wide of the mark, we have to say that the parables, both narrative and picture, contain clues that prompt us to read them in this imaginative way.

Another way of putting the matter is to say that Jesus is describing life in Galilee as it may be seen through God's eyes.

This is the theoretic frame within which I read both the parables and the aphorisms.

Part Two

LURKING BEHIND THE SAMARITAN

The Old Testament in Parable

The Good Samaritan

The Old Testament is posed as a problem initially for the church by its own constitution of the canon: it embraced the two Testaments in a single canon, but drew a line between them and marked the discontinuity by designating one the *Old** in contrast to the *New*. The Old Testament is also a problem by virtue of the conflict between Jewish and Christian interpretation. This tension has been heightened, furthermore, by the rise of the critical historical method. This method, which endeavors to let the Old Testament speak for itself, points back to but is not identical with Jewish interpretation. How the Old Testament may be appropriated by the Christian faith was consequently a problem for the church from the beginning, and has reappeared, under the impact of the historical method, as a theological problem of the first magnitude in recent times.[1]

Apparently from the very first, perhaps in the wake of the precedent of Jesus, the church undertook its own interpretation of scripture (i.e., the Old Testament) in support of its claim to the Old Testament as its own book.[2] In claiming the Old Testament as its own, the church was obliged to distinguish its interpretation from that of Judaism, and thus in the end to distinguish its understanding of scripture as scripture from that of Judaism. For an understanding of the scripture principle is contingent upon, or correlative with, a hermeneutic.[3] If the church subsequently set its interpretation of the Old Testament alongside that of Judaism, as a rival interpretation resting upon the same understanding of the

---

From *Language, Hermeneutic, and Word of God,* 1966.

*Editor's Note: For precisely the reasons that Funk is here raising, recent scholarship has tended to avoid using the term *Old* Testament, preferring instead Hebrew Scriptures or First Covenant. I have left Funk's usage stand as it represents the time period in which it was written and his arguments were exactly the type of impetus that has led to a shift in usage.

scripture principle, it did so at the peril of losing its claim upon the Old Testament. And the rise of historical criticism has tended to heighten the peril and make the claim more tenuous. In short, the church's right to embrace the Old Testament in its canon cannot be justified merely on the ground that the church, like Judaism, acknowledges sacred scripture.

The canonical status of the Old Testament was never actually a central issue in the church, except in those heretical movements, e.g., Marcionism,[4] which felt that the Old Testament could not be appropriated "on its own terms." It was what the Old Testament had to say for itself, assessed in the light of his own understanding of the Christian message, that led Marcion to reject it. But the unwillingness to appropriate the Old Testament "on its own terms" is reflected also by Christian orthodoxy, which sought to buttress its claim by applying a new hermeneutic. If, in retrospect, it looks as if the church read its own faith back into the Old Testament by means of allegory, typology, and the like, it should be recalled that this solution proved more viable than rejecting the Old Testament outright. That is to say, orthodoxy chose to do battle over the correct interpretation of the Old Testament rather than relinquish its claim to the scriptures of Israel.

Now that historical criticism has once again brought into the foreground the tension between the Old Testament understood "on its own terms" and Christian interpretation of it—that is, broadly speaking, between Jewish and Christian claims to the Old Testament—it is not surprising that, as an option to ignoring the Old Testament or rejecting it altogether, attempts are being renewed to interpret the Old Testament in a specifically Christian, or christological, sense.[5] Nor is it surprising that a strict historical interpretation of the Old Testament almost always has a Marcionite tinge to it when viewed theologically. To the extent that historical interpretation tends to coincide with Jewish interpretation, attempts to construct a specifically Christian interpretation gain urgency and vindicate themselves as efforts to save the Old Testament for the church.

Efforts to salvage the Old Testament for the church by means of christological interpretation, by whatever hermeneutical device, are bound to fail unless it is seen that hermeneutic is correlative with an understanding of scripture as scripture. Anyone who chooses to contest Jewish or critical historical interpretation, must also be prepared to contest the understanding of the scripture principle upon which these interpretations rest. For what scripture is cannot be divorced from how it is to be interpreted. The fact that the *what* of scripture is taken for granted makes the hermeneutical problem impossible of solution along any but traditional lines. And these lines have reached an impasse, with the weight falling on the Jewish side by virtue of the historical method.

The following essay is a preliminary attempt to approach the question from a New Testament perspective, without losing sight entirely of the theological problem. Specifically, it approaches the problem from the standpoint of Jesus' use of scripture in parable. Needless to say, the following study is based on previous considerations of the parable. However, taking up the problem of Old Testament interpretation from a New Testament perspective is not thereby justified. It has been said that critical historical interpretation tends to converge with Jewish interpretation on the assumption that the Old Testament was[6] a Jewish book. But historical interpretation cannot draw a line across history at the turn of the ages and insist that all historical interpretation of the Old Testament must draw on data from prior to that juncture as its basis. How Jesus and the primitive church interpreted the Old Testament also provides us with historical data—and Jewish data at that! These data must also be taken into account in historical interpretation.

From this it is not to be inferred that the hermeneutical methods of Jesus and various segments of the early church should automatically commend themselves to the church as viable solutions to the problem of Old Testament interpretation. Understanding of these methods is, of course, prerequisite to assessment. And understanding requires that hermeneutic and what is concomitant therewith, understanding of scripture as scripture, be brought into view. It is possible that by grasping the way in which Jesus interpreted scripture we shall come upon his hermeneutic and his understanding of scripture as such, which in turn may open the way to a reconsideration of how the church both understood and misunderstood Jesus' use of scripture. It is quite possible that the locus of the problem, when grasped in this way, will undergo a radical shift. The question may not turn so much on how Jesus or the church or Israel manipulated scripture, as on how scripture manipulated Jesus, the church, and Israel when brought into the context of the appearance of Israel's Messiah. In that case, understanding of the Old Testament does indeed turn on whether the Messiah has come, as the early church thought. An attempt to open the problem up from the side of Jesus' use of scripture in parable, if successful, may illuminate the contemporary theological problem as well.

The isolation of the parable within the Jesus tradition does not require further justification.[7] But the relation of scripture to parable is problematical, and it is to that connection that attention must first be given.

I

Scripture may be said to function in relation to the parable (including the rabbinic parables) in three ways: (1) as the text for which the parable is exposition; (2) as the source of the basic image or figure utilized in the construction of the parable; or (3) as the means of elucidating or enlivening the parable.

According to Jeremias, the primitive church introduced scriptural references and allusions into the parables of Jesus, usually in support of allegorizing tendencies (e.g., the parable of the Wicked Tenants), but there is scant evidence that Jesus cited scripture explicitly to any significant degree in the body of his parables. Hence, if only for this reason, the parable makes little or no overt and explicit use of scripture and scriptural allusion in the narrative body of the parable.[8]

It is a different matter to assert that Jesus drew upon Old Testament imagery in the construction of his parables, for in this case it is not a matter of scriptural quotation or allusion, but of dependence upon a common reservoir of images, of reference to a system of interlocking images and figures, known and meaningful in and of themselves to the hearer. The parable would then depend for its significance on the ability of the hearer to catch the overtones, to supply, as it were, out of the common heritage, the body of the image, which alone has the power to let the parable speak. Harald Riesenfeld has argued that the parables make use of a repertory of Old Testament images and motifs in a quasi-allegorical way,[9] with the consequence that the parables of Jesus are not really intelligible to someone not immersed in Old Testament lore. Riesenfield's student, Birger Gerhardsson, has attempted to make the case for the parable of the Good Samaritan in particular, not only that Jesus draws upon Old Testament imagery, but that he employs well-known rabbinic techniques of interpretation.[10] It is my intention to examine this effort more closely in due course.

It should be noted that the view advocated by Riesenfeld and Gerhardsson apparently runs counter to the widely held view that the parables are realistic in essence, that they reflect the everyday world. C. H. Dodd has put the matter well.

Each similitude or story is a perfect picture of something that can be observed in the world of our experience. The processes of nature are accurately observed and recorded; the actions of persons in the stories are in character; they are either such as anyone would recognize as natural in the circumstances, or, if they are surprising, the point of the parable is that such actions *are* surprising.[11]

Neither Dodd[12] nor Amos Wilder[13] wishes to press this characteristic too far: it is possible, both would allow, that now and then there are allegorical overtones in what is otherwise a completely human and realistic picture or narrative. Nevertheless, Wilder insists, "the impact of the parables lay in their immediate realistic authenticity," and to press the concrete, realistic images in the direction of allegorical ciphers "is to pull the stories out of shape and to weaken their thrust."[14]

If realism and allegory are occasionally compatible (extended allegory tends, as a rule, to weaken realism[15]), it is to be wondered whether secularity and allegory dependent upon the Old Testament stock of images can be reconciled, even occasionally. Lucetta Mowry has noted that the subject matter of the parables, with four exceptions, is secular,[16] and Wilder suggests that the naturalness and secularity of the parables points to something very significant about Jesus and the gospel, viz., that for Jesus human destiny is at stake precisely in "ordinary creaturely existence."[17] Ernst Fuchs puts it pointedly: "Jesus does not use the details of this world only as a kind of 'point of contact'; instead, *he has in mind precisely this 'world.'*"[18] If the secular world is the "field" intended by the parable, does the Old Testament stock of images belong to this world as part of its secular landscape? If so, what are the consequences for Jesus' use of the Old Testament?

This matter can be viewed from still another perspective. Assuming that Jesus is drawing upon a repertory of images belonging to the common Jewish heritage, is there anything determinative in this fact for his relation to the Old Testament? Could Jesus, for example, have drawn upon the Homeric metaphors with equal effectiveness, had his audiences been steeped in the Iliad and Odyssey? Or is the Old Testament the necessary linguistic school for the Christian faith? We are here touching upon the root problem of the relation of the New Testament to the Old Testament, which could be specified, to take one example, as the problem of typology. Even if it were established that there is *some* inner relation between the Old Testament images and the parable, it would still be necessary to inquire *what* this relation is.

This line of reflections may be arbitrarily terminated in order to note the first way, mentioned above, in which scripture may be related to the parable. The rabbinic parables are characteristically used in the exposition of scripture.[19] Gerhardsson is certainly justified in saying that one might antecedently expect Jesus to use the parable for this purpose also.[20] This is not often assumed to be the case, and indeed there is little evidence to indicate that Jesus did employ the parable in the exposition of scripture. One ostensible exception is the parable of the Good Samaritan in its Lucan context (Luke 10:25–37). It is just this point that is felt to provide the sharpest contrast between the rabbinic and Jesus' use of parables. Let Bornkamm summarize:

> The rabbis also relate parables in abundance, to clarify a point in their teaching and explain the sense of a written passage, but always as an aid to the teaching and an instrument in the exegesis of an authoritatively prescribed text. But this is just what they are not in the mouth of Jesus, although they often come very close to those of the Jewish teachers in their content, and though Jesus makes free use of traditional and familiar topics.[21]

It will now be clear that the relation of the parables to scripture in Jesus' usage is entirely problematic. Were it not for the position which the parables occupy in the tradition and the importance they are accorded by those of varying persuasions, one would be inclined to look elsewhere for light on Jesus' relation to the Old Testament. It would be possible, of course, to proceed *via negativa* and eliminate all possible contact between the parable and scripture. A detailed demonstration of this order would only be a tour de force, were it successful. It remains to examine with care those cases where the tradition has reported a connection between scripture and the parable, or where there is reason to suspect a connection not explicitly recorded. Attention will be devoted here exclusively to the parable of the Good Samaritan.

The reasons for selecting the parable of the Good Samaritan are two. In the first place, the Lucan context connects the parable with the lawyer's question about eternal life (Luke 10:25–28), which is initially answered out of the law. The parable would appear to be a midrash on the second part of the commandment. In the second place, starting out from the patristic tradition that the parable is a christological allegory, Gerhardsson has argued that Jesus draws upon the Old Testament imagery of the good shepherd (with its constellation of meaning), and employs well-known rabbinic techniques in debating the interpretation of the commandment with the lawyer in question. Together or singly, these could afford valuable clues to Jesus' use of the Old Testament and specifically to his hermeneutic. The balance of this essay will in effect be a study of the parable and of Gerhardsson's interpretation of it.

II

Gerhardsson first considers the parable of the Good Samaritan apart from its context.[22] The parable is not concerned with the injured man, but with the three persons who come across him, as the concluding question (Luke 10:36) shows. The challenge to the hearer is to identify the true neighbor: who is, of course, the Samaritan.[23] Adopting Jeremias' view that the parables of Jesus are marked by a polemic directed against the Jews, particularly the Pharisees and their scribes,[24] Gerhardsson reasons that the parable is intended as a criticism of the Jewish leaders.[25] It cannot be accidental, furthermore, that the parable exhibits such striking affinities with the shepherd motif found in the Old Testament, particularly in Ezekiel 34. The elements are the same: "The defenseless flock, abandoned by the false shepherds, given over to wild beasts, receiving the promise of the true shepherd."[26] The interpretation which suggests itself is therefore the following: the injured man represents Israel, the priest and Levite the religious leaders, and the Samaritan is the true shepherd (r'h y'sr').[28]

Is there any other support for this understanding of the parable? Indeed there is. It is to be found in the significance of the name, Samaritan (the significance of names is utilized in patristic exegesis as well as in the Jewish, including Old Testament, and early Christian tradition),[27] and in the double meaning of the root of the word [in Hebrew] for shepherd, r' or r'h.[29] Σαμαρίτης [Samaritan in Greek] represents [in Hebrew] šmrwny, derived from šmr, which means both to "watch over" and "to keep, observe." The intransitive verb can mean "to be a shepherd" (e.g., Hos. 12:12), the present active participle "shepherd" (e.g., 1 Sam. 17:20). Like rō'eh, šōmēr is used to designate God and his anointed. The Samaritan in the parable thus stands for the true shepherd, who is also the true keeper of the law.[30] In patristic exegesis it was a commonplace, beginning with Origen, to note that Samaritan meant watchman.[31] The patristic tradition, then, which universally interpreted the parable christologically,[32] has preserved under its "florid allegorizing" the original sense of the parable, viz., that the subject was Christ himself.[33]

Similarly, the Greek word πλησίον, "neighbor," represents the Hebrew word rēa'. The Hebrew word for shepherd is rō'eh. These words are graphically quite similar, and even their phonetic difference is slight in many forms; moreover, they derive from a single verb, *rā´āh*.[34] "It is not too rash to suggest," says Gerhardsson, "that this parable did not originally deal with who is the *true neighbor, rēa` (rē'eh)*, but who is the *true shepherd, rō'eh.*"[35] Such an interpretation is possible on the basis of the rabbinic rule that a word may be interpreted in its double significance.[36] The lawyer asked a question concerning the commandment (Who is my neighbor?) and received an answer about the true shepherd.[37] Such wordplay strikes the modern reader as grotesque, but it is quite in accord with the techniques of Jewish midrash, as exemplified, for example, at Qumran.[38]

The shift in meaning must have taken place before the parable took its canonical form, for the Greek word πλησίον [neighbor] preserves the secondary interpretation, which accords with the proclivity of the church for transforming the parables into didactic and paraenetical vehicles for its own situation;[39] the church would not need reminding of who the true shepherd was, but they would be interested in the lawyer's question! The secondary meaning was secured by the final imperative: "Go and do likewise."[40]

The Lucan context, in Gerhardsson's judgment, supports his analysis of the parable.[41] There is depicted a learned discussion of the law between Jesus (a διδάσκαλος, [teacher] *rby)* and a lawyer (a νομικός [rabbi]).[42] The discussion proceeds according to custom, including the use of rabbinic formulae and Hebrew. Since the rabbis were fond of the parable in the exposition of scripture, it is not surprising that the lawyer's question, which has to do with an *exegetical* point (what is the meaning of *rēa`* in the text?), evokes a parable as a midrash on the text. The transcript abbreviates the discussion (customary in the rabbinic literature), but the parable gives evidence that Jesus knew and used rabbinic techniques of interpretation. The conclusion is that the pericope, Luke 10:25–37, was a unity from the first.

The original significance of the parable, Gerhardsson believes, accords with the meaning of the pericope of the rich young man (Mark 10:17–21 and parallels), with which it has certain formal parallelisms:[43] the answer of the law as traditionally expounded is not sufficient; Jesus refers to scripture as the Messiah, i.e., gives his own interpretation, which means in the end that he interprets scripture messianically or christologically.[44] It is by no means clear how Gerhardsson gets from the former to the latter. Does the authority of the Messiah to reinterpret scripture imply that such reinterpretation, *eo ipso* [by itself], will be christological interpretation?

The formal affinity of Gerhardsson's view with that of Ernst Fuchs, who regards the parables as (veiled) self-attestations of Jesus himself,[45] and with the patristic view,[46] requires that these tendencies in contemporary scholarship be carefully distinguished from each other and from the patristic tradition. The differences are correlative with how one understands Jesus' understanding and use of scripture. It is not possible here to embark upon a systematic examination. It will be necessary, as a consequence, to restrict ourselves to a re-examination of the parable of the Good Samaritan with the problem of scripture in view.

III

The discrepancy between the formulation of the question ("Who is my neighbor?" Luke 10:29) and the question answered by the parable ("Which of these three proved neighbor?" Luke 10:36) is regularly noted. The disjunction may be epitomized as *"Quis diligendus?"* [who must be loved] (the lawyer's question) and *"Quis diligens?"* [who does the loving] (the question answered by the parable).[47] This hiatus has been advanced as an argument for divorcing the parable from its Lucan context,[48] but it has also been explained or minimized.[49] What is not often noticed is that the prevailing modern interpretation of the parable, i.e., that the parable defines neighbor as he who needs my help, is as much in conflict with the parable as is the lawyer's question.[50] The lawyer's question still tends to dominate the parable! Jesus' question, "Which of these proved neighbor . . .?" turns the lawyer's question around, if indeed the range to which "neighbor" is applicable is any longer the question at all.

Without a reformulation of the leading question or a recasting of the parable, the incongruity stands. It could even be said that the discrepancy is not alleviated by disengaging the parable from the lawyer's question. For his question continues to be the hearer's question. It should be asked, furthermore, whether the parable really deals with the subject of love as opposed to the object of love. Or are these options—subject or object—simply misleading?

It is methodologically sound to follow Gerhardsson in considering the parable initially in and of itself.[51] Quite apart from the Lucan framework it appears that the parable is devoted to the question of neighbor.[52] On the other hand, it is doubtful whether a moralistic interpretation does more than reflect the later interest of the church, which happens in this case to coincide with modern interests.[53] Jeremias has demonstrated the pronounced tendency of the tradition to convert parables with eschatological horizons into hortatory material.[54] Going together with a moralizing interpretation is the definition of the Good Samaritan as a *Beispielerzählung* (exemplary story). An exemplary story does not draw its pictorial element from a sphere other than the one to which its *Sache* [subject] belongs; it has no figurative element at all. "The 'exemplary stories' [Beispielerzählungen] offer examples = models of right behavior."[55] Exemplary stories do not, therefore, call for a transference of judgment as do the parables proper.[56] The Samaritan is just an example of a true neighbor (or, to follow the prevailing view, of the true love of one's neighbor), nothing more. Gerhardsson, in my judgment, has rightly challenged the validity of this designation,[57] although for what strike me as the wrong reasons.[58]

In comprehending the parable it is important to grasp how the hearer is drawn into the story. From what perspective is the parable told?[59] Initially at least, the account compels the hearer to identify with that nameless fellow jogging along the wild and dangerous road.[60] Straightway that fellow finds himself the object of a murderous attack which leaves him stripped, beaten, and half-dead. While lying helpless in the ditch, he is aware that the priest and Levite pass by with only an apprehensive glance. It does not matter to him whether their callousness can be excused or justified, and (as victim) lay listeners find their secret anticlericalism is confirmed. The priest or Levite hearers will, of course, be incensed. At this juncture lay hearers will anticipate the arrival of a benign layperson on the scene;[61] ecclesiastical listeners, muttering under their breath, will expect no less. In the teeth of just such anticipations, to the utter amazement and chagrin of every listener as Jew[62] (the previous dichotomy is bridged in an instant), a hated enemy, a half-breed, a perverter of true religion comes into view and ministers to the helpless victim who is powerless to prevent him.[63] While still in inner turmoil over this unexpected turn of events, the hearer is brought up short with the question: "Which of these three, do you think, proved neighbor . . .?" It is a question on which the Jew chokes. The lawyer in the Lucan account cannot bring himself to pronounce the name of that hated "neighbor," but he can hardly avoid the answer which the parable demands.

The Samaritan is undoubtedly the primary shock, although the behavior of the priest and Levite will raise preliminary resistance in certain quarters, nodding approval in others. The first sentences of the story evoke a silent "Yes, that's how it is" from everyone, but the clerics will already have begun their retreat with their own appearance. Nevertheless, the subsequent development overwhelms first reactions and brings the Jewish audience together again in a common crisis. Only the destitute and outcasts weather the second onslaught; they alone are untouched by the attack.[64]

When it is asked why Jesus chose the Samaritan as the central figure in the parable, it is simply not satisfactory to answer that the Samaritan is merely a model of neighborliness. For in that case the parable is reduced to a commonplace[65] and its bite completely vitiated. Rather, the Samaritan is the one whom the victim does not, could not expect would help, indeed does not want help from. The literal, i.e., historical, significance of the Samaritan is what gives the parable its edge. In this respect the Samaritan is a *secular* figure; he functions not as an esoteric cipher for a religious factor as Gerhardsson thinks, but in his concrete, everyday significance. On the other hand, the Samaritan is brought into a constellation in which he cannot be anticipated. It is this surprising, odd turn which shatters the realism, the everydayness of the story. A narrative begun with all the traits of an experience about which everyone knows, or assumes to know, is ruptured at the crucial juncture by a factor which does not square with everyday experience. The "logic" of everydayness is broken upon the "logic" of the parable. It is the juxtaposition of the two logics that turns the Samaritan, and hence the parable, into a metaphor.

Metaphor directs the hearer's attention, not to this or that, but to the whole background and foreground of the event by means of imaginative shock; it does so by virtue of the fact that it does not allow the figure or narrative picture to come to rest in the literal meaning. Metaphor seizes a focal actuality which it loosens from its moorings in everydayness in order to descry its penumbral actuality or field;[66] the latter is disclosed to the imagination by means of metaphor. If it is the literal meaning of Samaritan that provides the initial jolt to the everyday mentality embodied in the story, it is the nonliteral meaning that triggers, through the parable, a whole new vista—i.e., the penumbral field. In sum, comprehending the figure and the parable depends upon grasping the literal and nonliteral meanings concomitantly.[67]

The nonliteral or metaphorical horizon of the figure of the Samaritan and of the parable is suggested by the literal meaning and depends upon it. In this case, the Samaritan is both just a Samaritan and the one whom the hearers could not expect and do not wish to see on that road. The parable is both just a story of a good Samaritan and a parabolic metaphor opening onto a referential totality which is informed by a new vision of reality that shatters the everyday view.

Since the metaphor gives itself existentially to unfinished reality, so that the narrative is not complete until the hearer is drawn into it as a participant, the hearer is confronted with a situation in relation to which he or she must decide how to respond: am I willing to allow myself to be the victim, to smile at the affront to the priest and Levite, to be served by an enemy? The parable invites, nay, compels some response. And it is this response that is decisive for each hearer. Furthermore, since the parable is temporally open-ended, it is cast onto a plurality of situations, a diversity of audiences, with the consequence that it refuses ideational crystallization.[68] Every hearer has to hear it in *his* or *her* own way. The future which the parable discloses is the future of every hearer who grasps and is grasped by being in the ditch.

These considerations have prepared the way for a brief characterization of the other figures in the narrative. The victim is faceless and nameless, perhaps intentionally so, since every listener lands in the ditch. The poor traveler is literally the victim of a ruthless robber. So were the poor, the lame, the blind, and the others whom Jesus drew to his side. In fact, one has to understand oneself as the victim in order to be eligible. Furthermore, the victim is given true identity in relation to the three figures who come along the road. *How* each hearer views them determines who each is! The priest and the Levite, on the other hand, are those from whom the victim might have expected more. But they should also be considered from their own point of view. The priests and Levites in the audience can almost be heard, either protesting that they want to review the situation as the narrative pushes them by, or justifying or excusing themselves. They have the option, of course, of moving to the place of the victim or the Samaritan! In both cases the literal and metaphorical meanings must again be grasped concomitantly.

The parable has been considered thus far without raising the christological question. Gerhardsson's thesis compels us to ask whether Jesus appears in the narrative picture. Certainly not explicitly. The question can be rephrased: does Jesus appear in the *field* of the narrative picture? It would be a mistake to hasten to a positive answer. It should first be noticed that the question is restricted to Jesus, i.e., without reference to his messiahship. One is led to think, as Gerhardsson does, of Jesus as the physician, healer, shepherd who moves to the side of the destitute, tax collectors, prostitutes, sinners. The Samaritan is one who does not consider whether he has any business helping an enemy (it cuts both ways!); he does not cast an apprehensive glance around for the robbers; he does not calculate the cost or the consequences, anticipate a reward, or contemplate a result. To this extent Jesus stands behind the Samaritan. He is there in the Samaritan not as a messianic figure, but as one who lives in the "world," or under the "logic," drawn by the parable. It can of course be said that in this Jesus moves to God's side in relation to mundane reality, that he acts out of the vision of a world under "the jurisdiction of God's righteousness."[69] But to do so is to affirm that Jesus is declaring who God is, and that he is looking at the in-breaking of a kingdom nobody else sees.

If the latter is allowed to stand, then it could further be said that Jesus hovers behind the Samaritan also in the sense that he is the one whom his hearers could not expect and from whom they wanted no help, that is, so long as they refuse to be victims or to allow themselves to be helped by the alien. In that case the parable is christological, but not in the sense Gerhardsson takes it to be.

It should be recalled at this point that the parable ends by calling upon the hearer to pass judgment on the performance; no longer as victim, priest, or Levite, or even Samaritan, but as judge. From the point of view of the conclusion, the parable invites the auditor to take up a new position, this time in relation to the three named actors. Knowing the answer to the question posed hearers suspect that they have walked into the trap. Indeed they have. The parable is an invitation to comport oneself with reality in the way the Samaritan does. This should not be understood exclusively or even primarily as a moral demand to love neighbor; it is more a boon than a demand, more a grant that entitles the hearer to stake out an existence in the "world" of the parable, a "world" under the jurisdiction of God's righteousness. The right is granted by virtue of the language event which verifies the reality of that world. If, then, the hears are invited to "see" what the Samaritan "sees" and embark upon their "way," they are also invited to follow Jesus, for Jesus, as we saw, "appears" in the penumbral field of the parable as one who has embarked upon this way. Indeed, the parable bodies forth Jesus' "world," opening metaphorically as it does onto a "world" under the aegis of love. To put it succinctly, the parable is permission on the part of Jesus to follow him, to launch out into a future that he announces as God's own. In this sense, too, it is christological.

A final observation is necessary, for on it depends the "logic" set out in the preceding. Hearers are able to affirm the Samaritan and enter into his "world" only because they have first been victim: "We love, because he first loved us" (1 John 4:19).

IV

It is evident from the foregoing analysis that the parable cannot be rightly understood as a punning exegesis[70] of the Old Testament text as Gerhardsson proposes. While I would concur in his intuition that the parable requires a more adequate interpretation than modern exegetes generally have given it, and that the patristic tradition preserves, albeit in distorted form, its correct horizon, his own thesis is too ingenious, not to say palpably in contradiction to the mode of language of the parable as Jesus employs it. The real question is not the extent to which Jesus was influenced by his time and age,[71] but whether the language of Jesus, and hence his hermeneutic, is amenable to or shatters rabbinic categories.[72] The answer does depend, of course, on how one understands Jesus of Nazareth.[73]

More specifically, the everydayness (or realism) of the parable inveighs against Gerhardsson's view. On his view the narrative elements are merely ciphers. To the contrary, the metaphorical value of the narrative elements depends, paradoxically, on their everyday meaning for cogency. Gerhardsson is simply unable to cope with this aspect of the parable.

It is still possible, nevertheless, to inquire whether the parable is an interpretation of the Old Testament text (as in the Lucan context). In seeking an answer, it is necessary to begin again with the parable itself.

What is the prior question to which the parable addresses itself? Even without Luke 10:29, 36 f., I have noted, modern interpreters agree that the parable is devoted to the question of neighbor.[74] According to Bultmann, the point of the story lies in the contrast between the loveless Jew and the loving Samaritan.[75] Jülicher rightly points out that this contrast by itself does not yield the point, but rather the relation of the two to the anonymous man in need of compassion.[76] The priest and Levite represent the Jew who interprets the law correctly,[77] the Samaritan the unexpected one who misunderstands (sic) the law but understands the call of love. The parable therefore presents itself as a reinterpretation of the law on the authority of him who speaks the parable (cf. the "But I say to you" "I tell you" of the Great Sermon). The Lucan context is consequently not inappropriate to the parable.[78]

We may now consider the Lucan context. In contrast to Matthew (22:34–40) and Mark (12:28–31), who have Jesus answer the question of the first commandment, Luke puts the summary of the law in the mouth of the lawyer. Bornkamm thinks that such a summary of the essence of the law is alien to the rabbinic understanding of the law.[79] However that may be, the reduction of the law to the double commandment (cf. Matt 22:40) may well derive from Jesus. By attributing the summary to the lawyer, however, the possibility of relating the parable of the Good Samaritan to the commandment is opened up.[80] Whether or not the Lucan complex is original, the combination "brings the original sense of the double commandment of Jesus and thereby his understanding of what 'neighbor' means to expression in an incomparable way."[81] The question of the authenticity of the Lucan context is thus not decisive for a correct understanding of Jesus' intention with respect to the interrelation of commandment and parable. Luke or the tradition before him holds fast to the thrust of the parable by providing this context.[82]

It is appropriate, consequently, to consider the parable as an interpretation of an Old Testament text; specifically, of the double commandment. As an interpretation, the parable must be grasped with respect to its metaphorical field. The love of God or God's love (subjective or objective genitive) do not figure explicitly in the picture. The Samaritan does not love with side glances at God.[83] The need of neighbor alone is made self-evident, and the Samaritan responds without other motivation. At the same time, the narrative picture forces the hearer to take up the position of one in need of compassion. In so doing that person learns what "as thyself" means.[84] The hearer becomes the object of unconstrained, unmotivated mercy, at the point where one could not expect and perhaps was not willing to accept it. The narrative picture is therefore secular; God does not "appear."

While the need of neighbor is self-evident, the priest and Levite, as custodians of the law, pass by. Only the Samaritan answers the call of neighbor's need. What frees him to do so, while the other two are constrained to look away? It would be admissible to reply that the Samaritan simply saw and responded to the self-evident need of the victim in the ditch, were it not also the case that a Samaritan could not be expected to react in this way, and were it not also the case that the priest and Levite were confronted by the same pressing need. Manifest need does not of itself lay a claim on just any chance passer-by. The Samaritan, moreover, belongs to the parable (whether the narrative refers to an actual incident or not is beside the point), which means, to proceed from a trite point, that the Samaritan is there and behaves as he does by virtue of the parable. The triteness of the point should not be allowed to force the conclusion that Jesus is therefore merely telling a story. On the contrary, if the parable metaphorically discloses Jesus' world—the one he sees being invaded by love—then the Samaritan is there and behaves as he does by virtue of the parabolic world in which selfless response to neighbor's need is the thing to do, is taken for granted. The Samaritan in the narrative picture has this freedom, the freedom to risk all, to proceed with his love unhurried, deliberately. The parable itself gives him this freedom.

To say that the parable grants the Samaritan the freedom to act out of love is to shift the question to another sphere, viz., the sphere of language, and to direct attention away from the Samaritan to those who are listening to the story. The parable is indeed language and it has to do not with a Samaritan, but with Jesus' auditors. The parable as word leads, according to the Lucan context, to the call for action: "Then go and do the same yourself" (Luke 10:37). However misleading the moralistic interpretation of the parable may be, it has the virtue of calling attention to the event-character of what transpires in the parable and, as a consequence, of what is intended to transpire in the listeners. The deficiency of the moralistic view is that it does not grasp the primal word-character of the event. Remarkably enough, the Samaritan goes about his compassion wordlessly. For all that his act is no less language event. It is language event in that it "bespeaks" that which precedes, evokes, permits love. The Samaritan discloses in wordless deeds the world in which love as event is indigenous, a world that is made present, to those attending, in the deedful words of the parable. Ebeling puts the word-character of deeds succinctly:

> Man's deeds have word-character. It can be learned from them whether he has understood something of the situation in which he finds himself, or whether he completely misunderstands it. It can become plain from a man's deeds—more clearly and more convincingly than his words—what is in the man. A very ordinary deed can be uncommonly eloquent and significant. It can awaken hope and plunge into despair, it can—not in its immediate effect as a deed, but in its effect on the understanding, and thus in its word-effect—open up a whole world, but also destroy a world.[85]

Insofar as the Samaritan's deeds "communicate" his world to those attending the parable, i.e., insofar as his world arrives for them and they are led to it, the parable is a language event that shapes their future decisively. It is precisely its word-character that makes it an event of radical significance. As Jüngel puts the announcement of the parable, "The reign of God is as near you as the Samaritan to the one threatened by death."[86] The reign of God is as near as the parable, in which it may provisionally arrive. The parable thus forges an eschatological unity of promise and demand.[87]

It was remarked earlier that the parable draws a narrative picture that is wholly secular: neither God nor his Messiah "appears," and the Samaritan responds to the need of neighbor without ulterior reasons. Nevertheless, it must now also be said that the reign of love—to use a "secular" term—has drawn near for the Samaritan too, as it were. He has taken up his abode in a world where the plight of neighbor, in and out of itself, draws a net of love around the co-humanity of the two. Love's drawing near for him is thus language event. The con-text for co-humanity is established as love, not by virtue of any necessity attaching to neighbor's need, arising out of natural law, or attendant upon his own religious or moral drives, but merely on the basis that the man in the ditch becomes the occasion for love to come into play. The language event which grounds the Samaritan's action precedes the language event which the parable may become for its hearers. Only when language event has taken place, can language event take place. That Jesus belongs to the penumbral field of the parable as the one who lurks behind the Samaritan and dwells in his world provides the justification for reading the parable christologically: in Jesus God has drawn near as love, which gives Jesus the right to pronounce that drawing near upon the world in parable.

With respect to the Lucan context, it follows that Jesus does not allow the lawyer's question (and ours) to dominate the parable, for the lawyer's question is an effort to hold the question of neighbor at arm's length, and hence the force of the commandment. From the perspective of the parable, the question "Who is my neighbor?" is an impossible question.[88] The disjunction between question and answer, considered so grievous by Jülicher and those who have followed him, far from being inimical to the parable, is necessary to the point.[89] This means also that Jesus does not allow the law to dominate love as God's drawing near. Rather, Jesus proclaims the law in a context qualified by the event of divine love and interprets it with the help of the concrete instance of love's needfulness.[90] Jesus thus brings the question of neighbor near in its own right, i.e., as a self-evident question,[91] but makes it impossible to give the right answer except out of the event of grace in his own person and word. "The law now says [in the proclamation of Jesus], with your permission, look, I stand on the side of love! I allow you your righteousness. That is the sense, e.g., of the double commandment of love of God and neighbor (Mark 12:28–34 and parallel)."[92]

For Jesus the law labored under severe handicaps. It had been confined to a field in which God was ostensibly present but from which he was actually remote. The scribes and Pharisees sought to relate it to everyday existence in countless ways, but it grew less relevant with each step. Rabbinic interpretation of the law sought to engage the Jew, but ended by disengaging from reality. Jesus attempted nothing less than to shatter the whole tradition that had obscured the law. To put it in a way that is still enigmatic, but in the way the parable suggests, Jesus had to interpret the law in parable.[93]

The Good Samaritan
as Metaphor

Literary and biblical critics have always deemed it important to determine the kind of language being used in any text to be interpreted. In some cases this is crucial. For example, the argument over whether the tale of the Good Samaritan (Luke 10:30–35) is a parable or an example story can be settled only in conjunction with determining the nature of the language. The view advocated here is that the Good Samaritan is metaphorical and therefore not an example story (see the previous chapter in this collection). This understanding runs counter to both ancient and modern traditions of interpretation. John Dominic Crossan has joined the battle on the side of metaphor, while Dan Via has supported the older view with structuralist arguments.[1]

The Good Samaritan is a particularly interesting case because the story is felt to be a powerful symbol in the Jesus tradition, yet it is taken literally by most interpreters. Linked to this is the timely question whether metaphor is native to the modern positivistic mentality, or whether it constitutes an endangered species among classic modes of speech. In any case, the determination of the language of the Good Samaritan would be an important contribution to biblical criticism.

Traditionally, the parables in the Jesus tradition were taken either as example stories (models of right behavior) or as allegories (coded theologies). Even after the revolutionary work of Adolf Jülicher and his successors, the most influential of whom were C. H. Dodd and Joachim Jeremias, the parables were understood as example stories or as illustrations of a point that could have been made, without essential loss, in discursive, non-figurative language. In all these cases, the parables were understood literally: as example stories, they were taken as literally literal

From *Parables and Presence,* 1982.

and, as allegories and illustrations, they were understood to be literally figurative.

The literal understanding of figurative language implies that something conceptually known and statable is to be communicated by means of non-literal language: the figure is a vehicle for a univocal tenor. The metaphor, by contrast, is the means by which equivocal, because pre-conceptual, knowledge is discovered to both speaker (writer) and hearer.

The parable as metaphor thus has an altogether different locus in language, and it was as metaphor that the parables originally functioned, in my judgment. It is not possible to discuss here why, in the transmission of the tradition, the metaphorical horizon of the parables of Jesus—of all parables, not just the Good Samaritan— was lost. That is a very interesting question, however, and its answer might throw light on our own interpretive dilemma.

The parable communicates in a non-ordinary sense because the knowledge involved in the parable is pre-conceptual: it is knowledge of unsegmented reality, of an undifferentiated nexus, of a seamless world. Conceptual knowledge is knowledge of reality segmented, differentiated, classified. Knowledge communicated by the parable lies at the threshold of knowledge as commonly understood.

The parable does not, therefore, involve a transfer from one head to another of information or ideas about an established world. In the parable reality is aborning; the parable opens onto an unfinished world because that world is in course of conception. This means that both narrator and auditor *risk* the parable; they both participate in the narrative and venture its outcome. He or they do not tell the story; *it* tells *them.*

These generalizations, and others that could be made, are derivative; their source is a concrete example.

The parable of the Good Samaritan is commonly understood as an example story. Everyone knows its "meaning," including the synoptic writer, Luke, who included it in his Gospel. Jesus is asked: who is my neighbor? He answers: a neighbor is someone who helps another in need. The parable therefore makes the good Samaritan an example of what it means to be a neighbor. There is no figurative element in the parable, and the parable is taken as commending this kind of behavior.

It is quite possible that the parable can legitimately be read in this way. But I believe it can also be read as a parable, and specifically as a parable of grace. The primary reason for my conviction is this: *the parable does not invite the hearer to view it as an example of what it means to be a good neighbor.*

Every narrative is constructed so that the reader views events from a certain perspective. Put differently, a narrative is a device to make the audience observers.[2] The key question in determining whether the Samaritan is literal or metaphorical is how the parable places the auditors in relation to the events of the narrative.

A glimpse of the original register of the parable can perhaps be evoked by a fresh "reading" of the parable. By "reading" is meant "placing the auditor," by means of "criticism," so that he/she is enabled to attend the parable in the appropriate key. A "critical reading" of the parable is thus an effort to allow the narrative itself to "place" the hearer.

The parable runs as follows:

> This fellow was on his way from Jerusalem down to Jericho when he fell into the hands of robbers. They stripped him, beat him up, and went off, leaving him half dead. Now by coincidence a priest was going down that road; when he caught sight of him, he went out of his way to avoid him. In the same way, when a Levite came to the place, he took one look at him and crossed the road to avoid him. But this Samaritan who was traveling that way came to where he was and was moved to pity at the sight of him. He went up to him and bandaged his wounds, pouring olive oil and wine on them. He hoisted him onto his own animal, brought him to an inn, and looked after him. The next day he took out two silver coins, which he gave to the innkeeper, and said, "Look after him, and on my way back I'll reimburse you for any extra expense you have had."

The lead clauses in each section will indicate how the narrative places the auditor.

A fellow was on his way from Jerusalem down to Jericho. . . .

The first question is: who is this anonymous man going down the road? The question arises because the narrative is a piece of every-dayness which commands the immediate recognition and assent of the auditors. Naturally, this man is any Jew, like those in the audience, who has traveled that dangerous, precipitous road many times, or at least has heard stories of the robbers who lurk there. The listeners are anxious for him; they are not surprised when he is waylaid by robbers. The scene is well known and the listeners are able to respond with a certain recognition: "Yes, that's the way it is on the Jericho road."

The initial perspective therefore draws the listener into the narrative on the side of the victim in the ditch: they sympathize with him, shuddering at the danger because they know the story is true to life and, as a consequence, they take up a vantage point in the ditch to await developments.

From the ditch the victim observes

by coincidence a priest . . . went out of his way to avoid him . . .

As the man lying in the ditch, the auditors are nevertheless alert to what transpires next.

The listeners who are clerical or have clerical sympathies hesitate: they ask for a delay in the proceedings to consider whether they like the turn of events. They want to protest, not because the behavior depicted is not natural, but because callous indifference is being attributed to those who might have legitimate reason to act differently (ritual defilement, for example—let's disarm the point). But the story does not pause. It moves immediately to a new figure coming down the road.

The anti-clerical interests in the audience applaud. Exactly what one would expect of the clergy, they say to themselves.

It is to be noted that those belonging to the religious establishment identify with the priest and thus resent being so (rightly) represented. Those excluded from the religious establishment have their opinions of priests and so watch the priest pass by with glee—from the ditch. The auditors have now been divided into two groups: one retains the perspective of the victim, the other moves away—down the road.

Then

a Levite also avoids him . . .

This sub-scene reinforces the previous scene with its attendant reactions. The righteous have become angry; the religious outcasts begin to snicker. The first group is being herded down the road, reluctantly, on the other side; the second is lolling mirthfully in the ditch, having forgotten the beating and the robbery.

Neither group is prepared for

a Samaritan moved to pity . . .

The account of the Samaritan is relatively the longest part of the narrative and deliberately so. The Samaritan was the mortal enemy of the Jew because he was a half-brother. His appearance as friend sows confusion everywhere: all auditors are Jews. Particularly dismayed are those in the ditch, the religiously outcast, because they have been snickering and because they are now being lavishly befriended. A smile comes momentarily to the faces of the clerics as the spotlight shifts from them. But only momentarily. The narrator looks around to see whether a smile lingers on any face for more than a moment.

A Jew who was excessively proud of his blood line and a chauvinist about his tradition would not permit a Samaritan to touch him, much less minister to him. In going from Galilee to Judea, he would cross and recross the Jordan to avoid going through Samaria. The parable therefore forces upon its hearers the question: who among you will permit himself or herself to be served by a Samaritan? In a general way it can be replied that only those who have nothing to lose by so doing can afford to do so. But note that the victim in the ditch is given only a passive role in the story. Permission to be served by the Samaritan is thus inability to resist. Put differently, all who are truly victims, truly disinherited, have no choice but to give themselves up to mercy. The despised halfbreed has become the instrument of grace: as listeners, the Jews choke on the irony.

In the traditional reading of the parable the significance of the Samaritan has been completely effaced: the Samaritan is not a mortal enemy, but a good fellow, the model of virtuous deportment. Further, the auditors were no longer Jews but goyim. These are just two reasons the parable soon lost its original resonances.

To summarize: if the auditor, as Jew, understands what it means to be the victim in the ditch in this story, he/she also understands what the kingdom is all about.

Understand in the context of parable means to be drawn into the narrative as the narrative prompts, to take up the role assigned by the narrative. The parable is therefore also an invitation to comport oneself as the story indicates: it does not suggest that one behave as a good neighbor like the Samaritan, but that one become the victim in the ditch who is helped by an enemy. Indeed, the parable as metaphor was meant to be permission to so understand oneself. The metaphor is permission because it gives reality that shape.

The meaning of the parable cannot be made more explicit because it is non-literal: it lacks specific application.

The parable does not dictate the outcome: although auditors are prompted, they may be drawn into the story as they will. That applies both to those privileged religiously and to the religiously disinherited. The terms of the story, in other words, are not literal. Everyone is invited to smile. Anyone may move over into the ditch.

The "meaning" of the parable is the way auditors take up roles in the story and play out the drama. Response will vary from person to person and from time to time. The parable is perpetually unfinished. The story continues to tell itself, to "tell" its hearers.

It is possible, to be sure, to reflect on the parable as metaphor and endeavor to raise its meaning into discursive language. To do so on the basis of the reading just given, however, results in an abstract interpretation quite unlike the traditional meaning assigned to the parable. For one thing, the abstract language should retain some of the metaphorical quality of the parable itself. With these precautions in mind, the parable of the Good Samaritan may be reduced to two propositions:

1. In the Kingdom of God mercy comes only to those who have no right to expect it and who cannot resist it when it comes.
2. Mercy always comes from the quarter from which one does not and cannot expect it.

An enterprising theologian might attempt to reduce these two sentences to one:

1. In the kingdom mercy is always a surprise.

Part Three

Sauntering Through the Parables

The Leaven

Away-from-here as Destination

Biblical criticism is a species of literary criticism. If the range and function of literary criticism were clearer, that remark would be more illuminating than it is. Yet in spite of the ambiguity of terms, the correlation is suggestive.

Even the most rudimentary literary criticism ought to address two questions at the outset, basic questions that occur to the interested novice: Which writings merit my attention as a serious reader? How does my "reading" move from an uncritical to a critical level? A reliable guide to what is worthy of attention amidst the deluge of printed matter that assaults the optical nerves is alone worth the price of tuition. Even after the sorting has been made, it may not be immediately evident to all why a particular piece merits close reading and reflections. All of which is to say, how a piece, or text, is to be read and whether it is worth reading in the first place are not unrelated questions.

The literary critic, according to George Steiner, has these two functions: the first task is to "prepare the context of future recognition;" the second is to widen and complicate the map of sensibility.[1] The present reader is taught to see what is really there to be seen; failing the adequate transformation of present sensibility, the critic must lay the ground for delayed recognition. Criticism is a derivative enterprise, but without it the poet would not survive to be appreciated by subsequent readers.

The biblical corpus is large enough to warrant, even require, selective attention. And because it has suffered overattention, its language has been overlaid with tons of obfuscating debris. To change the metaphor, few literary compendia in the Western tradition have been so completely rinsed of resonances by the waters of endless repetition and uncritical interpretation. Is it possible to

---

From *Jesus as Precursor*, 1975, rev. 1994.

restore some of those resonances or cart away some of that debris? If so, what is the appropriate critical methodology?

One thing may be stipulated by way of anticipation: the methodology must be appropriate to the subject matter.

Away-from-here
The point of departure

The first question that naturally arises in connection with the interpretation of any text is: Where does one begin? Like the reticent apprentice approaching a computer for the first time, the student learning to interpret a text finds that the most difficult and foreboding task of all is "getting started." Once the opening hurdle has been cleared, however, most students are able to continue apace without fear of final failure, despite occasional faltering.

There is a point in the last remark: the way the task of interpretation is undertaken is determinative for the whole process. The *undertaking* anticipates what is to be *overtaken*. Methodology is not an indifferent net; it catches only what it is designed to catch. For this reason, phenomenology has been preoccupied with the methodology, but not as an enterprise independent of the subject matter. The slogan, "to the things themselves," suggests that the subject matter itself should be permitted to propose the terms of its unconcealment.

The question of methodology may be left vague for the moment. To return to the initial question: where does one begin? All interpreters begin where they must. *Interpreters must set out from where they are.* Where they are, of course, is their particular times and places in history in relation to the text under scrutiny.

The naiveté of this common-sense reply should not deceive. In the first, place, it is no easy matter to determine precisely where one is. Writing the history of the last fifty years is always the most hazardous task. The future of these years has not yet fallen out into the sunlight of historical distance. In the second place, the advice presupposes that where one is in relation to the interpretation of a given text involves a misunderstanding, or a non-understanding of that text. There would be no need for fresh interpretation were it not assumed that previous interpretation was in some respects inadequate or deficient.

To put the difficulties concisely: one is to set out from where one is, with the candid acknowledgement that one's current location cannot be defined with full precision; from that place one undertakes to move away from some unspecified misunderstanding or non-understanding in the direction of some as yet unspecified understanding. The as yet unspecified understanding must comport authentically with both the subject matter of the text one is interpreting and with the context in and for which the text is to be interpreted. A text without a context is a pretext.

To mark the way to this elusive destination the map has not yet been drawn. When the knowledge requisite to the map is in hand, there will no longer be any need for the map. Meanwhile, only the direction of the quest is certain: it is away-from-here, away from established understanding, which to some extent entails misunderstanding and non-understanding.

The real gravity of the dilemma may now be discerned: how can the text propose the terms of its unveiling when the terms themselves are dependent upon a glimpse of the text already unveiled? *Mis*understanding and *non*-understanding can give way to understanding only when the *mis* and the *non* are exposed by some new understanding.

Getting underway, consequently, is of crucial importance. The appropriate analysis will proceed circumspectly; it will endeavor to coax the text into betraying its own horizon by contesting the subject matter with the text. At the same time, it will look for the stray clue dropped inadvertently along the way, a by-product of the critical wrestling with the history of interpretation.

It may prove lucrative to advance these preliminary abstractions as a down payment on the analysis of a concrete text. Like everyone else, I would prefer a biblical text that is relatively free of ambiguities; but, alas, such a text is not to be found. Since ambiguity and complexity characterize every text, brevity will have to supply the virtue. For reasons that will eventually emerge, I have chosen for scrutiny the parable or similitude of the Leaven, taken from the Jesus tradition.

The parable of the Leaven is reported by Matthew and Luke in a form without significant variation:

> Heaven's imperial rule is like leaven
> which a woman took and concealed in fifty pounds of flour
> until it was all leavened. —Matt 13:33//Luke 13:20 f.

The parable is presumably derived from Q and is reported in both cases as a twin to the parable of the Mustard Seed.[2]

The Gospel of Thomas preserves a slightly different version:

> The Father's imperial rule is like a woman
> who took a little leaven,
> hid it in dough,
> and made it into large loaves of bread. —Thom 96:1–2

Most interpreters of Thomas hold that this version does not represent a significant alternative to the version found in Matthew and Luke.

In accordance with sound scholarly practice, and as a means of locating approximately where the modem interpreter is, one ought to begin by sampling the history of recent interpretation. Joachim Jeremias, the oracle of modern parable interpretation, who is read and quoted on both sides of the Atlantic, avers that the meaning of this parable, like that of the Mustard Seed, is that "out of the most insignificant beginnings, invisible to human eye, God creates his mighty empire, which embraces all the peoples of the world." For Jeremias the parable is a parable of contrast: the "tiny morsel of leaven" is "absurdly small in comparison with the great mass of more than a bushel of meal." The parable is aimed at overturning the doubts of those who hesitated to believe that God's domain could issue from the insignificant beginnings of Jesus' ministry. It is therefore what Jeremias calls a parable of assurance.[3]

Jeremias interprets the Leaven jointly with the Mustard Seed because, he says, the two are closely linked by content. He admits that their juxtaposition in the Sayings Gospel Q may derive from a collector or redactor. One may wonder whether the compiler of Q has not in fact skewed the interpretation of one or both of the parables by placing them together. In any case, Jeremias appears to have determined that the connection is valid.

In a somewhat earlier work, C. H. Dodd toys with the idea that the Leaven should be interpreted without reference to the Mustard Seed. If taken independently of its Q context, he claims, it means that Jesus' ministry is comparable to leaven working in dough: it works from within, without external coercion, "mightily permeating the dead lump of religious Judaism. . . ." If it goes with the Mustard Seed, then "the emphasis must lie upon the completion of the process of fermentation. The period of obscure development is over; . . . the Kingdom . . . has now come." In either case, Dodd's reading substantiates his thesis that God's rule is here and now present and effective.[4]

This sample of opinion may be augmented by notice of one other ranking scholar of parables.

Adolf Jülicher is the father of all recent parable interpretation. In his mammoth two-part work, published in 1899 and 1910, he not only reviews the history of interpretation but establishes the guidelines that parables are to be stripped of all allegorical overlay and interpreted in accordance with one point of the broadest possible (moral) application.[5]

For Jülicher's one generalized moral, A. T. Cadoux, another scholar of the parables, Dodd, and Jeremias all propose to substitute one particular point of historical application, namely, the point that best suits Jesus' historical setting. In other respects, however, they agree with Jülicher that the parables score a didactic point that can readily be reduced to discursive language. Put differently, they agree that whatever Jesus meant to say in his striking stories and enigmatic metaphors can be restated in prosaic terms suitable for Sunday School literature of the elementary sort. Once Jülicher launched modern interpretation on that trajectory, the search for that one elusive point of particular historical application has gone on relentlessly. However, the search has not resulted in substantial agreement about what that point might be.

With the rejection of allegory, the details of the picture or narrative were reduced to incidental features of the parable. Determine the point, it is said, and the details fall into place. But how is one to determine the point without first ascertaining what detail or which details are the vehicle of the point? According to Jeremias, the parable contrasts insignificant beginnings with great issue. The tiny morsel of leaven is thus contrasted with the huge mass of dough. How do we know that it is just these two details which convey the point, while the leaven and the dough themselves are incidental? Again, Dodd fastens on the process of fermentation as the clue to the point: like leaven working in dough, God's imperial rule works in the world or in Judean religion. Dodd has elected quite a different detail from which to adduce his point, and, one might suppose, with equal justification, since the process of selection appears to be arbitrary. Alternately, Dodd can fix on the leavened lump of dough as a sign of the kingdom's arrival. In either case, he is following Jülicher's fundamental maxim: one point corresponding more or less to one detail of the narrative or picture. Jeremias, by contract, often sneaks in two or more details in order to win his single point.

The only "single point" that seems clear from this diversity of interpretation is that the parable may have more than one entrance to its "meaning," more than one interpretive fulcrum to open up its sense.

Dodd and Jeremias are struggling with Jülicher's legacy without realizing they have been trapped by it. Instead of recovering the parable by discarding allegory, they have been thrown into anarchy: choose a detail, any detail, and draw the point. The point drawn is as reliable as the choice of detail, or as reliable as the (implicit) theology informing the point that prompts the choice of detail.

Jülicher's legacy is a trap because he was never able to escape from the allegory he so fervently rejected. For him and his successors parable interpretation is a form of reduced allegory; instead of many points corresponding to a variety of details, there is only one point corresponding to one, or a pair of details.

Parable interpretation is at an impasse. The way forward is away-from-here.

Away-from-there
Sedimented and refracted language

The ultimate point of departure in addressing a text is away-from-here, which is the interpreter's locus within the history of interpretation. The penultimate point of departure is away-from-there, which is the author's locus within his or her own linguistic tradition. The former has already been addressed. Attention may now be given to the justification and exposition of the latter.

As a tradition matures, its myths, symbols, and lexical stock, its semantic logic, are crystallized. The meanings evoked by the terms of a culture are sedimented. The crystallization and sedimentation of a tradition constitute the immediate background within which and against which one speaks or writes the language. If one simply traffics in the sedimented tradition, one merely repeats what is already contained in the language. Under these circumstances, the text produced is rightly interpreted within the framework of the sedimented or dictionary meanings of the terms.

The dictionary represents a tacit social compact to which all speakers must subscribe if they wish to speak intelligibly. Yet even the most halting speaker or writer has learned to manipulate a finite system of grammatical and semantic variables, so as to be able to produce, potentially, an infinite string of novel sentences. No speaker or writer, no matter how inexperienced, ever simply repeats what is already contained in the language. As a matter of fact, the semiliterate and illiterate constantly produce novel sentences in daily parlance that infringe the established grammatical and semantic conventions. Only the fully literate have any real prospect of trading in fully sedimented speech because only they are sufficiently familiar with the conventions to be able unerringly to rehearse them.

This point should be kept in mind as a rejoinder to those who hold that Jesus trafficked in the sedimented language of Judean religion *because he was unliterary*, perhaps even *illiterate*.

There is another reason sedimented speech is essentially unstable. A pure recapitulation of the tradition is a task of herculean, if not divine, proportions, as any good historian can attest. History does not pause sufficiently long to allow one to repeat even the same string of linguistic symbols without the temporal passage taking its modifying toll. What is said in one moment is modified when reiterated in the next by the same speaker just because the "I" of the speaker has shifted its temporal locus.

The unrepeatability of the tradition is a limiting concept of no little significance, but it is not the immediate issue.

The creative writer, in contrast to the hack or gossip, employs language as a means of refracting language. If one aspires to say something new, one must seek some exit from the vicious circle of sedimented meaning, and this exit is provided for by a deformation of the tradition. The writer cannot begin with new language, but must begin with the habituated language at hand, with the language learned at mother's knee. But that same aspiring poet may succeed in moving away from those sedimentations and finding a personal voice. The measure of success is commensurate with the degree to which one has infringed the semantic compact represented by the dictionary.

Away-from-there as the penultimate point of departure means, consequently, that the interpreter must work *out of* the sedimented tradition as received by the author of a given text. The interpreter must then work *into* the refraction or deformation of that tradition, as the author in question brings the tradition to speech afresh. What is distinctive about an individual speaker or writer cannot be known until both the *out of* and the *into* are identified.

These generalities should now be put to the test of a specific parable.

From this distance (from first-century Palestine) the parable of the Leaven looks featureless and flat. The simple sketch does not strike one as particularly poignant; in fact, it probably does not strike the modern reader at all. One may conclude that the parable is trite or insipid and let it go at that. Another possibility is that modern sensitivities have gone dead. On the other hand, if the parable itself has undergone domestication in the language tradition, then what is at issue is the deliverance of the parable into the hands, into the ears, of those who can hear it as though for the first time. How does one overcome the deafness that impedes first-time hearing?

Two procedures are immediately open. First, one may bury oneself in the primary literature, read parables of all kinds, read texts on leaven, baking, and the like, and even read texts that have no apparent connection with the subject matter of this parable. The object will be to reacclimate oneself to the sedimented tradition of that time and place, with a view to "listening in" on the lost resonances of our text. Secondly, one may scan the secondary literature for items which show us, "appear," but do not converge with the interpreter's view of the parable. Such items may prove to be important as clues to both away-from-here and away-from-there on the grounds that they have not been assimilated to what the parable is taken to mean. Ideally, one should combine the two procedures.

Consider the parable sentence once again:

Heaven's imperial rule is like leaven
which a woman took and concealed in fifty pounds of flour
until it was all leavened.

What items in the sentence stand out against the background of language sedimented "there"? Which items attract attention "here"? Which items show up as residual problems in the history of interpretation?

The scene is common enough. Anyone who has observed bread made, here or in the Near East, recognizes the scene for what it is: a piece of everydayness.

Well then, what clues are there beyond an undifferentiated common picture of a woman kneading dough for bread?

1. Even to the English reader the word conceal may sound odd in the context of putting yeast into dough. In what sense does she "conceal" the leaven? Jülicher is of the opinion that "conceal" may have struck Matthew as appropriate to the situation of Heaven's imperial rule in the world at the time he wrote: it is concealed from the eyes of most. However, Jülicher goes on to say that κρύπτω (kryptō) may also have been employed in a completely faded sense, meaning merely to *put* or *place in*. But the evidence he cites is slender.[6] The word normally conveyed the nuance of *conceal, secret, cover*. Other scholars avoid the question by averring that leaven is hidden in dough in the sense of disappearing in it, of becoming one with the dough it leavens. Dodd proposes that leaven is hidden in that, at first, nothing appears to happen;[7] it is there, no longer with its own identity, but without apparent effect. This view is perhaps supported by the final phrase: "until the whole was leavened."

We hear elsewhere in the language of Jesus of things pertaining to God's imperial rule being "hidden": the Father has *hidden* things from the wise and understanding (Matt 11:25; Luke 10:21); God's imperial rule is likened to a treasure *hidden* in a field (Matt 13:44); indeed the mystery of God's imperial rule is hidden in the parables themselves (cf. Mark 4:11 ff.). If hiddenness belongs to the essence of God's domain, as Günter Bornkamm maintains,[8] it is not surprising that the suggestion turns up in various contexts. In this case, the reader may have to do with a word deliberately chosen so as to vibrate in its context and thus attract attention, obliquely because metaphorically, to some horizon of the subject matter.

2. Although lost on the reader of traditional English translations, the unusual amount of flour (50 pounds) involved in "three measures"* would not have been lost on the original audience. The exaggerated amount has been a constant irritant to modem scholarship, especially to those who wish to affirm the everyday realism of the parables.

The precise value of the σάτον (*saton*) (Hebrew, *seah*) translated "measure," is not known. It may have amounted to as much as one and one-half pecks, or as little as two-tenths of a bushel. The total amount may then have been slightly more than a half-bushel, or slightly more than a full bushel. Jeremias estimates three *seah* as about fifty pounds of flour, or enough to make bread for more than a hundred persons. In any case, we have to do with a "party" baking, as C. W. F. Smith puts it, or with preparations for a festive occasion of significant proportions.

Jeremias takes advantage of the large amount of dough in contrasting it with the "tiny morsel of leaven," yet he suggests that the number "three" may be an eschatological touch added by Matthew and Luke. Support for the omission is afforded by the Gospel of Thomas, where the amount of meal is not specified. Perhaps the strongest argument for regarding the number as a gloss is that it constitutes a parallel to the "tree" in the Mustard Seed, which is almost certainly a modification of an original "shrub" or "bush," under the influence of the figure of the towering cedar in Ezekiel 17, 31 and Daniel 4.

These arguments are not without force. Nevertheless, there are even better reasons for retaining "three measures" as part of the original parable. These may be stated succinctly.

In the Mustard Seed, the smallness of the seed is emphasized, but not the size of the mature tree. The mustard plant constitutes a burlesque of the mighty cedar of Lebanon, a symbol for the mighty

---

*Editor's Note: "three measures is the literal and traditional interpretation, while "50 pounds" is the translation of Scholars Version translation.

empires of the earth. If the Leaven were precisely parallel, we would expect the smallness of the leaven to be emphasized. But that is not in fact the case. "Leaven" is not qualified at all. What is qualified is the unusual amount of dough, and this comports well with Jesus' tendency elsewhere to indulge in comic exaggeration (e.g., hiring laborers at the eleventh hour, the elaborate celebration for the lost son, the swollen size of the forgiven debt). That is to say, the parable of the Leaven is devoid of comic exaggeration if the amount of flour is secondary expansion.

Jeremias' suspicions were raised initially in this connection because of an Old Testament parallel. In Genesis 18, Yahweh visits Abraham by the oaks of Mamre in the form of three men. Abraham wishes to entertain his visitors with a "morsel of bread" on the occasion of this epiphany. He instructs Sarah to knead "three measures of fine flour" and from it make cakes (Gen 18:6).

A three-measure baking is thus suitable as an offering for an epiphany.

Gideon's experience at the oak of Ophrah parallels Abraham's at the oaks of Mamre.[9] Gideon prepares a kid—Abraham, a calf (Gen 18:7)—and unleavened cakes from an ephah of flour (Judg 6:19). An ephah is comprised of three *seim* or three measures. Again, the amount is suitable for the celebration of an epiphany.

It may also be noted in passing that when Hannah dedicates Samuel at the house of the Lord at Shiloh, she offers, among other things, an ephah or three measures of flour (1 Sam 1:24).

The everyday realism of the parable of the Leaven appears to be shattered, then, on the gross amount of dough—about as much as a woman could knead at one time—and the specific amount is intended to suggest that the occasion is no ordinary one, perhaps even an epiphany.

3. It has been remarked that three measures of meal is associated with the epiphany or with a thank-offering to the Lord. If this overtone is taken as a clue to the horizon of the parable, one is brought back abruptly to the curious choice of the central figure of the parable. In this connection, two texts may be recalled:

> And you are to observe the feast of unleavened bread, since on this very day I brought your people out of the land of Egypt. . . . For seven days no leaven is to be found in your houses; for if any one eats what is leavened, that person will be cut off from the congregation of Israel, . . . —Exod 12:17–20

This injunction was joined by a more general injunction to the effect that leaven was prohibited in connection with sacrifices and meal offerings (Exod 23:18, 34:25; Lev 2:11, 6:17).

The second text reflects the connotations the symbol of leaven conjured up in the New Testament period (1 Cor 5:6–8). Leaven was apparently universally regarded as a symbol of corruption.[10] So pervasive was this understanding of leaven, in fact, that a number of commentators have remarked of the parable of the Leaven: "an unexpected application of a familiar illustration."

The difficulty of taking a figure predominantly associated with the "infectious power of evil" in a positive sense has often enough been observed by modern interpreters. C. W. F. Smith insists that leaven cannot be reinterpreted in a positive sense, given the sedimented understanding of the figure. And for Jesus to refract the sedimented understanding of the term in his own disposition to God's imperial rule, would be to expect too much of Jesus' hearers![11] To this assertion must be responded: did Jesus allow his understanding of God's rule to be determined by the received tradition regarding that rule?

But Smith and others are unaware of the real difficulty attached to reading the leaven in a positive sense because they have taken only perfunctory note of the sacramental overtones of the three measures of flour. Only Ernst Lohmeyer has grasped the real tension inherent in the juxtaposition. For Lohmeyer the inseparable connection between "unleaven" and the holy was so intense that the parable of the Leaven could be understood only as part of an attack on temple and cult, an attack that comports with Jesus' displacement of the righteous and pious in Israel with the poor and destitute, the tax collectors and harlots: . . . "the tax collectors and prostitutes go into God's domain, but you (religious leaders) do not" (Matt 21:31). Such an attack represents an inversion of the symbol of the unleavened and thus a refraction of the sedimented language tradition: God's imperial rule arrives as a negation of the established temple and cult and replaces them with a sacrament of its own—a new and leavened bread.

It is just possible that his horizon is preserved less obliquely in the version in Thomas, where the woman makes large loaves (leavened?) out of the dough.

The proximity of the three terms, "leaven," "conceal," "fifty pounds of flour," within the confines of the brief sentence that comprises the parable, thus reverberate against each other and against the sedimented language tradition in such a way that the parable as a whole becomes plurisignificative. The terms are so subtly arranged that the unwary may well read it as a commonplace illustration of a commonplace bit of wisdom. But for those with ears alert to ironies, the parable triggers the imagination: the terms and the whole are set free to play against one another and against the tradition. Those who have ears hear strange voices.

Mode and Meaning

Listening in on the language opens the way for a consideration of mode and meaning. The words and sentences, when allowed to have their own say—against preconceived notions of what they mean—put one on the track of the subject matter, so to speak. But the subject matter is not something else, to be divorced entirely from the words. *What* the parable says cannot be simply divorced from the *way* it says. Form and content are wedded.

God's imperial rule may be compared to leaven which a woman took and concealed in fifty pounds of flour, until it was all leavened. The leaven suggests an inversion of the locus of the sacred: there unleavened; in God's domain, leavened. Concealed hints that the presence of God's rule is not overtly discernible. Fifty pounds of flour points to the sacramental power of God's rule, to the festive occasion of an epiphany. Over against the religious tradition into which Jesus was speaking, God's imperial rule arrives as an inversion, as a mystery, and as power.

If the subject matter is characterized as mystery, then the mode of communication, if it is to be faithful to the subject matter, must convey that mystery as mystery. It may be put more strongly: the proclamation of God's imperial rule cannot very well dispel the mystery without at the same time eroding the essence of that rule. The mode of communication must be commensurate with the thing to be communicated.

God's imperial rule *is* hidden. It does not arrive with observable signs, so that people can say, "'Look, here it is!' or 'Over there!' On the contrary, God's imperial rule is right there in your presence" (Luke 17:21). And God's imperial rule is proclaimed in parables, riddles, and dark sayings so that hearing, people hear not, and seeing, they see not (cf. Mark 4:12).

Furthermore, if God's imperial rule comes as an inversion of what everybody takes to be the case with the sacred, then the terms of its proclamation will of necessity represent a refraction of sacred tradition. The last shall be first and the first last; the tax collectors and harlots go into the God's domain but the righteous Pharisees do not. The mighty cedar becomes a lowly mustard shrub, the long-awaited messiah arrives incognito. The unleavened is leavened; the holy becomes profane and the profane, holy. In sum, God's imperial rule inverts the terms of the sacred and the profane.

If the mode and meaning of Jesus' language converge in both inversion and mystery, it may be anticipated that they will converge in power also. It is this convergence that has given rise to all the talk about language event. The conjunction of mode and meaning in power may be put concisely and provisionally this way: in the parables of Jesus God's imperial rule is offered only for what it is, namely, a venture of faith undertaken on the authority of the parable, in the power of the parable. The parable authorizes God's world into which it invites the hearer, and it empowers the hearer to cross over into that fabulous yonder.

World-loss and World-gain

What does the parable authorize? In traditional language but with deliberate ambiguity, it can be said that the parable authorizes the arrival of God's imperial rule. More precisely, the parable announces a world that is on its way, much as the imperial messenger in Kafka's parable is on its way.[12] For Kafka, the imperial messenger never arrives; in Jesus he has arrived all right, but his person and message lack the court credentials for which everyone looks. God's imperial rule is therefore heralded by a messenger and in a mode both of which are unaccredited, or accredited only on their own authority.

Messenger, mode, and message, consequently, are conjoined. If one is prepared, or at least disposed, to perceive the arrival of the one, then that person is prepared to perceive all three. For this reason, it makes perfectly good sense to speak of God's imperial rule as authorized by the parable in terms of any one of its aspects. However, the message may be singled out here as the focal point.

Günther Bornkamm, in the work already cited, gives this interesting summary of the message: "To make the reality of God present: this is the essential mystery of Jesus. This making-present of the reality of God signifies the end of the world in which it takes place."[13] Observe three features of this summary: (1) Jesus makes the reality of God present; (2) this making-present is a mystery; (3) the presence of God, or the arrival of God's imperial rule, brings an end to the world in which it arrives. Attention will be focused on the last, but in so doing, something shall be noted about the first two as well.

In what sense does the arrival of God's domain bring an end to the world in which it arrives? It is customary to think of the apocalyptic pictures drawn so fancifully by Daniel, Revelation, and the little apocalypse in the Synoptic Gospels.* It is probably not possible for the modern interpreter to understand the apocalyptic mode in anything like its original sense. However, the language of Jesus directs attention to a different dimension of the question and provides fresh perspective on the problem.

What was the world into which Jesus came? To say that it was a world of sticks and stones, like one's own, is accurate but not very revealing. It is more illuminating to observe what lived world dominated the scene; to inquire after the way in which the Jews of Jesus' time and place experienced reality; to ask what referential nexus constituted the horizon of all possible experience, including the experience of God's reign.

In posing the question in this form, we are posing a phenomenological question. When Edmund Husserl stated that the world is "always already there," he meant that no one experiences an object without at the same time experiencing the horizon within which the object is located; the object is the focal point of a backlying referential nexus to which it belongs as object. As Ray Hart has put it, it is the shift in horizons that prompts one to "perceive a cow as so many pounds of beef rather than as something to be worshipped."[14] But Husserl also meant that the perceiving consciousness is also "historically constituted: what is there is there in part as the history of consciousness has programmed it to apprehend."[15] The term "world," in a phenomenological sense, refers to the fundamental horizon or referential nexus within which consciousness apprehends and things are apprehended.

The religious world into which Jesus came—to limit consideration to one aspect of that world—was a world dominated by the law and the traditions of the fathers. The received world of Judean religion in late antiquity was programmed to guard the deposit of tradition once for all delivered to Moses and the prophets, and to preserve this tradition against the day when God would restore his people to their rightful place within the economy of world history. In the meantime, God was taken to have withdrawn into the confines of sacred scripture and its interpretation by the fathers, into the temple and its cultus, into its latter day surrogate, the synagogue, and into those customs which overtly set the people of God off from the rest of humanity. Within these confines Israel was to await, by faithful and patient observance of the law, the renewal of the ancient glory. The fullness of this glory would come, it was widely anticipated, in the near future.

---

*Editor's Note: See Mark 13.

Into this world Jesus burst with his herculean wrecking bar composed of parables and aphorisms. His message can only be understood as something designed to precipitate the loss of the received world of traditional religion in favor of the gain of the world of God's imperial rule. The world in which the scribes and Pharisees were at home was shattered upon a new world designed for the poor and destitute, the tax collectors and sinners. The righteousness of the Pharisees was devalued as confederate paper. The temple and cultus were swallowed up in new forms of celebration: eating, drinking, and dancing in profane style. Sacred scripture was either ignored or criticized, and the traditions of the fathers were set down as millstones about the neck. In short, the home world of Jesus' Galilee was turned upside down in the face of the new reality of God's imperial rule.

The trauma produced by Jesus' message for those whose home world was traditional religion is difficult to exaggerate; the resistance put up by those scribes and Pharisees, for whom the loss of this world was nothing short of apocalyptic, is difficult to appreciate fully. On the other hand, the joy of the religiously disinherited, the destitute, the maimed and the blind, was spontaneous. They had been invited to inhabit a strange, new, and alien world that demanded only that they celebrate its arrival as redemption from the past and openness to the future.

Meanwhile, the world of sticks and stones had not vanished in a cloud of apocalyptic smoke. To those who participated in God's imperial rule, however, the world took a new shape, its objects hung together in a new way, and the things themselves were transformed as by a miracle. Reality itself underwent a metamorphosis. To those who refused this new reality, the world was very much the same, though perhaps less secure around the edges. These looked in vain to see what Jesus saw; what all the shouting was about they took to be senseless mystery—and from their point of view, rightly so.

In the message of Jesus, the loss of received world, the mystery of God's imperial rule, and the making-present of the reality of God are coincident. In the parable of the Leaven the coincidence is marked by the juxtaposition of "leaven" (loss of received world), "concealed" (mystery), and "fifty pounds of flour" (the presence of God). The parable thus parsimoniously encapsulates the horizons of the message of Jesus. World-gain is made concrete, is particularized, "instantiated," as the philosophers like to say (which means "made into an instance of") by the parable, as a passage for all who care to follow him.

Resedimentation
Handing the tradition around and on

According to B. T. D. Smith, the parable of the Leaven probably owes its preservation to the fact that Christians saw in it a prophecy of the spread of the gospel and the extension of the church. It would be no little irony to learn that this parable was adopted by the church because its (concealed) meaning was misunderstood. The parable is not provided with a generalizing conclusion, as is the case with a number of other parables, so that one must infer how the later church understood it from some other premise. If the Leaven was joined to the Mustard Seed subsequent to Jesus, there is basis for the inference that the metaphorical overtones of the parable were soon lost and its meaning reduced to an illustration of the infectiousness of God's imperial rule. By the time of Ignatius (early second century c.e.), the figure of the leaven appears to have stood for the contrast between Judaism and Christianity. In his letter to the Magnesians, he writes: "Put aside then the evil leaven, which has grown old and sour, and turn to the new leaven, which is Jesus Christ. Be salted in him, that none among you may be corrupted, since by your savor you shall be tested. It is monstrous to talk of Jesus Christ and to practice Judaism" (Ign Mag 10:2f.). In this case, the fuller range of overtones, the plurisignificative character of the parable, has been lost, but the interpretation has preserved in ossified form the original contrast between the new faith and the old faith.

In the case of the Mustard Seed, we may observe how the burlesque of the mighty cedar of Israel in the original parable had faded, and the mustard plant converted back into a tree. This conversion may have been accompanied by additional emphasis on the smallness of the seed, as many interpreters, including Jeremias, believe. The Mustard Seed thus became at the hands of the church a parable of contrast, contrary to the opinion of Jeremias, who attributes this meaning to Jesus. In any case, the church "reinstitutionalized" the mustard plant, just as Ignatius "reinstitutionalizes" the leaven. "Institutionalizing" in this context means that the trauma of world-loss and world-gain has receded, and world, albeit in a new sense, is once again taken for granted.

It is inevitable that world-gain be freshly institutionalized or sedimented as it becomes established as tradition. In phenomenological parlance, tradition houses "received world," the circumspective horizon of all interpretation.

The emergence of world-gain is concomitant with what Ernst Fuchs calls language-gain. New language is generated at the threshold of any new world as the means of access to and habitation in that world. Such foundational language, as it may be termed, grants the rights of passage, but it also tends to linger on in sedimented form to become the eventual instrument of eviction. The rights of passage must perpetually be renewed at the price of a recovery of foundational language or the creation of yet another new language.

The sedimentation of foundational language has as its antidote one or more modes of secondary discourse, the function of which is to cast sedimentations, or tradition, back upon primary language and the experience of world-gain concomitant therewith. Failing appropriate modes of secondary language, primary or foundational language withers away in the dungeon of sedimented meanings until its pristine power is completely eroded by the vicious winds of common parlance. There is another possibility however: foundational language may die a historical death, given a radical shift in sensibility, in spite of all appropriate efforts to recover its horizon.

Foundational language is never totally lost to view within the continuity of a tradition. If the original language of a tradition has been forgotten, then the continuity of the tradition has been broken. The memory of an original tongue may grow extremely weak, as though its call were like the pealing of a distant bell. But the sedimentations will preserve that memory, though perhaps in a petrified form. It is for this reason that secondary analysis, like that undertaken in biblical interpretation, may rediscover the wave length of foundational language, as it were, by "listening in" on that language and its sedimentations, as though from a great distance. In stumbling around for clues in the texts of the Jesus tradition and the history of interpretation, the interpreter is endeavoring to locate the trajectory of the original language by attending to the ways in which that language has "fallen out" in its subsequent history. Once on the right wave length, the alert interpreter may hope to recover something of its original horizon.

As the parables were sedimented in the Jesus tradition, their potential as parables was stopped down, their metaphorical impact muted. The potential of the parable to evoke a fresh circumspective apprehension of the totality of what is there—a new world—was reduced to a specified meaning, a point, a teaching. This meaning or teaching could then be attached to the parable as a generalizing conclusion or be divorced from the parable and transmitted as a "truth." The point drawn from the parable diverts attention from the parable itself to what it teaches, and thus from the world onto which the parable opens to an idea in an ideological constellation, or, as we might also say, in a theology.

The loss of the parable as parable means the loss also of the cardinal points on the horizon onto which the parable originally opened. The dislocating impact of the parable's seismic inversion is lost and is replaced by contrast: it is no longer a matter of passage from world-loss to world-gain, but of the contrast between one world (e.g., pagan, Jewish) and another (Christian). The mystery is decoded as teaching or truth. The parable is mined for its moral and religious propositions. And the making-present of the reality of God is exchanged for belief in God. Conversely, the recovery of the parable as parable restores the original horizon, namely, the inversion, the mystery, and the power.

The fundamental question for the interpreter who wishes to recover the Jesus tradition today is this: is it possible any longer to recover the parable as parable? Or has there been such a radical shift in context that the original horizon of the parable is beyond recovery? The answer depends upon whether the foundational language of Jesus is any longer living tradition.

Technical and Essential Literacy

The analysis has come full circle. If the circuit has not been shorted, the return to the starting point will have occurred in another plane, and the circle will have become a spiral. Even so, success may not be imminent: an analysis of this type may turn out to be just one more opinion in the pantheon of opinions, unless or until it throws the interpreters back upon the text and leaves them there in solitude to confront the text without benefit of conceptual comforts.

Whether the parable of the Leaven, or any part of the Jesus tradition, is living tradition cannot be answered in advance. The line between life and death of symbols is far too fine for certainty. A death certificate may make demise legal, but it does not make it irreversible.

Such metaphors, if resonant, suggest that the Jesus tradition has taken on the appearance of death. What George Steiner says about the classics can be said also of the Christian tradition: it is not possible to edit classical texts or write commentaries on scripture within a few kilometers of Buchenwald without some premonition that these languages no longer speak. Steiner puts it in another way: "He who has read Kafka's *Metamorphosis* and can look into his mirror unflinching may technically be able to read print, but is illiterate in the only sense that matters."[16]

Edna St. Vincent Millay suggests as much and maybe more in these closing lines from sonnet lxvii, "To Jesus on His Birthday":

> The merry bells ring out, the people kneel;
> Up goes the man of God before the crowd;
> With voice of honey and with eyes of steel
> He drones your humble gospel to the proud.
> Nobody listens. Less than the wind that blows
> Are all your words to us you died to save.
> O Prince of Peace! O Sharon's dewy Rose!
> How mute you lie within your vaulted grave.
> The stone the angel rolled away with tears
> Is back upon your mouth these thousand years.

It is a living question whether proverbial postmodern souls, within or without the church, are any longer literate in the only sense that matters with respect to the foundational language of the Christian faith.

Appropriate criticism can teach one to read texts with larger eyes, but it cannot make literate. The text alone has that power. Biblical criticism, like other literary criticism, comes anon to the end of its way: from that point anyone who aspires to literacy must go on alone.

7

The Looking-glass Tree
Is for the Birds

The Cedars of Lebanon

The mighty cedars of Lebanon crown a magnificent spine of
mountains strung serpent-like along the shores of the eastern
Mediterranean. The snowclad peaks, proud and precipitous, fall
away into the azure waters of the sea on the one side, and into the
flat, burning mirror of the desert on the other. Riding this haughty
crest, sandwiched between water and waste, the muscle-bound
trunk of the cedar silently announces its stately grandeur. The
cedar does not want for nourishment or for admiration. Even royalty appears to pay court in the shadow of its branches, including
King Solomon, the builder, with his keen and covetous eye for its
splendid timbers.

Few Israelites could fail to be impressed by the towering height
and bulk of the Lebanese cedar. The prophet Ezekiel was no exception. So compelling did he find its spell that it inspired one of his
richer metaphors.

From the unreachable heights of the cedar—so Ezekiel's vision
runs (Ezek 17:22–24)—Yahweh will take a tender twig, which he
will plant on a tall and towering mountain, on the lofty heights of
Israel. Under the watchful eye of the Lord God, the young cedar
will wax and mature, will stretch forth boughs and bear fruit. It will
furnish a haven for birds of every feather, which will make their
nests in the shade of its branches. As Ezekiel conceives it, this tree
is not a real tree; it is an apocalyptic tree, the world tree, prepared
by God, under which all humankind will eventually gather.

The noble cedar, impervious and immovable, ageless and eternal—from a human perspective—symbolizes the secular powers of
the earth. From among the tender shoots of its majestic imperturb-

From *Jesus as Precursor*, 1975, rev. 1994.

ability, Yahweh will take the tenderest and from it produce a new cedar which will bring glory to Israel. The cedar of Israel, which will provide a place of rest—the final, definitive place—for all the peoples of the earth, will stem from the lineage of the secular powers: Yahweh will create his cedar out of the stock of the secular cedar, but will make it serve his own good purpose in his own good time: redemption for his people.

Since the cedar of Israel will exceed the secular cedars in nobility and grandeur, in strength and longevity, all the trees of the forest will learn that Yahweh brings the tall tree low and exalts the low tree, that he dries up the green tree and causes the withered tree to bud. The solitary cedar of Israel will displace the secular cedars, which will shrink, by comparison, into insignificance. "I the Lord God have spoken and I will act accordingly."

The Mustard Seed

> The disciples said to Jesus, "Tell us what Heaven's imperial rule is like."
> He said to them, "It's like a mustard seed. (It's) the smallest of all seeds, but when it falls on prepared soil, it produces a large plant and becomes a shelter for birds of the sky." —Thom 20: 1–4

The parable of the Mustard Seed (Mark 4:30–32//Matt 13:31–33/ Luke 13:18–21// Thom 20:1–4) is undoubtedly to be read against the background of the symbol of the mighty cedar, a symbol utilized not only by Ezekiel, but found also in Daniel 4 and elsewhere in the Hebrew scriptures. The interplay of Jesus' mustard plant and the tradition of the symbolic tree has to be considered initially, however, in connection with the history of recent interpretation. Modern interpreters find themselves struggling with the contrast between the figure of the lofty cedar and the puny plant. By observing this struggle, it may be possible to recover the full range of overtones resonating from the original contradiction.

The emphasis on the smallness of the seed—"the smallest seed in the world"—found in parentheses in Mark (4:31)

> To what shall we compare God's imperial rule, or what parable should we use for it?
> Consider the mustard seed: When it is sown on the ground, though it is the smallest of all the seeds on the earth,—yet when it is sown, it comes up, and becomes the biggest of all garden plants, and produces branches, so that the birds of the sky can nest in its shade. —Mark 4:30–31

and echoed by Matthew (13:32) and the Gospel of Thomas (20:3), is taken by C. H. Dodd to be a secondary expansion of the parable.[1] Luke's version, which omits this emphasis and is assumed to derive from the Sayings Gospel Q,[2] Dodd holds to be original. Accordingly, he suggests that the parable has nothing to do with the contrast between insignificant beginnings and great issue, but with the capacity of the shrub to afford shelter to the birds of the heavens. The parable therefore announces that the time has come when the multitudes of Israel, perhaps even of the gentiles, will flock to God's domain as birds flock to the shelter of the tree.

It is quite possible that Mark's parenthesis, and thus the emphasis on the minute size of the seed, is secondary, as Dodd thinks. However, Dodd fails to notice that the seed in question is the mustard seed in every version of the parable that has been preserved, and that the microscopic size of this seed, with or without emphasis, was already proverbial.

The oversight of Dodd coincides with an aberration of the original parable to be found already in the gospels themselves: In Mark the seed grows into the greatest of all *shrubs,* but in Matthew and Luke it becomes a *tree.* It is hardly speculation to say that the world tree of Ezekiel and Daniel has influenced the transmission of the parable in the gospels, and that it has also shaped Dodd's perspective.

> What is God's imperial rule like? What does it remind me of? It is like a mustard seed which a man took and tossed into his garden. It grew and became a tree, and the birds of the sky roosted in its branches. —Luke 13:18–19

The theological interest in making the parable conform to the prophetic (Ezekiel) and apocalyptic (Daniel) traditions has thus been at work on the one hand, in the tendency to play down the smallness of the seed and play up the size of the mature plant, in order to bring the figure back into the vicinity of the great world tree. The parable of the Mustard Seed simply resists that strategy.

Modern botanical interests have joined the game, on the other hand, in an attempt to salvage the "realism" of the parable. Rather than have the birds come and "make their nests" in the branches of a shrub, the botanizers want the birds to "light upon" or "roost" in its branches. It is of course the case that only Matthew (13:32) and Luke (13:19) speak of birds dwelling in the *branches;* in Mark's version the birds are able to make their nests in the shade of the shrub (4:32), while in Thomas the seed becomes a large plant and provides shelter for birds (20:4). The botanists know that mustard does not grow to tree size, although it may reach a height of 8 or 10 feet. It is an annual plant, moreover, which, although fast growing, and consequently mostly hollow, would hardly provide nesting places for birds in the early spring. It seems more reasonable, then, from a botanical point of view, to say that birds come and "roost" under the mustard plant during summer, attracted seasonally, as they are, to its shade and to its seed.

The text, however, is everywhere clear: birds come and *dwell* in or under the shrub. Whether preferred or not, the parable indulges in a bit of exaggeration, hyperbole, if you will, which every common hearer, who might have been expected to know something of the mustard plant first hand, would scarcely have missed: foolish birds to take up their abode in the short-lived mustard!

The difficulties inherent in the parable merely illustrate how poorly suited the figure is to the old cedar imagery on the one hand, and to modem botanical exactness on the other. The botanists are interested, of course, in saving the everyday plausibility of the parable. Modern theological interpreters, under the spell of Daniel 4, Ezekiel 17 and 31, are interested in asserting the literal figurativeness of the parable. The interpretation of Joachim Jeremias illustrates the second position well, when he writes of the parables of the Mustard Seed and Leaven as parables of contrast: "Their meaning is that out of the most insignificant beginnings, invisible to the human eye, God creates his mighty Kingdom, which embraces all the people of the earth."[3] God's imperial rule is symbolized by the "mighty" mustard plant, which provides a haven for birds from the four corners of the heavens! Ironically, Jeremias has recapitulated Ezekiel's allegory of the cedar of Israel, with hardly a glance in the direction of the parable of the Mustard Seed. Once a tradition of parable interpretation becomes domesticated, it is extremely difficult to dislodge.

Weeds and Seeds

Dodd sees the parable as depicting the growth of the tree up to the point where it can shelter birds. It is therefore an announcement that the period of obscurity for Jesus is at an end. At the time Dodd first wrote his famous book in 1938, he and other scholars thought they could arrange some events in Jesus' life chronologically. Most scholars today doubt that the gospels preserve any actual timetable of events, beyond the grossest features, such as birth-baptism-death.

Jeremias, on the other hand, thinks that the parable sets out the fundamental contrast between the beginning and end of a process, which, he claims, is the oriental way of viewing a story. He therefore takes the parable to affirm the miraculous power of God in the face of doubts that God's domain could issue from the mission of Jesus and his disreputable band.

Of the two, perhaps Jeremias more nearly seizes the parable as parable, but he, too, finally succumbs to the enchantment of the noble cedar.

The figurative meanings assigned by Dodd and Jeremias to the parable represent what might be called the melody. It is not so much that these are false notes in themselves, as that they are not being heard in concert with second and third level overtones. The images that lie behind and inform the parable from a great distance are not registering on the ear. Scholars engaged in history reconstruction tend to become tone deaf. Partial or limited hearing betrays a recurring proclivity on the part of interpreters to reinstate an allegorical understanding of parabolic texts.

When the parable of Jesus is set alongside the vision of Ezekiel, the first impression one gains by the juxtaposition is that Jesus has created a light-hearted burlesque of Ezekiel's figure: the noble cedar, which provides a haven for birds of every feather, is caricatured as a lowly mustard plant. And the first impression is not entirely wide of the mark. At second glance, however, the parable takes on the character of serious satire. Jesus appears to have grasped the final injunction of Ezekiel's oracle radically, "The Lord will debase the lofty tree and exalt the insignificant tree." Perhaps that is the reason he states, "Those who promote themselves will be demoted, and those who demote themselves will be promoted" (Luke 14:11// Matt 23:12). The noble cedar of Lebanon, as the hope of Israel, will be quite comparable, on Ezekiel's view, to the secular cedars of the world: both will suffer debasement. But when Jesus takes up the figure, it is to conform Ezekiel's new cedar—precisely Israel's future—to God's final dictum: all cedars, including Israel's proud hope, will shrink, and the insignificant tree, indeed the ephemeral mustard weed, will be made to bear Israel's true destiny.

The kingdom as Jesus sees it breaking in will arrive in disenchanting and disarming form: not as a mighty cedar astride the lofty mountain height but as a lowly garden herb. The kingdom is asserted with comic relief: what it is and what it will do, it will be and do, appearances to the contrary notwithstanding. It will erupt out of the power of weakness and refuse to perpetuate itself by the weakness of power, to translate into Pauline terms (1 Cor 1:18–31).

The mustard plant does offer a refuge to the birds of heaven, but what a modest refuge it is—in the eyes of the world. The contrast between insignificant beginning and glorious end is a pittance paid to the grandiose pretensions of human hope. An all-too-human hubris anticipates an island paradise as the sanctuary of final rest and is given a few clumps of earth—just enough to fill in a grave. The birds, too, have their metaphorical wings clipped: what odd birds they are to flock—in modest numbers—to the shade of a seasonal plant, imagining it to be their eternal home!

If the kingdom is extended in the parable with comic relief, it is in order to offer the kingdom only for neither more nor less than what it is. It is not the towering empire many self-deceivers hope for, but an unpretentious venture. As a venture of trust, it is, of course, potentially world-transforming: "If you have trust no larger than a mustard seed, you will say to this mountain, 'Move from here to there,' and it will move" (Matt 17:20). Trust is required because the vision that informs the venture runs counter to appearances. In its unostentatious way such trust has the power to reorder the face of the world.

The parable relocates God's domain where those who insist on the everyday world cannot have access to it apart from trust. The parable is full of promise and assurance, but these become available only in the context of what that domain really is: trust enough to cross over to that 'fabulous yonder' to which the parable beckons.

The Looking-glass Tree

The parable of the Mustard Seed intends nothing less than to transform the face of Israel's hope. The transformation of a tradition is much like moving mountains by word of command: both are equally difficult to effect because both are dependent upon the power of words. Hope and mountains both belong to the map of reality which unreflective souls take to be fixed and unalterable. Because of this god-like tenacity to cling to the habituated, inhabitants of the received world find world-transforming trust all but impossible to negotiate: human beings succumb instead to the comfort of the known world. We prefer a pedestrian world, the order of which seems immutable, to a wider world, one that is subject to the linguistic caprice of the poet and prophet, and thus open to an honest-to-God future.

Among those to whom the parable of the Mustard Seed was addressed were those who reckoned their chances of participating in Israel's hope, as traditionally understood, to be good. It was too much to expect them to abandon a reasonably certain future for themselves, even if they had to purchase that future at the expense of most of their fellow human beings. The risk was too great for them, the stakes too high: they were not about to be lured away from their dream—and certainly not by an unemployed teacher, an itinerant at that, whose every other sentence smacked of blasphemy.

On the other hand, those who had no future and no prospect of one were no doubt favorably disposed to a fresh pack of cards and a new deal, if not a new frontier. Any prospect at all was better than none. Yet they, too, found it difficult to risk the future, such as it was, on such a hazardous gamble. It must have been like inviting them to flee the debtor's prison and gallows by taking a leaky, short-masted, poorly provisioned frigate for the new world, on the condition that they would welcome aboard all and sundry who wanted to go, and face the prospect of an endless voyage at sea. There were few, even among the destitute, who were desperate enough to set out. Such is and always has been the power of the old hope that besets the human breast, even when that hope is certainly beyond reach. Now as then, breaking out of the perennial cycle of desperation, aspiration, risk, and refusal demands total resignation. As Bob Dylan sings it, "When you got nothing, you got nothing to lose."[4] Only then is escape possible.

The church, no less than Israel, is wont to stumble over its hope. It seizes, solidifies, and then takes possession of its hope in the name of divinely certified reality. In so doing, it merely converts the mustard plant back into a towering cedar. As regards that hope and its encapsulation in the tradition, the parable suggests the following items for reflection:

1. Whatever the Christian hope is, the form of its realization will come as a surprise to all who think they know what it ought to be.
2. The coming of God's imperial rule will disappoint the righteous, but be a source of joy to the religiously disinherited.
3. The certainty of hope is inversely proportionate to the certainty with which the resurrection of Jesus is held to be paradigmatic of the future.
4. The promise of the future is directly proportionate to the degree that one makes no claim upon the future at all.
5. The gift of the future is the gift of gesture: the parable is a gesture toward that 'fabulous yonder' that lies on the other side.

From time to time, one gets a glimpse of that other side from this side, through the looking-glass of the parable. Jesus advances the parable as an invitation to pass through the looking-glass. Permission to pass is granted by nothing more than the parabolic gesture, the sight-enabling word that occurs between and among average human beings.

On the other side things run the other way around: the mighty cedar is brought low and the humble herb exalted. On the other side: that is to say, in the world mirrored in the looking-glass of the parable.

The Narrative Parables
The Birth of a Language Tradition

The Christian movement embodied its extant traditions in the common tongue of the Hellenistic world, Koine Greek. Yet the language of this incipient movement was not simply congruent with the Greek vernacular as attested elsewhere, however difficult it is to define the difference. The emerging tradition adapted Greek to its ends, and Greek, for its part, took the tradition to its bosom. The union gave birth to a language tradition.

In pursuing the question of the specific vernacular in which the Christian tradition took shape—and to which it, in turn, gave shape—it is necessary to move as close as possible to the fountainhead of that language tradition. Chronologically speaking, it is probably in portions of the synoptic tradition attributed to Jesus that we stand closest to the tradition and language aborning in the new idiom. Within the Jesus tradition the major narrative parables will be subjected to analysis for the purpose of ascertaining whether the language of these parables bears the stamp of a linguistic tradition in process of formation.

The analysis will focus on one group of major narrative parables consisting of the the Vineyard Laborers, the Money in Trust, the Ten Maidens, the Dinner Party, the Samaritan, and the Prodigal Son. These parables each have three principal characters and comparable plot structures.

The analysis will move from the more general to the more detailed. The point will be scored wherever possible in English. In some instances it will be necessary to resort to Greek.

The major narrative parables give evidence of having been carefully composed and constructed.

From *Parables and Presence*, 1982.

There is first of all the matter of vocabulary. Words and expressions are used parsimoniously, as though drawn from a stock dangerously low. Vocabulary is the simplest: there are no freighted terms, only everyday words like *laborer, field, go, celebrate, five.* Abstract nouns are lacking. Some very common terms appear to be especially suited to the concrete realism of the parable: *vineyard, go away, slave.*[1] These few words come preciously to the tongue of the narrator, like water to parched lips in a city under siege. Or, to change the figure, words are polished like mirrors: an image is reflected in them unblurred.

Descriptors and adjectives are kept to a minimum; characters are defined by what they do. Feelings and emotions are mentioned only where essential. The background of persons and events is not made explicit but is left to the imagination. There is a penurious economy of words in depicting actions. Where details are given, however, they are concrete in the extreme. Such details often afford clues to the direction of the narrative. Direct speech is preferred to third-person narration.

The parsimony of words is joined by an economy of characters and conciseness of plot. Only the necessary persons appear. The plot is simple. Only two sets of relationships are developed, even in the full narrative, for example, younger son/father, older son/ father. Little appears in the narrative that is non-functional.

There is repetition by two's and three's, and occasionally more, with variation. Together with other forms of rhythm and assonance, this endows the prose of the parables with certain poetic qualities.

Some of these characteristics are common to folk literature of other types, but many appear to be specific features of the synoptic parables. It is of course difficult to attain certainty in every detail because of the editing to which the earliest traditions were subject.

The narrative or story line of the six parables is divided into three parts: opening, development, and crisis-denouement. The parts are signaled by certain surface markers hitherto unnoted by biblical critics.

The development and crisis-denouement are initiated, as a rule, by temporal sequence phrases. In the Money in Trust, the principle characters are introduced in two sentences (=opening), then the text reads:

Matt 25:16 *Immediately* the one who had received thirty thousand silver coins . . .

The crisis-denouement begins with:

Matt 25:19 *After a long absence,* the slaves' master . . .

In other words, temporal sequence phrases indicate where the two principal subdivisions of the parable begin.

The first temporal marker in the Ten Maidens comes after an elaborate opening:

Matt 25:6 *Then in the middle of the night* there was a shout . . .

And the brief denouement begins with the notice:

Matt 25:11 The other maidens *finally* come and say . . .

In the Vineyard Laborers the opening appears to be conflated with the development. The first temporal phrase appears in the first sentence.

Matt 20:1 [a proprietor] . . . went out *the first thing in the morning* . . .

The reason for this move is the long, repetitive development, in which the proprietor ventures forth to hire laborers five times. The opening is therefore incorporated into the development, which serves also to introduce the principals. The Vineyard Laborers is an exception in this respect, although openings elsewhere are sometimes minimal, as in the Prodigal Son.

The development in the Vineyard Laborers ends with verse 7. The crisis-denouement opens with these words:

Matt 20:8: *When evening came* the owner of the vineyard . . .

There can be no doubt about the division of this and other parables on the basis of temporal sequence markers alone.

The principal character, functioning as the axis of the story, so to speak, is introduced in the opening by a common noun: *proprietor, a man, someone.* As a rule, reference in the development is by pronoun or by zero anaphora. At the opening of the crisis-denouement, however, this same figure is reintroduced by a new common noun, that is, the participant is identified by nominal substitution. The *proprietor of* the Vineyard Laborers becomes *the owner of the vineyard* at the opening of the crisis-denouement. *A man going on a trip* of the first sentence of the Money in Trust becomes *the slaves' master* at the beginning of the third division. In the Dinner Party, *someone* becomes *a master* at the commencement of scene three. There are some exceptions to the rule, but in general a shift in identification indicates the beginning of a new division.

There is another type of marker that indicates, as a general rule, that the crisis or denouement has arrived. As the Samaritan comes down the road and sees the victim in the ditch, he is "moved to pity" at the sight of him (ἐσπλαγχνίσθη, Luke 10:33). When the host in the Dinner Party learns that the invited have rejected his summons, the closing scene opens: "Then the master of the house got angry . . ." (ὀργισθείς, Luke 14:21). Affective terms expressing compassion or wrath thus appear to mark the crisis or denouement.

The parable of the Unforgiving Slave belongs to another group of parables with a slightly different dramatic structure. There are actually two crises in the parable, one when the slave first encounters his master and the master "is compassionate" (σπλαγχνισθείς, Matt 18:27), the second when the master calls the slave to account for failing to "treat [his] fellow slave with the same consideration." On the second occasion, the master becomes "angry" (ὀργισθείς, Matt 18:34) and calls him a "wicked slave" (δοῦλε πονηρέ, Matt 18:32). In the Money in Trust, the master also calls the one talent slave "incompetent and timid" (πονηρὲ δοῦλε καὶ ὀκνηρέ, Matt 25:26) and deals with him angrily, although the term ὀργισθείς [EN: "angry"] does not appear.

The Prodigal Son can be read in two ways. The first episode can be taken as a parable in its own right. In that episode the father is "moved to compassion" (ἐσπλαγχνίσθη, Luke 15:20) toward his younger son when he returns home. The second episode can be read as the crisis-denouement going with the first episode as the development (the opening is very brief). In episode two, the older son is "angry" (ὠργίσθη, Luke 15:28) and will not join in the celebration underway.

The terms σπλαγχνίζω (moved to compassion) and ὀργίζω (angry) thus appear to be linked to the parable in a special way and are associated with the crisis or denouement. The terms are preserved in single tradition parables appearing in both Matthew and Luke.

According to Charles Taber, a carefully planned and executed narrative in Sango, an African language, involves precise doses of repetition mixed with novelty.[2] Repetition and novelty in exact measure appear to be characteristic of the narrative parables also.

In the Vineyard Laborers, Act I (the first division), scene i, consists of three sense lines or themes (Matt 20: 1–2):

(a) who went out the first thing in the morning to hire workers for his vineyard
(b) After agreeing with the workers for a silver coin a day
(c) he sent them into his vineyard

These three lines are repeated in scene ii with significant variation and in different order (Matt 20: 3–5):

(a) And coming out around nine A.M. he saw others loitering in the marketplace
(c) He said to them, "You go into the vineyard too
(b) and I'll pay you whatever is fair."

Scenes iii and iv are carried by a repetition of a fragment of the opening clause and what amounts to ditto marks:

(a) Around noon he went out again, and at three P.M. he repeated the process.

In the final scene, (b) is omitted, (c) is repeated from scene ii, and (a) is considerably expanded:

(a) About five P.M. he went out and found others loitering about (abbreviated from scene ii)
and says to them, "Why did you stand around here idle the whole day?" They reply, "Because no one hired us."

Note that the same thematic words and phrases appear: going out at *x* hour, loitering, hire, go, vineyard. Act I is then rounded off by (c).

(c) "You go into the vineyard as well."

It is difficult to get a clear impression of the repetition and variation in Act I without reading the lines aloud or setting them down on paper in a schematic arrangement and then examining closely. There is, first of all, the broad a/b/c pattern with the variations indicated above. Further, some phrases run like a thread through the entire act: εἰς τὸν ἀμπελῶνα (αὐτοῦ) ("into the [his] vineyard"): twice repeated in scene i, once in scenes ii and v, always at the end of clauses. In scene i the master ἐξῆλθεν ἅμα πρωΐ ("goes out first thing in the morning"); this phrase is repeated in scenes ii, iii-iv (καὶ ἐξελθὼν περὶ τρίτην ὥραν ["and coming out around 9 A.M."]; πάλιν ἐξελθὼν περὶ ἕκτην καὶ ἐνάτην ὥραν ["Around noon he went out again, and 3 P.M."]), with the elements in the same order. In the final scene, the order of the two principal phrases is reversed: "About five P.M. he went out" (περὶ δὲ τὴν ἐνδεκάτην ἐξελθὼν). The variation in phrase order after so much repetition invites renewed attention. And the expanded form of (a) with the omission of (b) in the final scene of Act I confirms that a significant development in the story is taking place.

Repetition and variation can be pursued, on a slightly smaller scale, through the parable as a whole.

In Act II, at the close of the parable, the owner of the vineyard singles out one of the grumblers and directs several remarks to him. In the first, "Look, pal, did I wrong you?" the verb ἀδικῶ ["wrong"] picks up a note struck in Act I, scene ii: "I'll pay you whatever is fair (δίκαιον ["fair"])." There is thus a play on δίκαιον/ἀδικῶ [*dikaion/adiko*] across a considerable expanse of narrative. The owner's second remark, "You did agree with me for a silver coin, didn't you?" renews a theme expressed in Act I, scene i: "After agreeing with the workers for a silver coin a day..." And these two initial closing remarks of the owner, "Look, pal, did I wrong you? You did agree with me for a silver coin, didn't you?" are also related to each other in that they both renew what was identified as theme (b) in Act I.

The owner next tells the protester to take his coin and be gone (ὕπαγε). Ὕπαγε recalls item (c) of Act I, which was twice repeated: ὑπάγετε καὶ ὑμεῖς τὸν ἀμπελῶνα ["You go into the vineyard too"]. The proprietor told them to go into the vineyard; now he tells them to get out. This represents still another verbal link between Acts II and I.

In what is probably the final remark of the owner, he says, "I intend to treat the one hired last the same way I treat you." The verb δοῦναι [*dounai*, "treat" or "pay"] picks up δώσω [*doso*, "I'll pay"] of (b) in Act I, scene ii: "I'll pay you whatever is fair." Meanwhile, the owner has instructed his foreman to "pay" (ἀποδίδωμι [*apodidomi*]) the wages at the beginning of Act II. The verb δίδωμι [*didomi*] represents a theme running through the entire parable. Moreover, the designation "last" for one of the workers hired at five P.M. goes back to the dichotomy also introduced at the outset of Act II: "... pay them their wages starting with those hired *last* and ending with those hired first." Subsequently, those hired *first* thing in the morning are referred to as "the first" (οἱ πρῶτοι), and they, in turn, call their lazy colleagues "the last" (οἱ ἔσχατοι). Again, there is wordplay on first/last in the second half of the parable.

The play upon or renewal of δίκαιον/ἀδικέω [*dikaion/adikeo* "fair/wrong", , συμφωνέω δηναρίον ["agree for a silver coin"], ὑπάγω ["get out"], δίδωμι ["pay"], πρῶτοι/ἔσχατοι [first/last] across a large expanse of the narrative gives the story a textual unity and subtlety that would not have been missed by the ear, difficult as it may be to catch by the untrained eye.

Some of the forms of repetition and variation indicated above are explored by J. D. Denniston in his work *Greek Prose Style*. In the final chapter, Denniston takes up various forms of assonance, which he defines as "the recurrence of a sound in such a manner as to catch the ear."[3] According to W. B. Stanford, the primacy of the spoken word in ancient Greek, and in other languages, before the age of printing had a significant effect on composition. Prose as well as poetry was composed by the ear rather than by the eye. Euphony therefore played a large role in Greek rhetoric and composition.

Matthew Black has endeavored to make a similar case for Aramaic.[4] He finds many examples of alliteration, assonance, and paronomasia (wordplay, pun) by translating portions of the New Testament back into Aramaic. His work confirms the importance of the ear for the common languages of Hellenistic-Roman Palestine.

The relation of sound to content need not be argued here. At the threshold of language—in *poiesis* in the root sense: the naming of the gods and in creation—it is taken for granted. It is no less obvious in the lullaby and the jingle, ancient and modern. In an age dominated by the eye, the precincts of the ear are mostly void. Yet for those laboring to say something unheard of in the common tongue, the ear must have been crucial. And one expects rhythm and assonance in folk literature, to which the parables are closely related.

Repetition and variation in themselves contain forms of rhythm and assonance: the parallelism of clauses with variation; the repetition of thematic phrases; the play upon theme words; and the like. It is not surprising to find such cadences and euphony in prose that borders on poetry. It is perhaps somewhat surprising that the parables exhibit other interesting forms of assonance involving the sounds of Greek.

Act I of the Vineyard Laborers concerns a proprietor who goes out to hire ἐργάτας [*ergatas*] "laborers," some of whom stand ἀργούς [*argous*] "loitering" in the ἀγορᾷ [*agora*] "marketplace." The use of these three terms exemplifies anagrammatic assonance (sound play on the same consonants in varying order). The juxtaposition of ἐργάτας / ἀργούς / ἀγορᾷ [*ergatas/argous/agora*] calls attention to Act I, scene ii: εἶδεν ἄλλους ἑστῶτας ἐν τῇ ἀγορᾷ ἀργούς ["he saw others loitering in the marketplace"]. In this line, in addition to ἀγορᾷ ἀργούς [*agora argous*, "loitering in the marketplace"], there is alternating alliteration with epsilon and alpha sounds (ε, α, ε, ε, α, α). This alliteration is continued in the first part of the next line: καὶ ἐκείνους εἶπεν, ὑπάγετε καὶ ὑμεῖς εἰς τὸν ἀμπελῶνα ["and he said to them, 'You go into the vineyard too'"], this time with ε [e] and υ [y]; the last phrase in the line of course renews a phrase already twice used. These two lines from scene ii thus exhibit at least three forms of assonance: anagrammatic assonance, alliteration of initial vowel sounds, and repetition of theme phrase.

The next line of scene ii runs: καὶ ὅ ἐὰν ᾖ δίκαιον δώσω ὑμῖν ["I'll pay you whatever is fair"]. The alliteration in δίκαιον δώσω [dikaion/doso "fair/I'll pay"] is striking in this context, especially when one recalls that δίκαιον [dikaion, fair] and δίδωμι [didomi, I pay] are both theme words, alluded to in the final line of the parable.

In Act II of the same parable, the protest of those hired first is introduced with the verb ἐγόγγυζον [grumble], itself an onomatopoeic word. And this is what they murmur:

οὗτοι οἱ ἔσχατοι / These guys hired last
μίαν ὥραν ἐποίησαν / worked only an hour
καὶ ἴσους αὐτοὺς / but you have made them equal
ἡμῖν ἐποίησας τοῖς βαστάσασι τὸ βάρος τῆς ἡμέρης καὶ τὸν καύσωνα / to us who did most of the work during the heat of the day.

The repetition of -οι -οι -οι / -α -αν -αν / -ους -ους [-oi, -oi, oi / -a, -an, -an / -ous –ous], called homoeoteleuta,[5] appears to reinforce the sound effect succession of the verb. In the latter part of the line there is a succession of sounds with terminal σ -ας, -οις –ος -ης [s, -as, -ois, -os, -es] (nine times), with a similar effect. And there is alliteration with β in βαστάσασι, βάρος.*

The kinds of assonance just noted undoubtedly occur, to a certain degree, in all levels of language—not just in poetry—when spoken by competent native speakers. The texture of the narrative parables is such that one has the impression they were "heard" originally in Greek by a competent native speaker.

The structural and surface evidence adduced from the parables is of more than one type. Some features may belong to deep structures which are translatable without essential loss into any language, for example, the law of the parsimony of characters in folk tales. Whether all deep structures are universally translat-

---

*Editor's Note: literally, "having borne the burden."

able is a question which cannot be broached here. Some surface features may be suited to either Aramaic (Hebrew) or Greek and readily translatable into the other language. Temporal sequence markers would presumably belong to this category. Many so-called Semitisms can also be explained either as translation Semitisms or as spoken Semitic-Greek.[6] Other features are difficult to account for on the basis of a Semitic (Aramaic or Hebrew) original, of which the Greek text preserved for us is a reasonably close translation. On balance, it seems to me that the major narrative parables provide ample evidence of having been composed in Greek.

J. Barre Toelken has suggested that the more significant aspects of Navaho coyote tales lies in their texture—in any *coloration* given a traditional narrative as it is unfolded.[7] He then cites Alan Dundes with approval: "the more important the textural features are in a given genre of folklore, the more difficult it is to translate an example of that genre into another language."[8] The texture of the narrative parables would make it difficult to achieve the same effect in another language.

The Greek of the parables strikes one not so much as translation Greek as Greek which has been thoroughly vacuumed for the occasion. The Greek of the parables is as clean of resonances as the German of Franz Kafka or the French of Samuel Beckett—both of whom were writing in a second language. Aramaic may well have been the first language of the narrator of the parables. However that may be, the composer employs Greek as though it were derived from a beginner's manual with only the immediate ordinary sense attached, just as Ionesco used beginner's English as the basis for his first play, *The Bald Soprano*. The Greek of the parables has been shorn of its rich history. Nevertheless, the unadorned and unnuanced simplicity of the style and diction marks an uncommon solemnity. The bare, uninterpreted act, such as a man going down from Jerusalem to Jericho, bristles with anticipation. The way the narrator manipulates this language is therefore not unlike the way Kafka polishes German or Beckett washes French.

These less tangible features are joined by more obvious traits, such as repetition with variation, and assonance in various forms. Taken together, they indicate that creativity has been inscribed into the parables both on the surface and at the depths. As Leo Spitzer claims, poetic genius touches the linguistic act at all levels.[9]

The conclusion to which these features point, then, is that the narrative parables were composed in Greek. This claim has long been thwarted by the assumption that a Palestinian tradition could not have taken shape in Greek. Now we have reason to believe differently. Further, from the distance of greater options, it becomes incredible that the original language of the tradition should have disappeared with only odd traces. Given the tenacity with which cultures and institutions cling to originating languages—the Latin church and French Canada, to cite only two examples—it is almost implausible that the Christian tradition took shape in Aramaic and then disappeared in that form in a few years or decades. Freedom from the earlier assumption and conclusion may permit us to examine the synoptic tradition with an eye to the ear.

There has been a steady refusal in this analysis to attribute the narrative parables in their Greek form to Jesus. Such an attribution is by no means ruled out. But the present argument extends just this far: the narrative parable tradition took shape in Greek, whether at the hands of Jesus or someone else, at some point proximate to the threshold of the Christian tradition.

CHAPTER

9

Parable, Paradox, and Power
The Prodigal Samaritan

As a consequence of the pioneering work done by Vladimir Propp on the Russian folktale, and the development of that work principally by the French structuralists, we can now say that there appear to be at least two basic plot structures possible in narrative literature. The narrative parables of Jesus seem to conform to one of them.

Propp defined the Russian folktale as any development proceeding from an act of villainy or a lack or misfortune, through intermediary functions, to marriage, reward, or the liquidation of the lack or misfortune. Such a three-phase development Propp terms a *move*.

In the Gospels, the healing miracle story appears to follow this general pattern. The healing miracle is developed out of a lack or misfortune: a sufferer is introduced, usually with some indication of the gravity of the malady (for example, a woman who had been infirm for eighteen years). This misfortune is overcome in the act of healing. The testimony of bystanders often serves as the conclusion, and this type of conclusion connects the narrative to its larger context in the Gospels: the witness to Jesus of Nazareth as a wonder worker.

The French structuralist A. J. Greimas has developed an analysis of what he terms the *contractual syntagm*.[1] In order to keep our terminology uniform, this type of plot will be called a *contractual move*.

The contractual move consists of three basic functions: contract, test, judgment. The contract is normally made between the hero and a superior power who has the authority to set the terms and to reward success or punish failure. The contract always comes at the beginning, the reward or punishment at the end. The test, obviously, must come between. No other order is possible.

From *Parables and Presence*, 1982.

The actors in this scheme are contractor/contractee, tester/tested, judge/judged. The six possible participants may in fact be represented by only two characters, the hero and the superior power. It is also possible, of course, to have two "heroes," one who fulfills the contract and is rewarded, the other who does not fulfill the contract and is punished. It is also necessary to have the same superior power running through the story, or implied in it, in order to have a narrative at all.

The contractual move as developed by Greimas appears to fit well the plot structure of most parables in the Jesus tradition.

The contract in the Ten Maidens is formed when the Ten Maidens take their lamps and go out to meet the bridegroom. Some go prepared and some do not. The test takes place when it is announced that the bridegroom is arriving. The imprudent maidens fail the test, the wise maidens are prepared and pass it. In the final scene, judgment is pronounced on the foolish ones through the closed door. The move—contract, test, judgment—thus serves as the plot structure of this parable and of the other narrative parables as well.

In identifying sets of participants and their interrelationships, and in identifying the basic plot structure of the parables, we have been trading in items too general to be discriminating. The analysis must be sharpened so as to be able to distinguish among specific parables—narrative parables only, it should be noted—and perhaps even grade them in relation to their literary quality, their power to draw listeners into their orbit, and the profundity of the message they bear.

The remarks that follow will be more readily appropriated if the results are presented in advance. I propose to demonstrate that the Dinner Party and the Vineyard Laborers are rather more sophisticated and compelling metaphoric instruments than the parables of Money in Trust and the Ten Maidens. Further, the Prodigal Son and the Samaritan are even more subtle and complex in spite of their evident simplicity: listeners are drawn into and captivated by them whether they will or not. In my view, the Prodigal Son and the Samaritan stand at the apex of Jesus' parabolic creativity; the Vineyard Laborers and the Dinner Party follow closely; by comparison, Money in Trust and the Ten Maidens are only fair representatives of the genre.

In the parables Money in Trust and the Ten Maidens, the determiner (D) is an authority figure. In the one case he is a landed master, in the other a bridegroom. It is this figure that sets the situation to which responders (R) respond. D also serves as the thread on which the story is strung.

The two respondents in the Ten Maidens are identified from the outset as wise and foolish. We do not have to wait to see how the story turns out; we know in advance that the foolish will do something unwise and be punished. There are no surprises. Furthermore, the wise maidens achieve something positive, something quite in accordance with normal expectations, to merit their designation and reward: they take extra oil along with their lamps for the vigil. The Ten Maidens is therefore heavy-handed: its message is hammered home unsubtly, like a commercial.

Similarly, Money in Trust introduces the listener to two groups of servants, one receiving plural valuables, the other a single one. Though they are not specifically identified in all versions at the outset as good and bad, the reader is reasonably certain that the number of valuables given in trust corresponds to the level of the servants' competence. We are therefore not surprised that the story turns out as it does. It meets common expectations. The trusted servants, moreover, do as we anticipate: they trade with the master's money and earn him interest. For this positive achievement they are rewarded.

These observations on the Ten Maidens and Money in Trust may be summarized in four points, to which a fifth and concluding point may then be added.

1. The determiner, or D, is an authority figure who rewards and punishes two sets of respondents in accordance with their behavior. D: it is this way because I say it is.

2. The two sets of respondents are identified as good and bad, wise and foolish, from the outset of the narrative.

3. Those who are rewarded merit their reward by achieving something positive.

4. The narrative affirms the hearer's everyday expectations: the story turns out as anticipated.

5. The last three features just enumerated make it possible for the hearer to hold the story at arm's length, to relate to it as a bystander rather than as a participant: (1) the hearer does not have to decide who the good characters are; (2) the good characters achieve something the hearer is expected to value (preparedness, thrift); (3) the story turns out as the hearer expects. This means that the Ten Maidens and Money in Trust are robbed of their provocative power: the hearer is not caught in a parabolic snare because there is no snare.

The Vineyard Laborers and the Dinner Party, together with the Prodigal Son and the Samaritan, constitute a group which may be termed *parables of grace*. In examining these parables, we must now distinguish functions from participants.

The Vineyard Laborers and the Dinner Party also present us with determiners who are authority figures. The owner of the vineyard and the host of the feast reward and include, rebuke and exclude, as does D in Money in Trust and the Ten Maidens. In respect of D, the second pair of parables is comparable to the first.

Those hired first in the Vineyard Laborers are prompted, by virtue of the full day's wage paid those hired last, to protest their treatment. This protest is lodged in accordance with the canons of everydayness, as observed earlier. Participant is not distinguishable from function: those hired first (first response = R1) give a justified response (= RJ, in this case, R1 = RJ)

In the Prodigal Son, the response of the older son is justified, expected, in accordance with contemporary standards (R2 = RJ). The noninvolvement policy of the priest and Levite in the Samaritan is prudent, safe, commonplace (R1 = RJ). Those invited to the banquet in the Dinner Party are expected to decline, given the responsibilities they shoulder (R1 = RJ); the hearer would be surprised if they didn't. In all these cases, one respondent in the story is marked as RJ: the one who is justified in protesting. Yet RJ is never treated in the story as he thinks he ought to be; RJ's expectations, and the expectations of all those dominated by everydayness, are frustrated. For RJ the story regularly turns in a tragic direction.

By contrast with RJ, the other respondent in these parables usually does not expect anything but is pleasantly surprised by the way things turn out. Because this respondent gets what is not deserved, the designation RG (recipient of grace) is given. For RG the story regularly turns in a comic direction.

Those hired at five P.M. in the Vineyard Laborers, the uninvited street people in the Dinner Party, and the younger son in the Prodigal are RG. It is no less evident that the victim in the ditch is the recipient of grace in the Samaritan.

1. As in Money in Trust and the Ten Maidens, D is an authority figure who rewards or punishes two sets of respondents in accordance with their behavior.

2. Unlike R1 and R2 in Money in Trust and the Ten Maidens, the two respondents in the parables of grace are *not identified in advance*. However, native responses prompt the hearer to identify RJ as the good and RG as the bad participants.

3. In Money in Trust and the Ten Maidens, the good characters are rewarded for positive achievements. In the parables of grace, the recipients of grace are either passive (street people in the Dinner Party, victim in the Samaritan), indolent (those hired at five P.M.), or wasteful (younger son). They appear to be rewarded in spite of non-achievement.

4. As a consequence of the two preceding points, it has to be said that the four parables of grace *do not confirm everyday* expectations. Indeed, those expectations are regularly frustrated. Grace, in fact, comes as a surprise.

5. Because these parables are realistic, the hearer is drawn into them by way of unstudied affirmation: the initial situation prompts the listener to affirm, "Yes, that's the way it is!" However, the parables take a turn in which that lazy affirmation is jarred and then upset. This turn intensifies the relation of the listener to the story: the hearer must now pay attention to see how the narrative turns out. Furthermore, the listeners will be disposed to join those who protest equal payment, if they consider themselves industrious and just, or they will smile if they have been sitting on their haunches in the marketplace all day. In sum, in these parables *listeners are provoked to choose up sides.*

It is for these reasons that the parables of grace may be taken to be more compelling, more provocative, more carefully constructed, and closer to the heart of the message of Jesus.

Two of the functions in the parables of grace have been identified as RJ and RG: the justified response and the recipient of grace. A third function in the parables of grace is the dispensation of grace or justice (IG/J = instrument of grace or justice) to common expectations. The preeminent function of the determiner in these parables appears to be to dispense grace and justice, and that involves a fundamental reversal in relation to habituated expectations. Just as the everyday or received order of things is undergirded by the initial realism of the parable and the hearer's unstudied response, so the new reality announced by the parable is sanctioned by D, the determiner around whom the whole story revolves.

Earlier, we were led to the question: is D always the instrument of grace and justice, as in the Vineyard Laborers and the Dinner Party? Or is this function, IG/J—and consequently also the functions RJ and RG—mapped onto the narrative in different ways? A preliminary answer was provided earlier in "The Birth of a Language Tradition," (see above chapter 8); we may renew it now with respect to the parables of the Prodigal Son and the Samaritan.

The parable of the Prodigal Son can be read in at least three different ways which will be sketched here in relation to both the participants and the plot structure.

In the predominant understanding of the parable, which for convenience may be designated Prodigal 1, the father is understood as the determiner and the two sons as contrasting respondents. In this reading, the division of the father's estate between the sons functions as the contract. The test consists of the way each son handles his inheritance, and the judgment consists of the response of the father.

Although this view of the Prodigal appears to have predominated in both ancient and modern times, two things may be said against it.

In the first place, the test or response of the older son is not related directly to his share of the inheritance, but to the reception of the younger son on the part of the father. Second, the father is not quite the thread on which the story is strung; the younger son appears to play this role.

Further, if we take the Prodigal as a parallel to the Lost Sheep and the Lost Coin, with which it is grouped in Luke, the first episode may be construed independently: the contract consists of the father giving the younger son his inheritance; the test is his performance in a foreign land; and the judgment is his repentance and reception by his father.

If the second episode is authentic—and some scholars hold that it is not—it is then necessary to understand the first episode as a whole as the contract, in relation to which the test of the older son is how he relates to his father's acceptance of the younger son's prodigality. And the judgment is the rebuke spoken by the father to the older son.

Read in this way, Prodigal 2 (to use a brief designation) is a complex parable, in the sense that one parable of the Lost Sheep type serves as the contract for another simple parable. The first simple parable as a whole serves as a constituent element in the second.

If this reading is correct, the structure of Prodigal 2 is unique among the parables of Jesus, so far as I can see.

In spite of its possible formal uniqueness, it is just possible that Prodigal 2 is, in fact, the more traditional reading.

A third reading of the Prodigal is suggested by the structure of the other three parables of grace. Recall that this formal structure is given its shape by a participant, D, who sets the terms of the narrative and runs like a thread through it. To D there are two contrasting responses.

If this formal structure is our sole criterion, it would appear that D is the younger son, and that the two contrasting responses are supplied by the father and the older son, as our observations on Prodigal 1 have already suggested. In this case, the contract, or the terms of the narrative, are set by the account of the younger son wasting his inheritance and then returning home to seek mercy. The test consists of how the father and the older son receive him. The judgment is not given as a separate item but is implied in the contrasting responses.

One difficulty with Prodigal 3 as a reading is that in the parables D is customarily an authority figure. There is thus a strong proclivity to interpret the father as D simply because the father is an authority figure. As an authority D means: it is this way because I say it is.

There are three good reasons for resisting this supreme temptation. The first is that the authority figure is not always a suitable model for God: for example, the doting father in the Prodigal and the master in a Shrewd Manager. To these could be added the Dinner Party: would God invite the socially respectable first and only then turn to the outcasts, as is suggested by the narrative sequence? In the Vineyard Laborers, would God pay a subsistence wage and insist on its justice?

The second reason has to do with interpretive consistency. If we read the father as a figure or model for God, should we not also read the other two participants as models? The older son is often taken, to be sure, as representing the Pharisees, so we have the equations: father = God; older son = Pharisees. In that case, what about the younger son? Should he not also be taken as the literal model of the sinner? In sum, those who take the father (and the older son) literally or figuratively are bound to take the younger son on the same terms.

The third reason is that there is one parable in which D is clearly not an authority figure: the Samaritan. In the Samaritan, D is the victim in the ditch. The parable calls on the Jewish man in the ditch to certify, even in his inertness, that grace has come, D = RG: it is this way because I have experienced it so. It follows, too, that D is not always the instrument of grace or justice. In others words, the Prodigal and the Samaritan open up new ways of understanding sets of participants and sets of functions. On the basis of the first four parables examined, it could have been concluded that the relationships between participants and functions are constant; the Prodigal and the Samaritan point to other and richer possibilities.

The reading of the Prodigal as Prodigal 3, which has not been proposed in the scholarly literature so far as I know, is suggested by the structure of the Samaritan. In both parables, D is a figure who has suffered misfortune. In both cases, D is the recipient of grace. The father and the priest and Levite are authority figures, but they are respondents. In one case, the father as R1 functions as the instrument of grace; in the other, the priest and Levite function as RJ, the justified response. And in neither case is judgment a discrete narrative item—by contrast with the Ten Maidens, Money in Trust, the Dinner Party, and the Vineyard Laborers.

That the Prodigal is carefully constructed is proved by the fact that it can be read in several ways. It is a narrative of no little subtlety. We are probably attracted to it by virtue of its structural ambiguities, even though we may tend to read it predominantly in one way. And finally, since there seems to be no way to arbitrate among the structural claims on this parable, the three ways of reading it would appear to contribute to its plurisignificative character as parable and metaphor.

The discussion of the Prodigal anticipates the analysis of the Samaritan in large measure.

On the formal side, D in the Samaritan is the fellow in the ditch: it is he upon whom the story turns. There are two contrasting responses, one by the priest and the Levite, the other by the Samaritan. The priest and the Levite are therefore R1, the Samaritan R2. With regard to parabolic functions, D is the recipient of grace and thus RG; R1 (priest and Levite) functions as RJ, the response to be expected; R2 (the Samaritan) is the instrument of grace, or IG. There is no explicit judgment, although IJ may be said to be implied, the Samaritan is therefore not heavy-handed, in contrast to the other narrative parables, including, perhaps, even the Prodigal (does the father function as IJ in relation to the older son?).

I must confess that reading the Samaritan in this way, indeed, reading it as a parable at all, runs contrary to the history of interpretation.[2]

The Samaritan as parable forces on its hearers the question: who among you will permit himself or herself to be served by a Samaritan? In a general way it can be replied: only those who are unable to refuse. Permission to be served by the Samaritan is thus inability to resist. Put another way, all who are truly victims, truly disinherited, truly helpless, have no choice but to give themselves up to mercy. And mercy comes from the quarter from which it is least expected. Grace is always a surprise.

As a parable the Samaritan is a very powerful instrument. It sets the message of Jesus in unequivocal terms for its audience. No one could mistake. It explains why IRS officials and prostitutes understand the kingdom, whereas theologians, Bible scholars, and professional pietists do not. It explains why a hated alien must be the instrument of grace. It makes pretense on the part of the listener impossible. No other parable in the Jesus tradition carries a comparable punch. The Christian community moralizes it in order to be able to live with it, and that is inverted testimony to its power.

Part Four

DISMANTLING AND RECOVERING

10

From Parable to Gospel
Domesticating the Tradition

The Samaritan

The Samaritan as parable

The parable of the Samaritan is usually understood as an example story. It is quite possible that the parable may legitimately be read in that way. But I believe it may also be read as a parable, and specifically as a parable of grace.

The parable opens with a man, undoubtedly a Jew, jogging down that treacherous road from Jerusalem to Jericho. He gets waylaid, just as we hearers familiar with local conditions expect, and because we are sympathetic hearers and Jews, we take up our place in the ditch with him. We anticipate further developments.

First the priest and Levite pass by. If we are anticlerical, as many common folk in those days were, we are delighted to have our opinions of the clergy confirmed. But the clerical hearers will want to interrupt the story to debate whether ritual defilement, prudence, or mercy take priority under the circumstances. The story, however, ignores the call for discussion and rushes on.

Developments have opened up a preliminary division in the audience: on the one side are the common folk and the victim in the ditch, modestly bemused at the course of events; on the other, the chagrined clergy, who suspect the narrative will give them a raw deal. Into this tension rides the Samaritan astride his ass. The suspicions of the clergy now turn to rage. And the *'am hā'āres,* the ordinary people, begin to desert the ditch: they, too, are taken aback at the turn of affairs.

The question thus posed by the story is a very simple one: who among you will permit himself or herself to be served by a Samaritan? As Jews it is a question on which we choke. But the

From *Forum* 1,3 (1985).

143

answer demanded by the story is unequivocal: the victim in the ditch is he who is unable to refuse aid. Put differently, the victim in the ditch is he who is truly a victim, truly disinherited, truly helpless, who has no choice but to give himself up to mercy. Further, that mercy comes from the quarter from which it can least be expected. In sum, grace is always a surprise.

In developing this reading of the Samaritan, permit me to make a series of observations relative to narrative content, audience, and the unfolding of the tradition.

Literal foundations

The Samaritan as narrative depends on terms that are heavily freighted with literal social, political, and religious meaning. Priest, Levite, and Samaritan are terms that resonate in every head, positively or negatively, with conviction. The term Jew is implicit in every line of the story, beginning with the opening line, "There was a man going from Jerusalem down to Jericho. . . ." And that road, too, is pregnant with expectations. The story thus rests on a stock of images that are current, cogent, and concrete.

The initial face of the story invites the hearer to take it in its everyday and literal sense. In other words, the narrative begins by affirming the received life-world. The listener nods, "Yes, that's how it is."

The everyday and literal sense of the narrative, however, is also laced with barbs. Some attendees are incensed. The senses that incense include the brusque treatment of the clergy and the complimentary picture of the Samaritan. Those who are offended withdraw from the narrative, so to speak; they do not permit themselves to be drawn into it. Refusal and withdrawal are occasioned by the literal sense of the narrative.

It may now be observed: those who refuse the narrative are those who identify themselves literally with participants in the story. Some Jews, priests, and Levites take themselves literally and so are offended. There were probably no Samaritans present. Had there been, they, too, would have suffered indignity.

Metaphorical proclivities

The Samaritan as narrative trades in the full concreteness of the everyday world. It is precisely that concreteness, taken literally, that offends. We must now inquire why the narrative is so constructed as to offend when taken literally. And we must ask whether there are clues in the narrative which inhibit the listener from taking it merely literally. Put differently, what prompts the hearer to look for non-literal overtones?

We may limit ourselves to two suggestions.

The first response of the Jewish audience is to affirm the everyday expectations associated with the Jericho road: hearers therefore identify with the victim in the ditch. The appearance of the priest and then the Levite causes the audience to divide over the issue of the clergy: some protest, others smile, depending on whether they are pro- or anti-clergy. With the hearers divided on what eventually proves to be a secondary issue, the Samaritan, an enemy of both parties, appears. This narrative strategy confounds a divided audience.

The first suggestion, accordingly, is this: the confusion of roles in the narrative itself inhibits literal identification. The narrative instructs hearers to be circumspect about those with whom they should identify, how they should react.

The second suggestion is less subtle. There are no warrants for the behavior of the Samaritan. Indeed, historically we expect Samaritans to be something less than hospitable to Jews. And the story provides no real motivation for his action. Antecedently, then, and within the story itself, the appearance and action of the Samaritan controverts natural expectations. As a consequence, the story moves beyond the realm of the everyday and takes on the character of fantasy: at least one character behaves in an altogether unexpected way.

The narrative, it was suggested, promotes a certain fluidity of roles. There is the ordinary Jewish hearer who will want, against all advice, to play the role of the Samaritan, perhaps even to be content as victim in the ditch; there is perhaps the rare priest who acknowledges the picture painted of his class or who dares to associate himself with the role of the Samaritan. In sum, hearers are prompted to receive new identities from the story, identities that do not coincide with their social identities in the everyday world. The story thus precipitates the transposition or migration of social roles.

The Samaritan is made to behave in a way that runs counter to normal expectations. Indeed, the narrative greatly exaggerates his willingness to help. Exaggeration and atypicality add an element of fantasy to the story: hearers can no longer believe their ears, as it were; their habituated reality sense is being called into question. In the world inhabited by the Jew, priest, Levite, and Samaritan of the story, things run the other way around, as in Alice's looking glass: the proud Jew is helpless; the hated Samaritan is helper; the clergy are devalued.

Once it is sensed that the parable is a fantasy—an order of reality that feeds on but ultimately contravenes the everyday world—it is but a short step to the view that the Samaritan is not about a stickup on Jericho boulevard at all; it is about a new order of things, a new reality sense, that lies beyond, but just barely beyond, the everyday, the habituated, the humdrum. Then the parable is understood as an invitation to cross over. One's ability to move will depend, of course, on the tenacity with which one holds to the received world, on one's willingness to cut the ties to comfortable tradition. The parable is pitted against the power of the proven. Victory does not come easily.

The Prodigal Father

In the reading of the Samaritan just given we have deliberately ignored the tradition of interpretation. We shall remedy that deficiency eventually. Meanwhile, the so-called parable of the Prodigal Son—perhaps better titled the Prodigal Father—is to be set down alongside the Samaritan and interrogated for the glimpse of the life-world onto which it opens. For this purpose we may best make an entrance through the portal of modern interpretation.

An asymmetrical hermeneutic

Joachim Jeremias wants to rename the Prodigal Son as the parable of the Father's Love.[1] He does so because he holds that the father is the central figure[2] and models God's love for sinners. Moreover, this parable is really a vindication of the good news Jesus proclaims in the face of critics, viz., Pharisees. As in the case of the other double-edged parables (e.g., the Vineyard Laborers), the emphasis falls on the second half, i.e., on the encounter between the father (God's love) and the older son (Pharisaic intransigence).[3] The parable is thus aimed at Jesus' Jewish critics; the son who is prodigal serves merely as the occasion for the justification of Jesus' good news for sinners.

The interesting aspect of Jeremias' reading of the Prodigal is that he concentrates on the two actants who are traditionally taken in a literally figurative way: the father in the story stands for God the Father, and the older son represents those who object to God's love for sinners, i.e., critics of the gospel. He is unable to make much of the younger son as profligate. Why is this so?

In connection with the Lost Sheep and the Lost Coin, Jeremias notes the definition of sinner that is operative in the Jesus tradition: a sinner is a person (1) who leads an exaggerated form of the immoral life (e.g., adulterer, prostitute, swindler), or (2) who follows a dishonorable calling (e.g., tax-collector).[4] The Prodigal fits this definition: he squanders all his property in loose living (Luke 15:13) among harlots (15:30) and winds up feeding swine (15:15–16) in violation of his religious heritage. If the father in the story is a model for God and the older son is a model of Pharisaic intransigence, why is the younger son not also understood as a model for the sinner? The answer lies in the literalizing proclivities of the community transmitting this tradition: it was quite willing to understand the father as God and the older son as the Pharisee, but it did not want to understand itself literally as the younger son, for, as the community of grace, the role of the younger son was its own role. There thus developed an asymmetrical hermeneutic: father and older son are taken literally figuratively; the character of the younger son is either taken quite figuratively or ignored.

The literal may also be defined as the confirmation of normal, everyday, unstudied expectations. The early church certainly wanted a father lavish with love; it believed its opponents to be as absurd as the older son in the story; but it did not want to understand itself as profligate. Indeed, the time soon came when it thought it may have merited God's grace (cf. Paul).

The literalizing of the tradition precipitates a hermeneutic of exclusion: parables and aphorisms in the Jesus tradition are so interpreted as to exclude subsequent redeemed readers from the tensions in the text. In sum, nobody gets caught in the snare laid by the text. We could also say: hardening (literalizing) of the terms goes together with hardening of the heart. And hardening of the heart permits the controlling interpreter to overlook undesirable features of the father in the story and to blunt several admirable characteristics of the older son.

Structural ambiguity

The literalizing tendency of the tradition also tends to brick over structural ambiguity. Such ambiguity of course contributes to polyvalence and hence to hermeneutical potential. The resolution of structural ambiguity is another form of control.

The Prodigal is normally taken, I assume, as a narrative in which two sons give opposite responses to their father. One is received back in spite of his response; the other is both affirmed and chastised because of his. On this reading, the story forms a triangle with the father at the apex, no doubt because he is an authority figure.

It may be argued that the figure who belongs at the apex of the triangle, so to speak, is the younger son. To his odyssey two opposing responses are given: that of the father and that of the older son. The reader is left to be drawn into the story on one side or the other: he or she may wish to play the role of the prodigal father or that of proper son. On this reading, the father corresponds to the Samaritan in that parable: the father cannot be expected to respond to the younger son as he does; indeed, the older son is correct—senility or something worse has seized the old man. But familiarity has fixed prodigal love as the property of God the Father, so that the story came to be read in only one way. The fundamental structural ambiguity has been resolved in a way in which risk is eliminated from the role of the father. The father is no longer prodigal and senile; he is literally figuratively God the Father. With that the parable loses its parabolic character, and the metaphorical functions of the two sons are destroyed.

Real and Unreal Relatives

It would possible to carry this analysis out for other narrative parables (Dinner Party; the Vineyard Laborers; Shrewd Manager; Unforgiving Slave), as well as for the picture parables (e.g., Leaven; Mustard Seed). I shall presuppose such analyses, several of which have been published elsewhere, in subsequent remarks. I should like, instead, to implement these observations by considering an aphorism set in a minimal narrative context, i.e., a pronouncement story. For this purpose, the pericope on true relatives (Mark 3:31–35//Matt 12:46–50//[Luke 8:19– 21]), which is a nearly pure example of the genre, will serve nicely. This narrative has been brilliantly analyzed by Robert Tannehill[5] and I draw freely on his work.

The text

It is necessary, first of all, to make a few pertinent observations on the text as it appears in Mark.

The phrase "mother and brothers" occurs no fewer than five times in this short text. In the pronouncement of Jesus it is used in a non-literal sense, but the terms are kept in close contact with the literal sense, from which the metaphorical usage draws its power. The narrative provides dramatic contrast for the play upon the literal and non-literal senses. Let us reconstruct: the mother and brothers of Jesus arrive at the throng pressed in about him and send word into him. He receives the report. While his family awaits without, he asks, "Who are my mother and brothers?"

The tension in this scene is heightened by the spatial proximity but physical separation of his mother and brothers, who are "outside." There are others about him, sitting there, who are "inside." The spatial arrangement is thus made to reinforce the metaphorical contrast.

The metaphorical use of the terms of relation is easily weakened. For example, there is often little blood left in the term "brother" for fellow Christians. But Jesus takes up with family ties in their literal, biological sense in order to win pervasive meaning for the metaphorical sense. To put the matter briefly, in the kingdom proclaimed by Jesus, the ties of fellowship are stronger than the ties of family. Family is to be forsaken for the sake of the kingdom. There is thus a radical reordering of values, relationships in the kingdom announced by Jesus.

Narrative information

The attitude of Jesus' mother and brother toward him is not indicated within the confines of the pericope itself (Mark 3:31–35). The brief story ends without the hearer learning whether Jesus' family was finally able to speak to him, and, if so, what they wanted. Indeed, the pericope provides no narrative information beyond the bare references required to set the stage dramatically for the pronouncement. The narrative thus has no interest in narrative information for its own sake.

In the context in Mark, however, it is stated that his family thought him mad ("they thought he was out of his mind") and so came to get him (Mark 3:21). The position of the Jewish authorities is clear: they hold that he is possessed by Beelzebub (3:22). To these two opinions given in 3:21–22 Jesus is made to respond in chiastic order in 3:23–30 and 3:31–35, respectively.

It is not clear why Jesus' family thought him beside himself. The conviction of the authorities is limited to his exorcisms (3:22; cf. 3:11), but that would be a harsh judgment if shared by relatives. It is possible that his madness, in Mark, is to be understood in light of the whole range of conflicts reported in 2:1–3:6 (healing of the paralytic; eating with tax collectors and sinners; fasting; breaking the Sabbath; man with the withered hand). In any case, in Mark 3:20–21, which is Markan editorial material, his madness goes together with all those things that led to his enormous popularity: the crowd came together and he could not even eat. It is thus all his conflicts with the authorities, especially those which involve healings or exorcisms, that lead to the opinion that he is mad. From his family's point of view, it may simply be that he permits himself to lead a style of life that does not permit him even to eat. This would square with a mother's concern for her son.

Two other possibilities suggest themselves. (1) Jesus' family may think him deranged because of the attitude he exhibits toward his own family: "Here are my mother and brothers," looking at the motley crowd in front of him. That Jesus subordinated family ties to other loyalties is evident from other texts, e.g., "I did not come to bring peace but a sword" (Matt 10:34–36//Luke 12:49–56). (2) Jesus' derangement may be a dramatic device or fiction, in connection with Jesus' effort, according to Mark, to subvert the tradition, to put it broadly. His broadcast conflicts with the authorities and his espousal of sinners make him metaphorically mad: he contests what everybody takes to be real.

It is possible, of course, that the madness theme is operative at several or all of these levels at the same time.

A parabolic act

We have explored these interpretive possibilities in order to set out the original horizon of the incident and to show what has happened to it in Mark.

We observed that the interplay between "mother and brothers" taken literally and the same phrase taken metaphorically sets up the dramatic tension and contributes to the force of the pronouncement. The intensity of the metaphorical meaning depends, moreover, on the proximity but spatial separation of Jesus' family. In the pronouncement, furthermore, the fundamental ties that serve as the glue of social structures are modified, or, better, reversed: in the received world family, in the kingdom, the fellowship of followers.

"Mothers and brothers" must migrate from the literal to the non-literal in order for the pronouncement to work. If the phrase is understood only literally, the pericope makes no sense at all. On the other hand, if the phrase is taken literally non-literally, the only persons in the world who cannot be Jesus' mother and brothers are his real mother and brothers (the basis of the contrast). And

Mark so understands the terms: they refer literally non-literally to the disciples, the community of faith.[6] And so Mark carries out his understanding, controls the meaning of the narrative, by making Jesus' mother and brothers into opponents, who seek to take him away and who are now and always "outside." By contrast, disciples now and always are "inside." The principle of arbitrary inclusion/exclusion is at work.

There is no hint of these developments in the brief narrative itself, beyond, perhaps, the generalizing legion in Mark 3:35 ("Whoever does God's will, that is my brother, and sister, and mother!"). So long as we limit ourselves to the narrative itself, we need not be misled by Mark's setting. We learn nothing about the disposition of Jesus' family from this pericope. At the conclusion of the scene, he may in fact have said, "Let my mother and brothers through, please." Or, the entire occasion may have been a fiction. It doesn't really matter because the narrative is true to the aphorism: the literal endows the metaphorical and then disappears into it; whoever wishes may be a relative of Jesus, including his relatives. The narrative and pronouncement do not come to rest in the disciples or anywhere else. Every gathering of victims in the ditch or profligate sons is subject to the pronouncement: "Here are my mother and brothers!" The pericope on true relatives is thus a parabolic act—a parable acted out, or an act turned into a parable.

The Domestication of the Samaritan

As promised, we return now to the history of interpretation of the Samaritan. The force of the Samaritan as first told depends on the interplay between the fiction, which assumes and trades in the habituated social world, and the roles the hearers assign themselves in that same world. As we noted, the story confirms typical aspects of that world and then confuses matters by reordering essential parts. Accordingly, the listeners are invited to consider their life-world anew. We must now inquire: what happens when there is drift or shift in the received social world presupposed by the parable?

In a situation in which the terms Jew, Samaritan, Levite, Jericho road have only faded or zero values, the fundamental tensions of the story are released: Jews and Samaritans no longer hate each other; there may or may not be the same pro- and anticlerical feeling; Jericho road is any street; and there may be no Jews in the story at all. Gone, too, is the inclination of the original (Jewish) hearer to identify with the victim in the ditch, and the Samaritan's fantastic behavior is buried under an avalanche of ignorant familiarity. An entirely new story emerges.

There is a nameless victim in some ditch or other. Two parties ignore the silent appeal for help. A third notices and is compassionate. The third is incidentally called a Samaritan, who, because of his act of mercy, is now called good. The story is told to commend his kind of behavior.

In this later version of the story with the same text, actants[7] in the parable have been generalized as victim, passerby, helper. Readers are surprised, not at the generosity of the Samaritan, but at the callousness of the clergy. Auditors view the story objectively: they listen without being drawn into it, without suffering the stringent claims placed on the original hearers. There is no transformation of social roles. A moralizing admonition may now be appended: "Go and do likewise."

The reading of the parable just sketched is derived, of course, from the context given the parable in the Gospel of Luke.

The Language of Jesus

The analyses of the Samaritan, Prodigal, and relatives will provide the basis, along with related texts, for a series of propositions relative to the language of Jesus and its destiny in the tradition.

The first and fundamental characteristic of the language of Jesus is this: *the language of Jesus is pervaded by tension.*

(*a*) We have already noted the tension occasioned by the *interplay between the literal and non-literal senses of key terms.* Jesus makes the proximity of real relatives play forcefully into his use of "mother and brothers" in a metaphorical way. He compels that lonely Samaritan to shout the significance of helper to the Jewish victim.

(*b*) In a similar way, *participants in and auditors of the narrative parables stand in tension with each other.* Those paid first and those paid last in the Vineyard Laborers represent a deep-seated conflict. Common folk auditing the Samaritan must have smiled knowingly at clerical indifference. The hostility of the older son breaks into the open in the Prodigal.

(*c*) Robert Tannehill has identified the *focal instance* as a form of non-metaphorical language that is nevertheless laden with tension. In the saying,

> When someone strikes you on the right cheek, Turn the other as well. —Matt 5:39b

Jesus selects a very specific but extreme example and then puts it in a series with other specific but extreme cases. A strike on the *right* cheek has very limited applications, if taken literally, so extremity and specificity suggest that the range of application is indefinite or open. This open-endedness is reinforced by the series setting: the series establishes a pattern which can be extended to other situations: left cheek, cloak also, second mile; give and lend; and other comparable situations.

(*d*) Turning the other cheek is possible. Keeping your left hand in the dark about what your right hand is doing (Matt 6:3) is, strictly speaking, not possible. Another form of tension in the language of Jesus is thus *hyperbole:* an injunction to do something one cannot actually do.

(*e*) Finally, the *antithetical statement* appears in a number of forms in the language of Jesus.[8] One form is the antithetical aphorism, as in Mark 7:15.

> It's not what goes into a person that can defile; rather it's what comes out of a person that defiles.

Such sayings tend to divide into two halves, one in a positive, the other in a negative, form. Word links often bring the tension into sharp focus. Conciseness, absoluteness, lack of qualifications contribute to the linguistic strain.

These very characteristics contribute to what Tannehill calls "a certain loss of conceptual clarity."[9] The saying does not specify what the things coming out of person are. Nevertheless, the term "defile" and the reference to what goes into person suggest that cultic food laws are the immediate context. The secondary commentary in 7:18–23 confirms the suggestion. However, the listener and the interpreter both miss the force of the antithetical aphorism if they limit the negative force to Jewish food regulations and the positive to the list of sins given in the commentary which follows (Mark 7:21–22). Rather, "It is the function of this antithetical aphorism to awaken a new dominant concern," to quote Tannehill.[10] In the first place, the concern for defilement is radically refocused; put differently, Jesus transcends the question to which the aphorism is a response. Defilement is henceforth to be viewed in a different horizon. In the second place, the saying is so focused as to present a direct challenge to the listener: one's customary perspective is being called into question; conviction is being challenged; life-world is under attack. Because the particular issue and its socio-religious matrix both stand in the dock, the auditor will experience the resolution as open-ended, emancipating, free: not what goes in, but what comes out. There is no immediate context for what comes out, of course, since there is no relevant reverse of what goes in. The auditor will therefore have to determine that context for him- or herself.

Answers transcend the questions

It will bear repeating: the tensive language of Jesus regularly transcends the question to which it is the response; his speech lacks clarity, his speech forms are laced with structural ambiguity, so that the auditor is thrown back on his or her own resources. As a consequence, listeners experience these absurd demands as radical but indeterminate. It is no wonder that the disciples and others found Jesus difficult to understand. In commanding folks to turn the other cheek, he was deliberately reversing one's natural tendency; to quote Tannehill again, this injunction "stands in deliberate tension with the way in which men normally live and think."[11] In his parables and in his other sayings, Jesus has the received life-world under attack; it is not easy to hear a challenge that subverts one's habituated reality sense, one's unstudied relation to things.

Crossing over

Both the form and content of the language of Jesus indicate that he announces a fundamental reversal of the human destiny. This reversal is related to expectations as informed by the everyday or received world. Moreover, this reversal is a perpetual state of affairs in the kingdom: whatever one comes to expect, to rely on, is perpetually refused; but to whoever expects nothing, who is truly profligate, who is a genuine victim in the ditch, the kingdom arrives as a gift.

Those who encounter Jesus' words are at liberty to take up with them as they choose. One may prefer the comforts, the securities of the habituated life-world and opt out of the parable or refuse the injunction. One may insist on justice and thus elect not to turn the other cheek. Of course, one may also be willing to settle for mercy. That means forever leaving home, forever forsaking cosmic comforts, in order to return. In that case, one is always crossing over to that fabulous yonder of Franz Kafka. The older son cannot come home because he never leaves; he clings to the certainties of the everyday and pouts because he has nothing to celebrate. The profligate, on the other hand, squanders his patrimony for the sake of a homecoming.

Jesus offers the new reality on the authority of the parable, as a comic inversion of received certainties. He does not coerce; he is no cosmic bully. The hearer is free to join the fantasy or not, as she chooses. God does not "appear" to force the issue. Although of ultimate seriousness, the issue is joined only in the full ambiguity of the metaphor, the hyperbole, the antithetical aphorism.

The whole matter could be summed up in still another way. The Pharisees are those who insist on their right to interpret the text, to tell the story as they see fit. The recipients of grace, on the other hand, allow the text to interpret them. They are the aim and goal of the parable.

Pharisees as Christian scribes

(a) In general, it may be said that the basic tension in the language of Jesus is relaxed as his words are passed around and on. A shift in historical context erodes the bite in terms like Samaritan and Jericho road, as already noted. But the purveyors of tradition, out of respect for it, will seek to fix or freeze the terms and this in a variety of ways. The pre-eminent Pharisaic proclivity is literality: where a literal reading is possible, be sure that it is the correct one. So the Samaritan is straightaway understood as an example story and the metaphorical horizon (and tension) of the original parable is lost. But the tradition seeks to be literal even when the text is patently metaphorical. For that reason, there is the overpowering tendency to make the prodigal father literally the model of God's love. And we thereby introduce an immediate sanction into the story; God is written quite literally into the narrative. The presence of deity tends to quell interpretive speculation.

Of course, Pharisaic control of the text may be exercised in other ways. To a polyvalent text one may simply add a clarifying interpretation, such as the context for the Samaritan or the list of defiling things coming out of person. The tradition may also be inclined to "remember" a text in accordance with its now fixed interpretation. Which is to say, the tradition may actually modify or edit the text to conform to its understanding. And, of course, a lively tradition will create new texts along superficially parallel lines, but without the creative tensions characteristic of originating language.

(b) Releasing the tension is a Pharisaic ploy to manage the text, to hold it at arm's length, in order to eliminate risk. So long as powerful texts like the parables or aphorisms of Jesus retain their own initiatives, there is the danger that those in whose house the texts have been domesticated—preserved and handed around and on— will be called on to be victims or perhaps put down as profligate sons. But the distance of tranquilized familiarity permits patrons of texts to insulate themselves from the ravages of root metaphors. In addition to the forms of control already sketched, insulation is generated by an asymmetrical hermeneutic, in which the Pharisees are caricatured, God is introduced out of the machine, and the insiders are protected from assault. In short, Pharisees are those who domesticate texts out of love for them. Domesticated texts are comfortable, like old shoes.

Lest we forget, it should be recalled that Pharisee in this context is a metaphor for all of us, then and now, who traffic in the Jesus tradition.

The Received World

In this study reference has been repeatedly made to the everyday life-world, the habituated world, the received reality sense, and the like. It will be both helpful and necessary to indicate the role this concept plays in what has been said and what remains to be said, for that role is central to the basic thesis.

In the phenomenological tradition stemming from Edmund Husserl, the concept of *Lebenswelt* or life-world has been a steady feature. The brief account given here follows the analysis of Alfred Schutz in his work, *The Structures of the Life-World*.

Received world as life-world

The everyday life-world, according to Shutz, is to be understood as that sphere of reality which proximate, wide-awake adults of sound mind take for granted.[12] This world is one in which the existence of other persons is assumed; these persons are further assumed to have relations to the same sphere of reality analogous to those I have. In fine, the world that is experienced in what Schutz calls the "natural attitude" is a social world. Moreover, it is historically pregiven for me and other persons: it was there before I was, so that at any moment the situation in which I find myself was only to a small extent created by me.[13]

The "natural attitude," i.e., the one that prevails under daily circumstances, involves the suspension of doubt concerning the reality and validity of that which is taken for granted. The suspension of doubt makes for parsimony of effort: one does not have to begin each day with root decisions regarding the structure of reality. Further, I trust that the life-world inherited by me and obtained from fellow persons will continue more or less as I know it. My stock of knowledge, which is derived from "sedimented group

experience that has passed the test,"[14] enables me to repeat successful acts, and adopt the "so forth" attitude, as Husserl put it.[15]

As actant however, I am not merely captive to an inherited or
habituated life-world: I do indeed operate within that world, but
also operate on it.[16] It is true that my tendency is to convert questionable experiences into routine experience, in deference to the
received world and because I am motivated by parsimony of effort.
Nevertheless, I do encounter novel experiences from time to time,
which cause me to see that my reference schemata are deficient. I
am able to manage novelty because my life-world floats in a sea
of indeterminancy; there are regions which simply lie beyond my
purview. I know that I can reinterpret but not change past events.
I know that many elements of my active life-world are unalterable.
Inherited structures form what appears to me to be a uniform plan,
to which I can repeatedly explicitly advert.[17] Yet I also know that
somatically mediated activity can modify what is imposed on me.[18]
I thus know that I can live out of a determinate past into an indeterminate future, but I also know that that future must relate to that
past as the "out of which."

My life-world is therefore perpetually in fine imbalance: it
evolves slowly, imperceptibly, in response to adjustments I am
forced to make to it and out of pressure brought to bear on it from
my fellows. It is in constant flux in spite of the fact that I experience
it as steady and determinate.

Other worlds

The natural attitude is characteristic of the normal, wide-awake
adult of sound mind. But life-world also embraces more than
everyday reality. People sink into sleep and enter a different world.
They go mad by making an exit from certified social reality. Older
people may revert to the naiveté of childhood. Furthermore, the
poet may transcend the natural attitude by means of symbols,
and we all lapse into fantasies or fictions. There are those creative
minds and souls who live, not in the natural attitude, but mostly in
a symbolic or fantastic world.

Secondary life-worlds

J. R. R. Tolkien, in a particularly provocative essay on fairy tales,
has suggested that the true fairy tale or fantasy creates a secondary
world which prompts the reader to suspend doubt about its reality. The suspension of doubt about the secondary world generates

a reversal of the suspension regarding the ordinary life-world. The result is a competition among worlds.

A secondary life-world provides a horizon of meaning to which I can repeatedly explicitly advert. It may be supported by a community of believers who share the fantasy. That new world stands over against the received life-world and vies with it for ascendancy. To be sure, the reigning life-world always regards itself as *true*, i.e., as permanent. It therefore discredits new fantasies in advance. However, the establishment of a new fantasy demonstrates the magic beyond truth: all our worlds are fantasies. A fantasy is thus nothing more or less than a circumspective totality of significations to which we give ourselves.

The Domestication of the Tradition: Theses

The foregoing tentative sketches of the form and content of the Jesus tradition together with some observations regarding its immediate destiny in the tradition will provide a somewhat limited but I believe adequate basis for a more sweeping depiction of developments.

For the sake of brevity, this section will take the form of a series of propositions, followed in some instances by brief commentary.

(*a*) The parables and aphorisms of Jesus constitute a fantasy: the creation of a secondary world called the kingdom of God, which is the good news or truth about the then regnant primary world.

(*b*) The kingdom arrives in the language of Jesus for those for whom it is fantasy. The fantasy of the kingdom certifies the kingdom as the ultimate reality. This has the effect of making the ordinary life-world deceptive, false.

(*c*) The parables and aphorisms of Jesus are not self-referential; he does not appear in the phenomenal field of his own language. Rather, Jesus stands in the penumbra of his language as one who heralds the miraculous arrival of that kingdom. Further, God is not immanent to the fantasy of the kingdom in the parables and aphorisms of Jesus. The kingdom certifies itself in its presence because it brings and is a new sense of the real, a new life-world.

(*d*) The sanctions and rewards belonging to the kingdom are intrinsic: the kingdom is its own reward, like love. The kingdom is therefore extended with comic relief: the mustard plant replaces the mighty cedar.

(*e*) In the transmission of the Jesus tradition several things transpire simultaneously: (1) the tension in the language of Jesus is released; (2) the terms of that language are assimilated to previously habituated categories so that Jesus is made to compete within a pregiven life-world; (3) Jesus is painted into the narrative picture as the certifier of the new reality; (4) God is made immanent to the process; (5) these developments lead to the disenchantment of the fantasy, so that the arrival of the kingdom is pushed off into the future; (6) the messiah must then return to achieve what he did not achieve the first time through.

(f) The first linguistic step in these developments was the creation of the pronouncement story: a saying set in a minimal narrative context. Some pronouncement stories are true to the parabolic and aphoristic base, but once Jesus "appears" it becomes easier for the form to become self-referential. Self-reference means that attention is being diverted from the kingdom as fantasy to Jesus as the future bringer of the kingdom.

(g) The second linguistic step is the miracle story in which Jesus is now being assimilated to secular categories: he is a thaumaturge temporarily suspending the processes of the received life-world. In other words, rather than creating a new fantasy he is taken as an alchemist changing base metals into gold.

(h) In stories about Jesus or legends he is further assimilated to the previous tradition: he belongs in but is superior to other memorable leaders in the received tradition. Rather than subverting the tradition, he competes with it.

(i) The primitive community soon painted itself into the picture as the community of faith (in Acts, for example). By so doing, it gave itself the charge of causing that tradition to be assimilated to what that community already knew. But its faith knowledge interfered with the horizon of the original Jesus tradition, in which everyone, including Jesus himself, risked the arrival of the kingdom. The community no longer submitted itself to the insider/outsider test, but assumed that it was perpetually inside.

(j) The gospel form is not itself a further stage in the same linear development. It is rather a compromise in which the community of faith gives expression to its life-world and then embeds Jesus in it, while recalling, at the same time, elements of the original tradition which contradict that life-world. In other words, when translated into life-worlds, the Jesus tradition clearly contravenes the tradition of interpretation that was superimposed upon it.

This observation permits a generalization: the strength of a really lively tradition is reflected in what that tradition remembers against itself. A weak tradition assimilates fragments of experience and memory entirely to what it already knows—the received world. A powerful tradition feeds on glimpses of other worlds, spheres of reality aborning.

The gospels embody paradoxes and anomalies, which means that they arrest and even reverse the trend visible in the miracle stories and legends: the words of Jesus are an uneasy memory in tension with the emerging secular faith (faith that squares with interpretive categories of the received world).

(k) The kerygma with an empty center is a fully mythologized expression of the faith of the primitive community. To describe it as having an empty center means that it concentrates on the pre-existence and incarnation, on the one side, and the death, resurrection, and exaltation, on the other, without remarking the originating Jesus tradition that underlies that conviction. It is mythological in the sense we have been using the term: the Christ as God's messiah and the deity itself are thought to be immanent to the life-world of the community. The terms of the kerygma are drawn from both the Jewish and hellenistic world and are mostly assimilated to those worlds. However, Paul recognizes the danger presented by assimilation and strives to avert it by reforming the categories. He does so out of deference to the Jesus tradition but without invoking it directly, probably because it was controlled by his opponents. The gospels do invoke the Jesus tradition directly and fill in the empty center; it is probable that Mark represents only the center without a mythological frame.

Beyond Demythologizing

It has taken forty years for the issues Bultmann raised in his 1941 essay on demythologizing to come clear. It is time to put these issues in proper perspective in order to be able to move beyond them. By doing so, we will be able to pay homage to an important era of biblical scholarship from a distance and chart a firm course into the future rather than continue to drift, blown about by minor squalls.

The language of Jesus

The Christian faith is rooted in the language of Jesus rather than in the primitive Christian kerygma or the Easter event, contrary to Bultmann. To sum up the previous argument, parable, aphorism, and parabolic act are the threshold opening onto the new reality, the fantasy, called the kingdom. The first community of faith went across this threshold and found itself—for brief moments—in the fantasy of the kingdom. Having glimpsed that never-never land, it desired to locate it in space and time, i.e., in relation to received categories of experience, and thus give an account of it. But it took no notice of how it had gotten there, other than its memory of Jesus as the declaimer of revelatory words. For this reason, it superimposed its own explanations, derived from a prior life-world, on the Jesus tradition, which it tended to assimilate to its own understanding. In spite of its predominant tendency, the community remembered Jesus' words as the locus of revelation, even in the face of its own expectations linked to a more or less conventional messianic hope. Its hope was essentially mythological: God was immanent and the end-time was imminent, but in the language of Jesus the kingdom did not suffer comparison with habituated apocalyptic hopes. Modern scholarly efforts to locate Jesus within the Jewish apocalyptic of late antiquity only indulge the proclivities of the primitive community and contravene the bedrock of the Jesus tradition. The latter indicates that the language of Jesus is non-mythological: God is not immanent to the fantasy of the kingdom nor is the consummation of history.

The kerygma and Easter

Both the kerygma and the Easter event are derivative in relation to the language of Jesus. The Easter event represents the conviction that the power of the Jesus tradition lives on, just as the kerygma draws its precipitator, the teller of parables and aphorisms, into the phenomenal picture and then writes the community of faith as the witnessing community into the picture as well (cf. 1 Cor 15:3–5). The kerygma is thus a fully mythologized expression of faith. To put the matter more tellingly, in the kerygma everything becomes explicit, except the ground of faith, viz., the language of Jesus. But an empty center was required because a non-mythological center would have contradicted the mythological frame.

Contrary to Bultmann, the kerygma does not require demythologizing in the face of the modem, scientific worldview; it requires demythologizing in the face of its source and ground, the revelatory language of Jesus. Had Bultmann not chosen to rest his case for the Christian faith on the message of the primitive church, he might have been willing to complete his demythologizing program. As it was, he demythologized everything but the word of God; that he still consigned to the Holy Spirit and thus guarded it from the ravages of modernity. But Jesus does not resort to anything outside the domain of his secular life-world: his message does not trade in mythology at any level.

The sociological movement

I do not wish to impugn the instincts of Bultmann that led him rightly and inevitably to his demythologizing program. As long as one takes a worldview or a life-world as the criterion of what may be believed, demythologizing as he advocated it becomes necessary. But Jesus did not appeal to his received life-world, except to shatter it. We may assume that the fantasy of the kingdom shatters every life-world as the locus of shelter from the ultimate claim. It follows that the modern, scientific worldview cannot be the criterion against which the fantasy of the kingdom is to be measured.

Those who advocate the criterion of dissimilarity as a means of identifying the core of the Jesus tradition are therefore on the right track. If in parable and aphorism Jesus is pointing to a radically new life-world, he is simultaneously breaking with the old. We do not have to resort to theory to recognize the point; we may derive it from his words themselves. On the other hand, some workable theory to account for this phenomenon may prove helpful.

Howard Kee concedes that the objectivity of the dissimilarity position is commendable. "But," he continues, "the result is to detach Jesus from any recognizable life-situation capable of being reconstructed historically. This approach is a kind of historical-methodological docetism."[19] He reasons further that "a responsible historian cannot assume in advance that there was a radical disjunction between a figure of the ancient past on the one hand and the conceptual-cultural antecedents shared by his contemporaries on the other."[20] That appears valid enough, but then he posits the opposite assumption: "the assumption of cultural continuity holds true whether the subject under investigation is Jesus or Mark."[21]

To the sociological movement as exemplified by Kee it may be rejoined that continuity may take the form of "out of which" as well as the form "within which." We all operate on our life-worlds as well as within them, and it is our efforts to find our own voices, to establish discontinuity, that characterize us as individuals. It may be true of most of us that we are prosaic enough to live mostly within a received frame of reference. That does not make us interesting. It may be true that Jesus stands in full continuity with his "conceptual-cultural antecedents," but in that case he would not be very interesting. As Alfred North Whitehead has said, "it is more important that something be interesting than true."

To be sure, discontinuity cannot be assumed; it can be accepted only on unequivocal evidence. And it is this evidence which the parables and aphorisms of Jesus offer in abundance.

The sociological movement advocates the habituated life-world of Judaism in late antiquity as the criterion of a non-docetic Jesus. Bultmann proposed the modern worldview as the criterion. Neither is satisfactory. As one endeavoring to burst the seams of his inherited world, Jesus should be permitted to establish his own criterion.

The history of ideas

The ascendency of life-world as a category of historical judgment is an improvement over the history-of-ideas approach, which is exemplified in its acute form by Millar Burrows, *An Outline of Biblical Theology*. But even Bultmann, the advocate of existentialism, trades predominantly in ideas. His treatment of the message of Jesus in his *Theology of the New Testament* utilizes rubrics such as "Jesus' Idea of God"[22] and "the Messianic Consciousness of Jesus,"[23] as though Jesus' "ideas" were determinative. Indeed, Jesus' "ideas" are mostly put into the record by his interpreters. For this reason, the quest of the historical Jesus can be renewed only as a quest aimed at the life-world inspired by the fantasy of the kingdom, in relation to the habituated life-world which functioned and functions as its "out of which."

Language and event

Ray Hart, my colleague of many years, has characterized imaginative discourse as language at the lowest level of abstraction.[24] Like a true philosopher, he thus defined it in relation to the philosophical norm of intellectual discourse: discursive language. Nevertheless, he goes on to say that imaginative language is the overlay of language and event so closely that the two cannot be discriminated: language permits event to occur and event gives language its tongue.

Imaginative language as revelation is to be understood quite differently from theological language as revelation. The latter offers concepts as the content of revelation, while the former is illumination that enables sight; in imaginative discourse, the mind is not so much informed as formed.[25] If we may use a theological category as a metaphor, we may say that "God" is the pre-primordial, the before of our being, the seeing of our sight. "God" thus does not "appear" in the phenomenal field of the parables because "God" is the metaphor that constitutes the fantasy of the kingdom.

The language of Jesus as the house of faith

The conviction of the primitive church was rooted, not in the so-called historical Jesus, but in his life-world, the world he recognized and celebrated as the fantasy of the kingdom. The fantasy of the kingdom is that to which both Jesus and the first disciples gave themselves; they both risked their sanity (the certainty of the habituated world) on that fantasy. The imaginative discourse of Jesus is therefore the house of faith: in it faith lives and moves and has its being. This holds true even when that faith gives account of itself in a totally different linguistic key.

This view of matters represents a radical shift in the locus and character of revelation and the methodology appropriate to its study. The quest of the so-called historical Jesus can only be a quest of the parabolic Jesus, parable understood as speech-act. But even the phrase, parabolic Jesus, is misleading. The object of the quest is actually the life-world onto which the parable opens, viz., the fantasy of the kingdom. That life-world, that fantasy, is there by virtue of Jesus' imaginative discourse, which should be understood, not as belonging to him, but as the locus of transactions between self and world, community and world, world and self and community. In sum, his imaginative discourse, his parable, is the house of faith.

The irony of success

We have been speaking in an altogether too cavalier way of the renewal of the quest, although now relocated. We should nevertheless take care that the danger signals are properly heeded. Among many we can observe only one, the pre-eminent danger.

It may be thought that the first danger to which the quest is open is that it will discover a Jesus who is wholly compatible with its active life-world. That threat is ever immanent, but it is not the first danger. The ultimate threat is that such a quest, if executed faithfully, will discover a Jesus that is unpalatable, distasteful, inimical to the tradition to which he belongs. That is a danger because it will be fundamentally disruptive to the community of faith. On the other hand, the kingdom of which Jesus spoke was fundamentally disruptive to the community of faith to which he addressed his parables. If our hermeneutic is not to be asymmetrical, our methodology should correspond to the primary text: the measure of success may thus be the extent to which this quest contravenes the tradition to which it belongs. Put theologically, the strength of the tradition lies in its power to invoke its memory against its own proclivity to domesticate the tradition.

Jesus

The Silent Sage

The Jesus Seminar has concluded that twenty-two authentic parables of Jesus have been recorded in the gospel tradition. Although the gospels have probably not preserved the actual words of Jesus, it is entirely possible that the evangelists have retained the original plot in most cases. The authentic parables are:

1. The Leaven (Luke 13:20–21//Matt 13:33//Thom 96:1–2)
2. The Samaritan (Luke 10:30–35)
3. The Shrewd Manager (Luke 16:1–8a)
4. The Vineyard Laborers (Matt 20:1–15)
5. The Mustard Seed (Thom 20:2–4//Mark 4:30–32 //Luke 13:18–19//Matt 13:31–32)
6. The Lost Coin (Luke 15:8–9)
7. The Lost Sheep (Luke 15:4–6//Matt 18:12–13//Thom 107:1–3)
8. The Treasure (Matt 13:44//Thom 109:1–3)
9. The Prodigal Son (Luke 15:11–32)
10. The Corrupt Judge (Luke 18:2–5)
11. The Dinner Party (Thom 64:1–11//Luke 14:16–23 //Matt 22:2–13)
12. The Pearl (Thom 76:1–2//Matt 13:45–46)
13. The Assassin (Thom 98:1–3)
14. The Unforgiving Slave (Matt 18:23–34)
15. The Leased Vineyard (Thom 65:1–7//Luke 20:9–15 //Matt 21:33–39//Mark 12:1–8)
16. The Rich Farmer (Thom 63:1–3//Luke 12:16–20)
17. The Money in Trust (Matt 25:14–28//Luke 19:13–24)
18. The Powerful Man (Mark 3:27//Matt 12:29//Thom 35:1–2// Luke 11:21–22)
19. The Pharisee & Toll Collector (Luke 18:10–14)
20. Seed and Harvest (Mark 4:26–29)

From *Jesus as Precursor*, rev. ed. 1994.

21. The Sower (Mark 4:3–8//Matt 13:3–8//Thom 9:1–5 //Luke 8:5–8)
22. The Empty Jar (Thom 97:1–4)

The parables, which Jesus tells as though he were hearing them, are undoubtedly the primary receptacle of his vision. The striking feature of the parables is that in them Jesus does not speak about what his first listeners—and his subsequent listeners—expected and expect him to speak about. (Our expectations dictate the range of our hearing: we have great difficulty hearing anything outside that range.) Jesus does not speak about God in his parables, he does not develop a doctrine of God, he does not speak about himself, he does not proclaim his messiahship, he does not predict his passion and death, he does not claim that he is about to die for the sins of humankind, he does not predict that history will soon end, he does not depict a last judgment, he does not picture supernatural beings, or miracles, or even exorcisms, and he does not commission his disciples to form a church and conduct a world mission. On all these topics of burning interest to people in his day, to his disciples of the second and third generations, and modern readers of the gospels, he was and is simply and startlingly silent.

In his parables he does speak about a robbery on an isolated road, about shrewd business managers, about day laborers in a vineyard, about the wild mustard plant, about lost coins, sheep, and wayward children, about secret treasure and fantastic pearls, about assassins and strong men, about baking bread, about a dinner party, about leased vineyards, about prayers in the temple, about rich farmers and money held in trust, about sowing seed, and about an empty jar. All mundane topics, everyday particulars, often caricatured or exaggerated, regularly with surprising endings open to audience participation.

On the basis of his parables, we might conclude that Jesus rarely spoke about religion at all. Insofar as religion figures as subject matter in his stories, it appears to be part of the secular landscape, something that one stumbles across the same way one observes a woman carrying a jar on her head or a farmer prodding a donkey along the path. Readers of the gospels speak glibly about the religion of Jesus because his followers created a religion about Jesus. It is not at all clear that religion concerns Jesus.

There are also approximately sixty-eight authentic aphorisms of Jesus, depending on how one counts couplets and clusters. The Jesus Seminar has attempted to identify and isolate the voice of Jesus on the basis of a voice print defined by the predominant forms of his remembered speech—parables and short, pithy, poignant one- and two-liners. The aphorisms and proverbs are not significantly different from the parables in the subject matter they address. It is true that Jesus speaks occasionally about God, for example, in the one-sentence prayers collected into what we know as the Lord's prayer (Luke 11:2). He refers to the Creator's care for the sparrows and lilies (Luke 12:6–7, 22–24, 27–28) and he compares God's graciousness to that of human parents (Matt 7:7–11). In these and other references to God, Jesus is not adopting a metaphysical creed—or preparing the way for one—but observing the world as he sees it—as though it were in an intensive care unit run by his Father.

That perspective, in fact, is the difference. In Jesus' world, God is not an object, not even a person, whom one can observe here and there by keeping one's eyes open. When Jesus speaks about God, he is only observing his unseen God at work, he merely notes what God does. God himself or herself does not enter his field of vision.

Nor does Jesus speak about himself in his aphorisms. The apparent exceptions are sayings in which he is at war with Satan, with evil powers. He remarks:

> I was watching Satan fall like lightning from heaven. —Luke 10:18

This statement parallels another, similar remark:

> If by God's finger I drive out demons, then for you God's imperial rule has arrived. —Luke 11:20

Jesus does not actually claim to be driving out demons, but suggests that if he does, God is acting through him to overcome evil powers loose in the world. In both statements he is an observer; in the second he is also an agent, but this is as close as he comes to claiming exceptional agency for himself.

At his trial, according to the gospels, the ranking priests brought a long list of charges against Jesus. Pilate tried questioning him. "Don't you have some answer to give?" he asked Jesus. But Jesus stood dumb. Pilate was baffled.

In this pathetic scene (Mark 15:4–5), his accusers address numerous questions to him. He is either unable or unwilling to answer. Perhaps he hasn't heard. In any case, the silence enrages his foes and puzzles the stoic Pilate. Although the scene is undoubtedly the creation of the evangelist, it may well reflect the disposition of Jesus to questions that fell outside his field of vision. Who he was and what he had been sent to do belong to terrain that was unexplored and unexplorable for him. The Fellows of the Jesus Seminar accordingly have been skeptical of the authenticity of all *I am . . .* or *I have come to . . .* statements.

A little earlier in the narrative (Mark 15:2), Pilate asks, in disbelief, "You are the king of the Jews?" Jesus gives an ambiguous answer, which can be translated, "If you say so," "You said it, I didn't," or "The words are yours." The title, in fact, is derived from the sign Pilate had put over the cross (John 19:19).

Jesus does give what appear to be vacillating, equivocal answers to some questions. And he not infrequently poses riddles. Both reflect his unwillingness to speak, to give advice, to define.

It is frustrating, even exasperating, to be faced with someone who will not give a straight answer. When asked whether it is permissible to pay the poll tax, Jesus counters, "Pay the emperor what belongs to the emperor, and pay God what belongs to God" (Mark 12:17). When asked why he eats publicly with sinners and toll collectors, he responds, "Since when do the able-bodied need a doctor; it's the sick who do" (Mark 2:17). The behavior of Jesus' disciples and those of John is contrasted by some officials. They ask him, "Why do John's disciples fast but yours don't?" He replies, "The groom's friends can't fast while the groom is present can they?" (Mark 2:19). Jesus' disciples apparently harvested handfuls of grain on the Sabbath while walking through a grainfield. The officials thought that was improper. Jesus responds:

> The Sabbath day was created for Adam and Eve,
> Not Adam and Eve for the Sabbath day.
> So, the son of Adam lords it even over the Sabbath day. —Mark 2:27–28

In this sweeping response, Jesus takes his critics back to creation. He gives the appearance of humankind a higher priority in the order of things than the creation of a seventh day of rest. Answers of this type subvert the question to which they are ostensibly the answers. Questions about table fellowship, fasting, Sabbath observance are trivialized by the frame into which they are inserted.

Jesus has some questions of his own to ask. "If salt becomes bland with what will you renew it?" (Mark 9:50). That question, we must suppose, has an obvious answer: either salt cannot be renewed or it can be renewed only with more salt. It is the obvious on the lips of the sage that gives pause. But to what sphere of human experience and endeavor does it apply? "Since when is a lamp brought in and put under a bushel?" he inquires, as though his listeners didn't know the answer (Mark 4:21). "Since when do people pick grapes from thorns or figs from thistles?" he asks innocently (Matt 7:16). Of course they don't and they can't. The occasion on which and the reason for which he made this pronouncement have been lost. His mother and brothers come to take him home but can't get to him for the crowd. He asks of the circle around him, "Who are my mother and my brothers?" (Mark 3:33–34). When he is accused of exorcising demons in the name of Satan, he asks: "How can Satan drive out Satan?" to the consternation of his interlocutors (Mark 3:23–26).

Then there are the paradoxes. How can we explain them? "The last will be first and the first last" (Matt 20:16). "Whoever tries to hang onto life will forfeit it, but whoever forfeits life will preserve it" (Luke 18:33). "When you give to charity, don't let your left hand in on what your right hand is up to" (Matt 6:3). These are impossible combinations. They express a contradiction in terms. They may embody some profound truth, but we are left without explicit clues to that truth.

In spite of ambiguities, in spite of parody, hyperbole, paradox, and injunctions impossible to heed, the invitation to cross over is clear. Jesus' parables invite; they constitute open invitations. But they are not explicit. When we ask, "Do we have your permission to cross over?" Jesus does not answer. When the young man with real money wants to know what he must do, Jesus assigns him the one thing he can't and won't do, as though he took some delight in creating an impossible gulf to span. Or perhaps he was just pointing to the lack of commitment underlying the question asked by the wealthy inquirer. We cannot tell. When Jesus is asked who he is, when it is demanded of him to tell on what authority he does these things, he counters with a riddle, or with a metaphor, or with a paradox. In sum, he refuses to answer. His listeners can reject his answers, they can stop their ears against his alluring tales, but they can't tolerate his silence. When Jesus advises, "No one knows the exact day or minute; no one knows, not even heaven's messengers, not even the son, no one, except the Father" (Mark 13:32), we cannot abide his refusal. We demand to know. We will know. We will twist and torture ancient texts until we come up with the answer Jesus himself refuses to give. For not to know humiliates. Human pride is at stake. Another name for that is human hubris—the demand to have a peer relationship with God. Adam and Eve were ejected from the Garden because divine silence was not good enough for them.

CHAPTER

Jesus

A Voice Print

Jesus was a wandering teacher of wisdom. His voice emanates from a compendium of parables, aphorisms, and dialogues the Jesus Seminar has isolated from the mass of tradition that accrued to his name. In those sayings, and correlative acts, we can occasionally catch sight of Jesus' vision, a vision of something he called God's domain. Visions come in bits and pieces, in random stunning insights, never in continuous, articulated wholes. Yet from these fragments of insight we can begin to piece together some sense of the whole. Together those fragments provide us with glimpses of the historical figure. Since his vision was neither more nor less than a glimpse, the best we can hope for is a glimpse of his glimpse.

The Aphorism

Jesus was a master of the short, pithy witticism known as an aphorism. We need to distinguish an aphorism from a proverb.

An aphorism is a proverb-like saying that subverts conventional wisdom. "An apple a day keeps the doctor away" is a proverb. It expresses conventional wisdom; it affirms what everybody already knows. "Let the dead bury the dead" is one of Jesus' most difficult aphorisms. An aphorism subverts or contradicts conventional, proverbial wisdom. "Let the dead bury the dead" attacks the fundamental obligation to care appropriately for the dead, and it does so by suggesting that many living are in fact metaphorically dead.

Oscar Wilde was a well-known aphorist. One of his best: "We wouldn't be so concerned about what people thought of us, if we realized how seldom they do."

Flannery O'Connor was asked over and over again if she thinks the universities stifle writers. Her response, "Perhaps, but they don't stifle enough of them."

From *Profiles of Jesus,* 2002.

Halford Luccock, who taught homiletics at Yale University for many years, was once asked, "How many points should a sermon have?" To the question he replied, "At least one."

The Parable

The parable is a fantasy—a fantasy about God's domain, an order of reality that feeds on but subtlety transforms the everyday world. It is about an order of reality that lies beyond, but just barely beyond, the everyday, the humdrum, the habituated. In that case, the parable is also an invitation to cross over, to leave the old behind and embrace the new. The ability to cross over will depend, of course, on both the tenacity with which one holds to the inherited scheme of things, and on one's willingness to cut the ties to comfortable tradition. The parable is pitted against the power of the proven. Making the transition under such circumstances does not come easily.

The options Jesus offers his audience consistently run counter to their normal way of looking at life. Both his parables and aphorisms regularly frustrate the expectations of his hearers. Jesus develops a consistent rhetorical strategy that matches the content of his message. First, he depicts and then distorts the everyday world he and his Galilean neighbors inherit and inhabit. We shall refer to that world as the received world. Second, his parables and witticisms transform and transcend that world. He adopts and then distorts the received world in order to hint at a new horizon. The result is a fleeting glimpse of what lies beyond the boundaries of the everyday; his language and deeds constitute a knothole in the cosmic fence.

Before we attempt to summarize the content of his vision, we should explore this strategy. It will telegraph valuable hints about the content of his vision.

1. His language is concrete and specific. Jesus always talked about God's domain in everyday, mundane terms—dinner parties, travelers being mugged, truant sons, the hungry and tearful, toll collectors and prostitutes, a cache of coins. He never used abstract language. He made no theological statements. He would not have said, "All human beings have sinned and fallen short of the glory of God." He would not have confessed, "I believe in God the Father Almighty." It never occurred to him to assert that "God is love." Jesus did not have a doctrine of God; he had only experience of God.

2. Typifications. Jesus makes use of typifications to which everyone in his audience could have given immediate assent. Travelers get mugged on the Jericho road. A manager embezzles from his employer. A woman loses a coin on the dirt floor. A judge is corrupt. A friend knocks on the door at midnight and asks for bread. A truant son asks for his inheritance and then blows it on wine, women, and song in a foreign land. People nod their heads in agreement with these generalizations.

3. Unlike other teachers, he does not cite and interpret scripture. He does not debate fine points in the law. He makes no theological statements. He would not have said, "God is the ground of being" or even such a simple thing as "God is love." He does not make philosophical generalizations. He would not have said, "I think, therefore I am," or "Homo sapiens is the only animal that has language."

4. He does not make personal confessions nor are his stories and witticisms self-referential. It is inconceivable that he said, "I am the way, the truth, and the life; no one comes to the Father except through me." On the contrary, his discourse is focused exclusively on the banalities of the everyday world.

5. Although his language was drawn from the mundane world around him, he did not have ordinary reality in mind. His language is indirect; it is highly figurative or metaphorical. We know the parable of the Leaven is not about baking bread. The Dinner Party has nothing to do with social etiquette or with seating patterns at a banquet. The Mustard Seed and the Sower are not about gardening. The Shrewd Manager is not advice about business practices. His admonition to lend to those who can't pay us back is not about banking practice. While he invariably speaks in mundane terms, about what appear to be trivial or trite matters, his listeners know he has some other, much more significant subject in mind.

6. They know that for several reasons. They know because his exaggerations, his caricatures, resist literal interpretation. Three people are invited to a dinner party; they refuse at the last moment to come; hundreds from the street are then herded into the hall. The discrepancy is fantastic. A slave has a debt of ten million dollars cancelled, but he is unable to forgive a debt of ten dollars. The contrast is ludicrous.

7. Moreover, he frustrates ordinary expectations by reversing what we anticipate will be the case. When he proclaims, "Congratulations, you hungry! You'll have a feast," he is countermanding expectations. In the parable of the Vineyard Laborers,

those who work only one hour are paid the same wage as those who labored the entire day. We do not think that is fair. In the parable of the Prodigal, the truant son is welcomed home like royalty, when we think he should have been reprimanded and chastised.

8. He makes free use of parody. The parable of the Empty Jar in the Gospel of Thomas is a parody of the jar of meal miraculously replenished by Elijah for the widow of Zarepath. The Mustard Seed pokes fun at the image of the mighty cedar of Lebanon employed by Ezekiel as a symbol for the mighty kingdom of David.

9. Parody is a form of humor, to be sure. But Jesus indulges in other forms of humor. In the parable of the Lost Coin, the woman spends the value of the coin she has just recovered in celebrating her good fortune. The shepherd recovers the lost sheep and promptly announces a celebration, which probably involved the slaughter of a sheep. When sued for your coat, Jesus advises his followers, give up your shirt to go with it. That would of course leave them naked. Jesus' listeners must have laughed at these travesties on sober speech.

10. He often combines the literal and the figurative in order to create tension. "Give to everyone who begs from you" is an example. His listeners knew they should practice acts of charity, but how could they respond positively to every request without financial ruin?

11. Jesus was plied with questions, to which he never gave a direct answer. "Should we pay taxes," he was asked. "Pay the emperor what is due the emperor and pay God what is due God" was his ambiguous but not evasive response.

12. Jesus may be described as a comic savant. He was perhaps the first standup Jewish comic. A comic savant is a sage who embeds wisdom in humor, a humorist who shuns practical advice. "If someone sues you for your coat, give him the shirt off your back to go with it." That is not practical advice: to follow it is to go naked. Comic wisdom refuses to be explicit.

Yet in the stories he tells, the sage constructs a new fiction that becomes the basis for his or her own action and the action of others. The contours of that fiction are ambiguous in order to frustrate moralizing proclivities; they are also open to multiple and deeper interpretations as a way of keeping them open to reinterpretation in ever new contexts. Our task is to follow their lead and figure out what meaning to give them in our own circumstances.

13. This way of speaking about the kingdom of God is necessary because God's domain is not immediately observable. Jesus

employs tropes or figures of speech drawn from the sensible world to speak obliquely or indirectly, and therefore metaphorically, about another realm. His followers remember him warning them repeatedly, "Those here with two good ears had better listen." What he was trying to convey was subtle and covert. He was undermining the immense solidity of the received world with a vision of an alternative reality. His words communicate in a non-ordinary sense. The knowledge he communicates is pre-conceptual; it is knowledge of reality unsegmented, of an undifferentiated nexus, of a seamless universe of meaning. In his parables and aphorisms is embedded a world coming into being.

13

The Mythical Matrix and God as Metaphor

Scientific and historical knowledge acquired over the past four centuries has eroded traditional Christian dogmas. We have been stripped of the symbolic universe that furnished our mythical home for more than two millennia.

On the one hand, scientific knowledge has discredited the old mythical matrix in which Christian affirmations were conceived. The old geocentric worldview died in the arms of Copernicus, who published his heliocentric theory in 1543. Giordano Bruno was burned at the stake in 1600 for his view that the earth revolved around the sun. Galileo was condemned in 1632 and forced to recant. It has taken four centuries for Pope John Paul II to admit that heaven is a metaphor. In a recent telephone interview, 21% of those interviewed said they believe the sun revolves around the earth. An additional 8% said they didn't know which revolved around which. We have been slow to conclude that there is no place for a God to dwell "up there" in the far reaches of space and no concept of deity adequate to what we now know of the physical universe. The best we have been able to do is to shrink God back inside the new physics, the theory of relativity, and quantum mechanics. That has left us with a God who is homeless.

On the other hand, the historical-critical study of the Bible has eroded claims made by and on behalf of the Bible. The erosion began with Genesis, but in recent years, the quest of the historical Jesus has raised theological questions concerning the so-called Christ of faith to crisis level. It has done so by further divorcing Jesus of Nazareth from canonical representations of him. The perceived gap between the historical figure and the way he is represented in the narrative gospels has grown rather than diminished. Orthodox affirmations about Jesus as the Christ have become increasingly difficult to square with the results of the quest, just as

From *Forum* new series 3,2 (2003).

the doctrine of God has been repeatedly whittled down to accommodate new notions of reality.

We did not elect to pass from one age to another. We did not willfully abandon the symbols and myths that once served Western people well. But those symbols and myths are gone. They linger on, to be sure, in cultural eddies, especially in North America, owing to a receding level of literacy in both the Bible and the sciences. But they have lost their cogency.

We are not responsible for the demise of the symbolic universe because mythical worlds are socially produced and only collectively abandoned. We can trace the history of their rise, for example, in ancient Israel and in the early Christian communities. We can also trace their modification and decline.

Because symbols and myths are social products, we cannot adopt or abandon them arbitrarily. But we can track their trajectories. It is worth knowing where we are in the life cycle of a symbol system. And we know these larger trends will eventually take all of us with them. However, we also know that we can deflect or modify the direction of their rise and development by exerting concentrated, focused social pressure. Christianity did just that when it borrowed the tribal traditions of Israel and turned them into trans-ethnic symbols, and eventually into cosmic myths. In our case, we are faced with a new and more formidable challenge: we shall have to replace the old symbols and myths with new ones appropriate to the global age we are now entering. That is a herculean task, one might even say, a task for the gods.

There are those, I know, who think we can salvage the old symbols by assigning them new meaning. And there are those who think we can undo the trends set in motion by the Enlightenment. I doubt that we can do either. Symbols come with meaning attached, and I do not believe it possible to reinstate aspects of the old symbolic universe for the sake of the old myths.

I am not among those who think the Enlightenment was a bad thing. The Enlightenment brought us tolerance for alien forms of faith, created the secular state to referee the conflicts between warring religious factions, established the priesthood of all believers, and created a middle class with a powerful work ethic that is the foundation of all modern democracies. And the Enlightenment made the empirical sciences possible by discrediting the church as a reality authority.

Still, I am filled with a sense of foreboding. Many Associate members tell me they are engulfed by waves of isolation, loneliness, and impotence. The literacy levels in matters both religious and scientific has fallen to a dangerous low. The introduction of religion into politics may inspire new religious wars sponsored by the state. In a democracy, people cannot be both ignorant and free, as Thomas Jefferson once said. Moreover, the institutions we might have expected to assist with the transition are either unprepared or are unwilling to do so; rather, they are beleaguered and defensive. I am saddened that many of our colleagues in colleges and universities have elected to sit out the struggle in the comfort of their carrels. Beyond these matters, I am alarmed at the prospect of having to negotiate new shoals as globalization increases. The explosion of the world's population and the confrontation between the world's faith traditions means that political, economic, and social problems may overwhelm us.

The dilemmas we face were confronted by pioneers and precursors, whose struggles with the mythical losses require recognition. I intend to do that, briefly, in the first section. Then I will recognize the demise of the Christ myth in its orthodox form. Its demise has been raised to crisis level by the quest of the historical Jesus. The passing of the old God myth has advanced more slowly but on a broader front. That will be the topic of the third section. Finally, I propose to explore the possibilities of a faith that bridges our need to know scientifically and historically and our need to form symbols and create myths. I will undertake that by considering God as a metaphor. The one thing that has not changed for us is that we still live by our myths.

A warning: Do not expect too much. The task I have set for myself is broad and deep. I aspire only to make a beginning.

Pioneers and Precursors

We have precursors in the struggle honestly to confront the decay of the old affirmations as we cross the threshold of the third millennium. Some of the most important ones are:

David Friedrich Strauss, *The Old Faith and the New*, 1872

Rudolf Bultmann, *New Testament and Mythology*, 1941

Paul Tillich, *The Shaking of the Foundations*, 1949

Dietrich Bonhoeffer, *Letters and Papers From Prison*, 1953

John A. T. Robinson, *Honest to God*, 1963

Lloyd Geering, *God in the New World*, 1968

Don Cupitt, *Taking Leave of God,* 1980

John S. Spong, *Why Christianity Must Change or Die,* 1998

David Friedrich Strauss, the author of the first critical life of Jesus (1838), serves as the paradigm for what has happened to scores of biblical and theological scholars during the last two centuries. Strauss is representative of Protestant thought from the beginning of the nineteenth century to the present, and increasingly of Catholic and Jewish religious thought as well.

The crux of the matter for Strauss was that he could no longer believe in a transcendent, personal God who intervenes supernaturally from time to time in the course of nature and history. His skepticism did not arise arbitrarily from a willful desire to disbelieve. It was the result of the emergence of an acute historical consciousness, of the desire to know what really happened. He sought to substitute a rigorous investigation of Christian origins and the contents of religious consciousness for a supernatural revelation and the infallible magisterium of the church. Of course, investigating the past was nothing more than probing the religious consciousness of persons from other times and places who were deemed highly spiritual. To get to the contents of Jesus' consciousness, he had to isolate and set aside layers of obfuscation posing as piety.

A century after Strauss, **Rudolf Bultmann,** perhaps the greatest biblical scholar of the twentieth century, and another German scholar of deep conviction, argued that the primitive Christian gospel with its mythical framework had become untenable. We can no longer accept the ancient worldview in which the gospel was encased, he said, because it contradicted our reality sense, which after all is dictated by the modern worldview. If we are to continue proclaiming the Christian gospel, we must "demythologize" it. By that he meant that we must translate its mythical elements into modern terms so its real message can be understood.

According to Bultmann, we can no longer accept the ancient cosmology that posited a heaven above as the abode of the gods and a hell beneath as the domain of Satan. We know the earth is not the center of the galaxy, and we are no longer convinced that the universe was created simply for our benefit. We do not believe in demons and spirits that determine the fate of individuals. Our world has been swept clean of the astrological deities once thought to inhabit the heavens and haunt springs, wells, and outhouses. We no longer think history will come to an abrupt end at the hands of an angry or vengeful God. We do not accept the view that death is punishment for sin; we are inclined to the view that death is part of the natural order. And we find incredible the monstrous notion that God would kill his own Son in order to atone for the sins of humankind—propitiation by proxy, as it were. And we do not believe that the resurrection of Jesus involved the resuscitation of a corpse or functioned as the doorway to another world and eternal life.

To ask people to believe in this set of outmoded propositions, Bultmann insisted, is to drive thinking people away from the gospel and the church. His solution was to translate the essence of the old-time gospel into modern categories. As it turned out, the solution he proposed lasted only for a short time, probably because he came too early in the evolution of secularism, and because he held on to some elements of the old mythical worldview in spite of his protestations to the contrary.

Paul Tillich published his *The Shaking of the Foundations* in 1949 and theologians the world over began immediately to talk about God as the ground of being. Tillich had moved God from the heavens into the depths, which meant, among other things, the depths of the human psyche. Meanwhile, **Dietrich Bonhoeffer's** *Letters and Papers from Prison* appeared posthumously in 1953 after he was hanged by the Nazis in 1945, just as the war ended. One can draw a straight line from those two books to the controversial bestseller (aren't all theological books that pioneer new ways of thinking controversial?) *Honest to God,* issued by **Bishop John A. T. Robinson** (1963).

On the other side of the world, **Lloyd Geering** had just been acquitted in a Presbyterian trial for heresy (1967) when he published his book in this same tradition, *God in the New World* (1968). Professor Geering had challenged the orthodox interpretation of the resurrection and had suggested that human beings do not possess immortal souls. The storm that broke over his work in the press and on television had the effect of transforming the religious scene in New Zealand.

In 1980, **Don Cupitt,** Dean of Emmanuel College, Cambridge, resumed the discussion of the God question begun by Bishop Robinson. His provocative book was entitled, *Taking Leave of God.* In his book, Dean Cupitt argued that "an objective metaphysical God is no longer either intellectually secure nor even morally satisfactory as a basis for spiritual life." He was subsequently invited by the BBC to make a six-part television series in which he described the transition from a traditional "realist" religion to what he termed "nonrealism." This series and the book created along with the series were entitled *The Sea of Faith*. That was the beginning of the Sea of Faith movement in Great Britain.

On the American side of the Atlantic, **Bishop John Shelby Spong** published his revolutionary book, *Why Christianity Must Change or Die*, in 1998. As a bishop of the Episcopal Church, he stood in a long line of Anglican bishops and theologians who had dared to reopen theological issues long since considered closed. Bishop Spong had earlier attempted to deliver the Bible from fundamentalism; he had challenged the literal interpretation of the virgin birth of Jesus; he came out in support of women and homosexuals in the official life of the church; and he challenged the understanding of the resurrection of Jesus as the resuscitation of a corpse.

This line of radical thinkers could be extended almost indefinitely beginning with the Enlightenment and its aftermath and continuing into the twentieth and twenty-first centuries. It is evident that the alienation felt by Strauss and Bultmann, Geering, Cupitt, and Spong, has been shared by dozens of others, inside and outside the churches.

To this cloud of witnesses, I add a single voice from among the Associates of the Jesus Seminar.

One of the Santa Rosa local Associates of the Jesus Seminar recently confessed that in a period of about two years he recently came to sartori-like clarity on two basic issues. He is now convinced that God does not exist, at least not as God is commonly understood, and he is certain that consciousness does not continue after death. He went on to say that no particular event triggered these revelations. It is just that for him the whole incredible façade of traditional religious belief suddenly collapsed under its own weight. Initially, he confessed that he felt betrayal, anxiety, fear, even terror, as he became aware of the immense loss. But then, when the dust had settled, he began to feel serenity, exhilaration, happiness, and complete freedom. His confession he thought of as a declaration of independence from the tyranny of the old concepts, rituals, narratives, agencies, and institutions. At the same time, he discovered to his utter surprise that he still cared about the same things as before. That was also a revelation. That he was still devoted to the same standards of behavior and the same causes meant that the old dogmas were not the foundation or the inspiration of his deep convictions. His experience is not unique; it has been paralleled by countless others during this same period.

The Demise of the Christ Myth

The consequences of the collapse of the mythical matrix of the Christian creed became most obvious in affirmations about Jesus as the Christ. John Hick traces the effect of historical research and theological reflection on the doctrine of the incarnation in his book, *The Metaphor of God Incarnate* (1993). We have just noted how that doctrine declined in the work of New Testament scholars and in private confession. It is time to sum up.

Most statements in the second article of the Christian confession, known as the Apostles' Creed, have become incredible. The second article has to do with Jesus as the Christ. The only uncontestable elements are the declarations that Jesus of Nazareth suffered under Pontius Pilate and died by crucifixion. These are hard, cold facts. Everything else is dependent on the mythical matrix, which is bound up with an ancient worldview that has been steadily passing away.

That second article is the story of a redeemer figure who drops in from *another world*, is identified by his *miraculous birth*, performs a few *miracles*, and then dies on the cross to absolve humankind of sin and guilt. After his death, he *ascends to the heavens* whence he came; the story tells us that he will come again to sit in *cosmic judgment at the end of history*. There we have the essential elements: a visitor from another world, miraculous birth, miracles, ascension, end of history. We have experienced the breakup of the symbolic universe in which this part of the creed was conceived.

The loss of credibility for the framing worldview means that elements of the creedal story have peeled away one by one until there is virtually nothing left. We are left with a Christ that has become unbelievable.

We no longer believe Jesus was born of Mary without the benefit of male sperm. We no longer think he could perform miracles like walking on the water or calming the storm. We are relatively certain that his resurrection was a grief vision. We believe the empty tomb story is a late and fictional attempt to certify his bodily resurrection. The ascension of Jesus into the heavens is a fiction.

We doubt that Jesus died to atone for the sins of humankind, resulting from Adam's original error. We are convinced that Jesus did not intend to establish a new religion, appoint clergy, or inaugurate celibacy. In sum, Jesus of Nazareth contributed very little to the development of what emerged as orthodox Christianity.

These are the conclusions of the Fellows of the Jesus Seminar after fifteen years of conversation and debate. The Fellows were doing no more than taking the work of our precursors to their logical conclusions. While some of us may want to contest one or the other of the individual items, it is clear to one and all that the ancient mythical matrix has collapsed and left us with empty slogans that the churches continue to rehearse without any warrant other than tradition.

In the judgment of many believers and non-believers today, the essential dogmas of the fundamentalists and the TV evangelists are items that belong to the museum of Christian dogmas: in the judgment of Jack van Impe, the items that define Christianity include the divinity of Jesus, the virgin birth, the blood atonement, the physical resurrection, and the second coming. That Jack van Impe, Jerry Falwell, and Pat Robertson, along with others, control the airwaves only indicates the extent to which the popular tradition has been split off from the trunk of the tradition. The decay of the old symbols has progressed to such an extent that many theologians, biblical scholars, and now clergy, no longer find such dogmas even interesting enough to discuss.

The Passing of the God Myth

The decay of the Christ myth has made the problem of God acute. After all, Christian theologians have traditionally held that Jesus is God, as the second person of the trinity. If Jesus is not the Son of God, then we may have to revise our notions of God. However, the old concept of God has suffered erosion in and of itself.

Creator of heaven and earth

Darwin's *Origin of Species* became the spearhead of the first frontal assault on the reliability of the Old Testament and the doctrine of the special creation. Around the turn of the twentieth century, Professor C. A. Briggs of Union Theological Seminary was tried for heresy and defrocked by the Presbyterians for interpreting the Genesis account as a myth. Nevertheless, Genesis died as a literal account and God was being made redundant as creator.

The erosion did not begin, however, with Darwin and Briggs. Bishop James Usher (1581–1656) was counting up the generations from Adam to Jesus about the same time that Galileo was looking through his telescope and confirming what Copernicus already knew, viz. that the sun did not rotate around the earth. Special creation goes together with the notion that the earth and human beings are at the center of the universe: the universe, it was believed, is geocentric and anthropocentric. Darwin made it necessary to imagine hundreds of thousands of years for *homo sapiens* to evolve. Darwin's theory has been supported by the new physics, which estimates that the earth is approximately 4.5 billion years old. The universe as a whole is probably 15 billion years old. Human beings arrived relatively late on the scene. If there is a living creation myth, it is probably the Big Bang theory. That theory is no less mythical than the Genesis account. Yet the Big Bang does not accord humankind a privileged place in the scheme of things. Moreover, our record as custodians of the biosphere we inhabit has not done much to commend us as superior life forms.

The creation story in Genesis has been the focal point of controversy for more than a century. The history of the controversy illustrates how tenacious has been the effort to preserve traditional views of God, and the Bible. That history also illustrates how inevitably conservative defenders of the Bible have been forced to retreat. While they cling to special creation in principle, they have gradually moved the event back in time.

I will return to evolution and creation later when we consider God as the guarantor of a moral code.

God as interventionist tyrant

The old God of Israel was essentially a tribal God. God had chosen this particular people to favor and often intervened in the course of events on their behalf. To be sure, he sometimes intervened to punish them. But the Israelites were bound to Yahweh and Yahweh to them by covenant. The relationship between the two was a distinct disadvantage to the Canaanites, Egyptians, and Babylonians, except that they had their own tribal deities in turn. It was a war of the gods.

Christians inherited this former tribal God, who had been converted to a universal monotheistic God by the great prophets. But the old God had been conceived in the era of absolute monarchies, when emperors and kings had unlimited power. Monarchs demanded constant worship and praise, as tyrants are wont to do. The chief metaphors for Yahweh were derived, as a consequence, from the protocols common to royalty. God was the lord of lords and king of kings, epithets later transferred to Jesus of Nazareth. And the realm where God ruled was called the *Kingdom of God.* Our creeds and confessions, psalms and hymns are loaded with language derived from the ancient royal court.

A conflict arises, however, when the old tribal deity, who intervenes in history on a small and often personal scale, is juxtaposed with the universal God of law and order, of justice and fair play, who was introduced by the great prophets of Israel. Yet it is the inflated tribal deity that has survived in Christian tradition: that God answers prayers on behalf of certain petitioners, performs miracles now and again, supplies little banes and blessings to individuals and favored groups, as Don Cupitt has put it.[1]

That God is a relic of the small-scale tribal deity of the earlier layers of the Hebrew Bible. And as a monarch, this deity is subject to flattery and bribes. A God who is discriminatory, inconstant, capricious, or arbitrary is not adequate even for our paltry human sense of justice and fair play. Yet the tribal deity survives in popular and ecclesiastical piety because the large God of physics, biology, astronomy, and philosophy seems too abstract and remote to be influenced and bribed. Yet for us to believe in God, we must have a God who endorses and supports justice for all, impartially, without favoritism, relentlessly, and without fail.

Jesus' notion of God seems to have gone beyond the old tribal deity, although we cannot be sure he openly included the gentiles in his kingdom movement. But he does suggest that God sends the rain and causes the sun to shine on one and all, without respect to moral condition. He appears to hold the view that the sins of the fathers are not visited on sons and daughters generation after generation. He would not have endorsed Augustine's view that humans are all sinners as a consequence of Adam's fall. Jesus' God, on the contrary, is a God of compassion, who has special affection for the poor, hungry, mournful, and persecuted. The kind of favoritism Jesus supports is merely a way of leveling the playing field. And Jesus' God apparently cannot be influenced to act differently.

God of the last judgment

The creator God stands at the beginning of history, while the interventionist God meddles in history midstream. Traditional views of God also picture God as bringing history to a conclusion. That is the God of the apocalypse, of the last judgment. In sum, God is there before, during, and after.

Just as the temporal span of the past increased exponentially under the tutelage of the new physics, so the future of the planet and the solar system seemed to extend indefinitely into the future. Now scientists tell us that in about four billion years the sun may burn out and life forms on earth may die from want of warmth and light.

Of course, new apocalyptic possibilities arose with the invention of the atom bomb and we gradually became cognizant that a meteorite might wipe us out just as one apparently made the planet uninhabitable for the dinosaurs. Yet these threats do not cause us to lose much sleep worrying about them. They did not and do not function in the same way as the seven seals revealing the four horses of the apocalypse. The seven bowls of the wrath of God are remnants of the old vindictive tribal God.

The predictive possibilities of the apocalypse continue to capture the popular imagination of the literalist Christian right, but they have long since been lost to biblical scholars and educated clergy. In all the years I taught in theological seminaries, I was never asked to teach a course on Revelation. Indeed, I was not able to awaken any interest in the Apocalypse in the Jesus Seminar as we approached the end of the second millennium, when a public statement might have eased the anxieties many seemed to be experiencing.

The God of the apocalypse and the second coming of Christ no longer occupies a central play in our mythical heavens.

The homeless God

As the unemployment rate for God grew, God was also out looking for someplace to dwell in the universe. The God "up there" in the heavens became the God "out there" beyond the edge of the universe as our notions of space and time enlarged. We learned in due course that there is no "out there," just as there is no "up there." So God lacked a home.

Faced with this dilemma, creative theologians found a place for God's domicile in the depths. Paul Tillich called those depths the ground of being. God was at the bottom of things. This move was encouraging news for mystics, who had always claimed they could discover God by looking inward. However, Freud and Jung came along and put paid to that scenario by pointing out that the God of the depths might be no more than the projections of the human self. After all, we cannot be sure that what we see in our interiors is anything more than our reflections at the bottom of a deep psychic well. And mystics have never been able to come up with a description of their encounters with God that they can agree on.

Theologians pursued this course by converting theology into anthropology. They interpreted all statements about God as statements about ourselves: statements about God are really claims about human beings. This strategy was the crowning achievement of existentialism and neo-orthodoxy that reigned in the period between the great wars. It also survived after the second war long enough to anoint a new generation or two of young theologians, myself included.

The God of the depths gave way eventually to a new concept of God made possible by the new physics. From the new physics we learned that mass is the equivalent of energy, and with that a new approach to the God question was opened up. Rather than think of God as an object or thing among other objects in the universe, or think of God as the ground of being, theologians proposed that God was a form of energy diffused throughout the universe.

Panentheism became the new name of the game: locate God and explain what God does. Process theology developed the doctrine of internal relations, which held that God both influences the course of events and is influenced by them. Although God transcends the physical universe in some sense, God is also contingent—what God does is limited or dependent on what others do.

Put differently, the notion of God was "decentered." Since God now has no intrinsic mass—God is no longer understood as a thing—God can therefore be distributed throughout the atomic world. On this view, God does not suspend the laws of nature from time to time or interfere supernaturally in the course of events, but indirectly attempts to influence how things turn out. God is at the mercy of the laws of nature and the course of history. This new concept of God is correlative with the principle of indeterminism.

God still stands for the order and rationality of the universe, but also for the strains of chaos disrupting order and rationality. God has to take lumps along with the rest of us. A personal God, much preferred by many, has been turned into energy and spread over the infinite reaches of space.

God as primary datum

The core of the problem of God owes to the fact that God is not a primary datum for acquiring knowledge of the world. We do not know God directly; no one has seen God or heard God or smelled God. We "know" God only mediately or indirectly. (I am aware that many claim to have known God directly and immediately, but can we find one person who has adduced one single new fact from that experience?)

The Bible never pictures God. In fact, it is a form of idolatry to make an image of God since God is invisible. God never appears. Even Homer tells us that the immortals can appear to mortals only in disguise. The trick is to be able to tell when meeting a mortal that one is in fact actually encountering a deity.

The invisibility of God means that we are dependent on those who claim to have an indirect experience of God, or to have "seen"

God in some metaphorical or non-literal sense. Or to have had a "communication" from God. An experience of God, or a revelation from God, are interpreted experiences. That is because there is no such thing as an uninterpreted experience. Communications from God, analogously, must be ineffable, since God presumably does not speak a particular human language with all its limitations.

Christians believe that Jesus of Nazareth had experience of God. So far as we know, Jesus did not claim to have seen God or to have had a direct communication from God. But he does claim to know the will of God. We will return to this point later.

God as human creation

When Karen Armstrong writes a history of God, she is doing no more than tracing the creation of God by human beings in three religious traditions. The Israelites created Yahweh. Muhammad created Allah. And the Christians created the trinity.

Jack Miles award-winning book, *God: A Biography,* sketches how God was understood at various periods and by different authors in the history of Israel. In other words, these volumes are histories of what human beings have imagined God to be.

It has been very difficult for us to acknowledge that we made it all up. Mark Twain once remarked, the Bible tells that God made us in God's image, but we have more than reciprocated. We not only made God in our image, we took one further step: we made ourselves the product of the God we had created. And we gave ourselves a special place in the order of things by inventing a geocentric solar system and assigning ourselves the prerogative of naming all the other creatures of the earth. That only illustrates the extent to which human beings are capable of deceiving themselves. The task we now face is monumental: we must convince ourselves and the rest of humanity that the earth is not ours to plunder. We can do that only by creating a new myth in which human beings are one with nature. We must see that our future is bound to the future of the biosphere and everything in it.

God anxieties

Like children, most of us want to know who is in charge of the universe. We want someone to impose rules of behavior and belief on us. That desire opens the door to tyrants and God. We prefer to think of God as *in loco parentis*—a surrogate parent. That may be the reason we call God father. But God steadily refuses to interfere in human affairs and tell us what to do.

We need to feel at home in the universe without parental assurances that we can have the order without the chaos. Since God won't do it, we need to take the responsibility for ourselves, for each other, for truth, and for the planet.

What lurks at the margins of the creationism debate is the notion that God's character is the foundation of morality. Why do the evolutionists promote Darwinism, asks Dr. D. J. Kennedy on his Sunday morning television program? Why, because they want to get rid of God. And if they get rid of God, they have gotten rid of the basis of morality. Then they can do anything they want. (Am I to believe that everyone who accepts evolution as a theory does so because he or she endorses moral anarchy?)

The final nail in the coffin of the old tribal deity is the discovery that belief in God is not the foundation of morality. In truth, the residue of conviction that the old tribal deity provides miracles and answers prayers undermines morality and justice at their foundations. Moral issues can no longer be settled by claiming that this is God's will. Belief in God's will produced the craze that sent thousands of women to their deaths as witches beginning in 1231. The claim to know God's will prompted the condemnation of Galileo in 1632. Belief in God's will inspired the wars between Protestant and Catholic in Europe and more recently in Ireland. The claim is hollow that religion and belief in God are the foundation of morality.

The conviction that belief in God is the foundation of the moral code also underlies the doctrine of rewards and punishment. I have yet to meet someone who is an advocate of punishment—of eternal suffering in hell—who thinks that he or she deserves that fate. That makes the doctrine self-serving: punishment is for you; reward and eternal life is for me. How can I not be suspicious?

A Faith for the Future
God as metaphor

A faith to bridge . . .

What we need now is a faith to bridge our need to know scientifically and historically and our need to form symbols and create myths. The empirical sciences and history have robbed us of our old symbols and myths in the Western world. Yet symbols and myths provide us with an integrated vision of the world and our places within that world. We cannot do without them. The question now is: can God and Jesus continue to help us in our dilemma?

A faith for the future . . .

We need a new vision, one that will accommodate the adjustments we will have to make as we enter the global age. It is too early to say yet of what that vision will consist. In any case, it will emerge in the imaginations of storytellers and poets, artists and architects, and perhaps even a theologian or two.

Visions do not come to us whole. They come in fragments, glimpses, glimmerings, caught in the tail of the eye.

Spirituality in our time consists in glimpse training. We have to cultivate the glimpse. Disciplined observation, meditation and openness to the world permits us to see through, or around, the lumpy, opaque, heavy, obstinate obstacles that limit sight and impede progress. Glimpse training entails the quest for salient insights. It also requires imagining how those insights form a cogent whole. If we are successful, we will weave those elements into a new story, a new myth, and perhaps a parable or two.

God as metaphor . . .

If God has a role in the new vision, it will be as a metaphor. As a metaphor God can function as an integrating symbol. As a metaphor, God is a symbol that unites or encompasses all spheres of our reality. There is nothing that falls outside the single divine domain. Mystical visions regularly confirm that the universe is one, that it really is a universe and not a multiverse.

Metaphors of transcendence . . .

God may continue to be useful as a symbol of transcendence. Transcendence means that God is more than the world. Transcendence means that there is more to the world than meets the eye. Things are not what they seem. The really real must lie in some other dimension. Yet we must not fall back into literalisms when invoking God as metaphor. As a metaphor, God must represent some dimension of human experience. Let me suggest four such dimensions.

First, God is the symbol for acute self-transcendence. We are inclined to deceive ourselves, to hide from the truth. An omniscient God reminds that we cannot hide. God knows everything; God will find us out. That is a very useful symbol that points beyond ordinary self-consciousness, and thus to a critical dimension of human experience.

Second, God is a metaphor for the oncoming future, for the fund of possibilities the future lays on the present. Because we live into our futures, God is the invitation to explore those possibilities and make the most of them.

Third, God is also the metaphor for a revisionist past. The old terms for this were forgiveness and redemption. God stands for the second chance. Because God is omnipotent, God can undo the past, provide us with the opportunity to start over.

Finally, God is the metaphor for the Beyond of the beyond. We know that we will eventually acquire new knowledge that will change present perspectives. We know there is a beyond to present knowledge, although we may be tempted to think we have reached the ultimate stage. A few physicists today think they may be close to the fundamental building blocks of reality. That may be no more than scientific hubris. God also stands for the ultimate limit, the final horizon, the Beyond that we will never see. Space is curved, we are told, so we cannot see too far ahead, so we cannot see to the edge of the universe. God stands for our finitude: we will live and die without ever knowing the ultimate truth about ourselves, about our world. God guards us from the ultimate temptation: the temptation to think we are gods ourselves.

Metaphors of immanence . . .

Theologians have traditionally said that God is both transcendent and immanent.

God is also a metaphor for immanence. Immanence expresses the idea that, in spite of God's transcendence, the divine is nevertheless intimately related to the world. In our imaginations, we are inclined to think that the temporal reflects aspects of the eternal, that the finite has an infinite side.

The immanence of God is thought to be expressed in nature—just look at the sunset—or in human beings. Christian theologians have been in the habit of saying, if you want to know what God is like, look at Jesus of Nazareth. We now know that Jesus is not literally God. Yet Jesus allegedly represents the way God is related to the world. Both the acts and words of Jesus have been taken as indicators of the character of God. When the fathers of the church developed content for the character of God, they did not consult their abstract christological formulations; they consulted the words and deeds of Jesus. And that is the reason we must go on to ask what bearing the results of the quest have on the God question.

Jesus and metaphors for God . . .

Jesus of Nazareth still offers some promise as a guide to a faith for the future. He is a cultural icon of considerable residual power. He is a world class sage, along with the Buddha, Mohammed, Moses, Lao-tzu, Confucius, and others. There is no reason we should not enlist him in our cause. But we must free him from the creedal and scriptural and experiential prisons in which we have incarcerated him.

The insights of Jesus of Nazareth provide us with a paradigm that may prove fruitful for our transition to the global future. We should consider Jesus' vision of the kingdom of God as clues to the immanence of God.

The world as God's domain is a symbol. It is a symbol that binds all of humanity together, and is thus a symbol suitable for the global age. But the symbol itself doesn't tell us much about the character of that kingdom.

However, the vision of Jesus does. His vision is made up of a compendium of discrete but related insights expressed in aphorisms and parables. Together they constitute a vision of what the world is like when it is seen for what it really is, that is, when it is actually under the direct aegis of God.

Jesus' insights are predominantly metaphors of immanence. He occasionally suggests the transcendence of God by comparing God with the emperor, for example. And he refers to the domain of God as the *Kingdom* of God. In such allusions, he is drawing on the old metaphors for God derived from the royal court. But he overwhelmingly employs figures drawn from everyday life to represent God's imperial rule.

Jesus' parables and aphorisms—his predominant forms of discourse—talk about God in everyday, mundane terms: dinner parties, truant sons, vineyard laborers, toll collectors and prostitutes, a cache of coins. His language was concrete and specific. He never used abstract language. He made no theological statements. He would not have endorsed the ontological argument for God. He would not have said, "All human beings have sinned and fallen short of the glory of God." It would not even have occurred to him to generalize that God is love. Jesus did not have a doctrine of God; he only saw God at work in the commonplaces of life.

Although his language was drawn from the mundane world around him, he did not have ordinary reality in mind. His language is indirect; it is highly figurative or metaphorical. We know the parable of the Leaven is not about baking bread. The Mustard Seed and the Sower are not about gardening. His admonition to lend to those who can't pay us back is not about banking practice.

His language is directed to the everyday, the received world, but not in its ordinary senses. What he sees is hidden in the intersections of daily activity and in the world of nature. God's presence is there, but human beings lack the eyes to perceive it. Just about all of the metaphors Jesus employs for God are metaphors of immanence. Jesus experiences God, not as remote from the world, but as everywhere present in the most ordinary events.

His vision integrates all the dimensions of the world in one seamless whole. Yet his vision consists, not of abstractions or generalities, but of concrete images. We are told that God's domain is peopled with the poor, the hungry, the mournful, the downtrodden. God watches over the sparrows and counts the hairs on human heads. Anxieties about food and clothing reflect the lack of trust in the goodness of God—and neighbor. God's love is expressed through the love an enemy has for a victim. God sends sun and rain on bad and good, just and unjust, indiscriminately. God is like the father who would not give a son a stone when he was asking for bread.

Jesus insisted that following him meant subservience and service. He asked no favors, no titles, for himself. He celebrated life at every opportunity. He sponsored an unbrokered relationship to God. These are a few of the insights that comprise his vision.

God's domain in a global age . . .

If we extrapolate from these features, it is clear that his vision of the world as God's domain is global in its reach. By insisting that to cling to life is to lose life, his vision transcends self-interest. He advocates love of the enemy, which means that God's domain transcends the tribe, the ethnic groups, and the nation. He no longer sponsors the male patriarch who dominates the family. He embraces all genders and ages. His notion of the kingdom is transhuman since its includes the birds and the flowers.

His views are transbiblical, transchristian, and even transreligous. He seems not to be bound by what the Bible says, and I see nothing in his vision that calls for a parochial religion like "churchianity." He appears not to require religion at all.

The vision of Jesus, when translated into terms appropriate to our own time and place, moves from our present of unfulfilled promises to a future of partially realized hopes within a horizon of trust. That vision offers some hope for our collective future on planet earth, especially if taken in concert with the wisdom of other sages and visionaries from our own and other cultures.

Notes

Introduction: Movements

1. Achtemeier, *An Introduction to the New Hermeneutic*, 1969.
2. Schmidt, "It All Began with Grammar," 8.
3. Dodd, *Parables*, 1.
4. Harnack, *What is Christianity?*, 15.
5. Crossan, *Raid on the Articulate*, 115; Scott, *Hear Then the Parable*, 46–47.
6. Dodd, *Parables*, 10.
7. Gowler, *What Are They Saying About Parables?*, 19–25.
8. See Miller, *Apocalyptic Jesus*, 6–11.
9. Rohrbaugh, "A Peasant Reading."
10. See Tannehill, 165–71
11. Funk, *Poetics*, 293; see esp. 292–94.
12. Wilson, in *The Creation: An Appeal to Save Life on Earth*, writes a letter to an imaginary Southern Baptist preacher who is pleading for creation. I can only imagine the wonder of a conversation between Wilson and Funk. They could have bridged the gap between science and religion and crossed over.

Chapter 1: Parable as Metaphor

1. Dodd, *Parables*, 16.
2. The bare definition is expanded as indicated (Dodd, *Parables*, 16–18).
3. Dodd, *Parables*, 22–24; cf. Bultmann, *History of the Synoptic Tradition*, 182f., 191f.; Cadoux, *The Parables of Jesus*, 45ff., 56ff., 118, 127, 139f., 197.
4. Bultmann, *History of the Synoptic Tradition*, 198.
5. An "exemplary-story" *(Beispielerzählung)* is a parable involving no figurative element at all (Bultmann, *History of the Synoptic Tradition*, 178). According to Bultmann the Good Samaritan, the Rich Fool, the Rich Man and Lazarus, the Pharisee and the Publican are examples of this (178f.). See further below, chap. 8, p. 76.
6. Cadoux, *The Parables of Jesus*, 19f., doubts that Jesus ever interpreted his parables. Jeremias (*Parables*, 105) is cautious: eight parables end abruptly without explicit application; originally the number must have been considerably greater, as is shown by the Gospel of Thomas, where only three parables are provided with an interpretation. Dodd (27f.) believes there were some applied parables in the traditions underlying the Gospels. But he draws back from attributing these to Jesus himself, while allowing that in some cases they reveal how the parable was understood "by those who stood near to the very situation which had called it forth" (29). Cf. Bultmann, *History of the Synoptic Tradition*, 182ff., who also wants to reserve judgment in specific cases, but is willing to concede that the tendency of the tradition was to supply applications.
7. Bultmann (*History of the Synoptic Tradition*, 182) distinguishes between point and application: the point is the *tertium comparationis*, the point at which the image touches the subject matter.

8. The question of what constitutes an application is to be left open. A rule of thumb might be: must listeners make the transference of judgment for themselves?

9. Cf. Jeremias, *Parables*, 48ff., 110ff.

10. Cf. Dahl, "Gleichnis und Parabel II," 1618.

11. Jeremias' book unquestionably gives the impression that he wishes to set aside all accretions to the original parables as secondary; that these accretions more often than not obscure the real point of the parable in its original context. Whoever draws from this the conclusion that Jeremias regards the interpretive work of the tradition not only as obscuring the original context and point, but also as fundamentally misconceived, should ponder his remarks on p. 48: "Thus, by the hortatory application the parable [of the Unjust Steward] is not misinterpreted, but 'actualized'. ... It is not a question of adding or taking away, but of a shift of emphasis resulting from a change of audience." It is consequently a question of whether the church at various points in its history *correctly* grasped the parable in relation to its own situation; this question cannot be determined merely by recovering the original context, though that is certainly the first step. On the other hand, it is more problematic whether the church was justified in canonizing particular applications along with the parable itself.

12. The difference between a metaphor and simile, as is often noted, is that in the latter the comparison is made explicit by *as* or *like*.

13. Dodd, *Parables*, 18.

14. Wilder, *Language of the Gospel*, 80.

15. The formal distinction between a simile and metaphor is being raised to a substantive difference for the sake of convenience. The formal distinction, in fact, is not always discriminating, nor are simile and metaphor commonly restricted to the senses here indicated. The convention is introduced so as not to have to write each time, "metaphor understood as. . . ." Cf. Wilder, *Language of the Gospel*.

    Wheelwright (*The Burning Fountain*, 93ff., 106ff.; *Metaphor and Reality*, 70f.) enjoins us from making anything of the syntactical distinction between simile and metaphor. One can accept the points he is making, i.e., that the grammatical difference is not discriminating, that simile and metaphor belong to the same spectrum, without being deprived of the use of the terms in rather different senses. In fact, Wheelwright appears to give to the simple simile something like the meaning I have suggested (*The Burning Fountain*, 106f.), while reserving the term metaphor for simile plus plurisignation (i.e., significative at more than one level).

16. Barfield, "Poetic Diction and Legal Fiction," 52.

17. Metaphor, of course, may "rediscover" a point previously made but now lost, which is what makes it impossible to draw a hard and fast line between metaphor and simile.

18. Lewis, "Bluspels and Flalansferes," 36–50.

19. Ramsey, *Models and Mystery*, 9ff.

20. *Models and Mystery*, 48.

21. *Models and Mystery*, 48ff.

22. Barfield, "Poetic Diction and Legal Fiction," 66.

23. Barfield, *Poetic Diction*, 16, referring to Wittgenstein's *Tractatus Logico-Philosophicus*.

24. Barfield, *Poetic Diction*, 16f., 113 n. 1, 131 n. 1; "Poetic Diction and Legal Fiction," 66f.

25. Wheelright, *Metaphor and Reality,* 37.
26. Heidegger, *Being and Time,* sec. 33 (pp. 195–203).
27. Cf. Wheelwright, *The Burning Fountain,* 63.
28. Cf. the remarks of Hart ("Imagination and the Scale of Mental Acts," 15): "All mental powers are tethered to the concrete event, for what is offered them, but reason has the longest stakeline. Its capacity for universality is its capacity for farthest removal. And reason removes from the concrete event, we said earlier, by means of cataleptic pauses or stations. Reason places the event under 'arrest.' Reason assumes that an event is a closed affair, a delimited base from which solid ideas may arise and to which they apply; that its significance is its closure, not the new field of potentiality it opens and opens upon. The concepts of reason are abstract just because they are abstracted from a stable referent."
29. On the distinction between "sharp" and "soft" focus, see Wheelwright, *The Burning Fountain,* 62–64.
30. Hart, "Imagination and the Scale of Mental Acts,", 16.
31. "Imagination and the Scale of Mental Acts,", 20.
32. "The world, like Dionysus, is torn to pieces by pure intellect; but the poet is Zeus; he has swallowed the heart of the world; and he can reproduce it as a living body" (Barfield, *Poetic Diction,* 88; cf. 115, 191).
33. Barfield, *Poetic Diction,,* 88.
34. It might be pointed out in this connection that even the poets, according to Cleanth Brooks, do not always understand the function of metaphor correctly. Some, e.g., A. E. Housman, hold that metaphor is a mere surrogate, a rhetorical gilding, an alternate way of saying something, and not the necessary and inevitable way ("Metaphor and the Function of Criticism," 133f.).
35. Barfield, "Poetic Diction and Legal Fiction," 67.
36. Barfield, "The Meaning of the Word 'Literal,'" 49.
37. Wilder, *Language of the Gospel,* 92. Cf. Tillich, *The Protestant Era,* 107f.; *Systematic Theology,* 122–26.
38. Wheelwright, *Metaphor and Reality,* 37.
39. Attention will be given subsequently to the "realism" of the parables.
40. Cf. Heidegger, *Being and Time,* 199ff.
41. Wheelwright, *Metaphor and Reality,* 45–69, develops the notion of "tensive" language at length.
42. The possibility of the death—and birth, rebirth—of metaphors and symbols qualifies these formulations. Insofar as theology is bound to the "language event" of its infancy, it cannot easily consign the revelatory images of its infancy to the flames. If it does, it may find that it has come unhooked from its own historical ground. On the other hand, it is a question whether theology can deliberately keep the historic images alive.
43. Hart, "Imagination and the Scale of Mental Acts," 17.
44. "Imagination and the Scale of Mental Acts," 6.
45. Cadoux, *The Parables of Jesus,* 12.
46. *The Parables of Jesus,* 13f.
47. For a further discussion of this see Funk, *Language, Hemeneutic, and Word of God,* 175–82.
48. Cadoux, *The Parables of Jesus:,* 45.
49. Cf., e.g., Bultmann, *Jesus and the Word,* 31ff.
50. Cadoux, *The Parables of Jesus:,* 197.
51. Jeremias, *Parables,* 145.

52. See further Funk, *Language, Hemeneutic, and Word of God*, 175–82 and notes.
53. The formulation is Bultmann's (*History of the Synoptic Tradition*, 191f.).
54. Wilder, *Language of the Gospel*, 29.
55. On the parable as riddle, cf. Farrar, *A Study in St. Mark*, 241f.; Dibelius, *From Tradition to Gospel*, 256; Vincent, "The Parables of Jesus as Self-Revelation," 84.
56. Barfield ("Poetic Diction and Legal Fiction," 52f.) also places simile on the same gamut to which metaphor and symbol belong.
57. Dodd, *Parables*, 25. He is writing here of Jülicher's "broadest possible application." The effect of Jülicher's method of making the parables empty out into a general principle, he writes, is "rather flattening."
58. Jeremias, *Parables*, 100.
59. *Parables*, 102.
60. Wilder, *Language of the Gospel*, 80, n. 2.
61. Indicating comparison, which corresponds to Aramaic 1^e. For the various forms of this phrase in the New Testament and the rabbinic literature, see Jeremias, *Parables*, 100f.
62. Jeremias, *Parables*, 101.
63. *Parables*; cf. Clayton R. Bowen, "The Kingdom and the Mustard Seed," 562–69.
64. Cadoux, *The Parables of Jesus*, 50ff. (the quotation is found on p. 52).
65. Jülicher, *Die Gleichnisreden Jesu*.
66. Cf. Dodd, *Parables*, 24; Jeremias, *Parables*, 18f. Further, Bultmann, *History of the Synoptic Tradition*, 198f.
67. Jeremias, *Parables*, 19.
68. Dodd, *Parables*, 18f., 24ff.
69. Dodd, *Parables*, 26–33; Jeremias, *Parables*, 21f. and *passim*.
70. Jeremias, *Parables*, 19; cf. Dodd, *Parables*, 25f.
71. Jeremias, *Parables*, 115.
72. Jeremias, *Parables*. Cf. Dodd, *Parables*, 197. Dodd guards himself more in this respect than does Jeremias.
73. It is interesting to note that in the first English edition of Jeremias' work (New York: Charles Scribner's Sons, 1955 = 3d German ed., 1954), with respect to the parable of the Laborers in the Vineyard, Jeremias writes: ". . . the question arises whether our parable has teaching as its object. None of the detailed parables of Jesus consists of mere teaching" (25). This point is missing from the revised edition (cf. 36). But even in the earlier formulation Jeremias has in mind the contrast between "mere teaching" and the parable as "vindication of the Gospel" (1st Eng. ed., 27; cf. 2d ed., 38). He is thinking, of course, of the way in which the church converted the parables, which originally had a debate context, into devices for instruction. Such a shift was inevitable, given the change in context. While the proclivities of the church in handling the parables have emerged clearly enough in his study, Jeremias never, so far as I can see, challenges the view that the parables were ideational in Jesus' hands. He gives us the contrast between *ideas* formulated in debate and *ideas* drawn out of the parables for catechetical purposes.
74. Bultmann, *History of the Synoptic Tradition*, 199.
75. In support of the line being taken here, it could be pointed out that Jeremias has had difficulty with his "few simple essential ideas":

between the third (1954) and sixth (1962) editions of his work he found it necessary to enlarge the number of interpretive categories (from eight to ten): In addition, he sometimes finds it necessary to list a particular parable under more than one rubric (suggesting that the single idea may not be so single after all). It is not always easy, furthermore, to distinguish among his categories. These observations are intended only to point to the difficulty of confining the parable in the straitjacket of a single, simple idea.

James M. Robinson implies a similar criticism of Jeremias, et al., when he states that, "The parables will therefore by the very nature of the artistic form provide us with a correct response to a situation whose historical pole is completely devoid of concrete historical details" ("Jesus' Understanding of History," 20).

76. E.g., Fuchs, *Zur Frage nach dem historischen Jesus*, 141f.

77. Jeremias, *Parables*, e.g., 22, 114.

78. Dodd, *Parables*, vi–vii.

79. Dodd, *Parables*, 195.

80. The significance of the critical historical method for determining the original import of the parable, and thus for providing a control over reinterpretation, must be emphasized, owing to the criticisms of Dodd and Jeremias being developed here. On the one hand, Dodd and especially Jeremias, in correcting Jülicher, have insisted on the crucial importance of the situation for parable interpretation. The direction in which Jesus aims the parable and the particular context in which it is heard have everything to do with its original meaning. James Robinson has summed the matter up well: "When . . . one disregarded the speaker's intention and provided only an aesthetic or literary interpretation, one did violence to the inherent nature of the subject matter under investigation and to this extent failed in one's task as an interpreter. Interpretation has frequently taken its point of departure from the beginning or the end of the parable, looking upon it as a whole, undifferentiated along the way by a point of existential involvement on the part of the hearer. Thus a false perspective of continuity, of normal unbroken progression, of process under law as revealed by the world of nature, has been forced into the parable as a factor dominating the interpretation. This exegetical foreshortening is corrected when the parable is approached from the flank, i.e., from the position of the intended hearer and the point in the parable to which such a hearer is expected to attach himself" ("Jesus' Understanding of History," 18f.). The original meaning of the parable is thus to be grasped in relation to the locus from which it is spoken and the locus from which it is heard. Without losing sight of this point, on the other hand, it is possible to claim (a) that the nature of the parable as metaphor has not been properly grasped, and (b) that the two loci have been too narrowly defined.

81. Dodd, *Parables*, 18–21, esp. 19. Cf. Bultmann's analysis of the style of the parable, *History of the Synoptic Tradition*, 187–92, for the laws of parsimony of detail.

82. Dodd, *Parables*, 21.

83. Barfield, *Poetic Diction*, 201, suggests that allegory involves a more or less conscious hypostatization of *ideas*, followed by a synthesis of them. Allegory may, of course, make use of previously created material, in which case allegory is a rationalization of mythical or other language.

84. See Dodd's definition given in full at beginning of this chapter.
85. Dodd, *Parables,* 21; cf. his *The Authority of the Bible,* 144–48.
86. Jeremias, *Parables,* 23.
87. Wilder, *Language of the Gospel,* 81ff.
88. Jeremias, e.g., calls attention to the "bad farming" represented by the parable of the Sower: the farmer sows indiscriminately. Yet, because the farmer sows *before* he ploughs, he sows the entire field—the path, among the thorns, and on rocky ground, as well as on the good ground. The parable thus depicts a convention in Palestinian agriculture (*Parables,* 11f. and n. 3).
89. Wilder, *Language of the Gospel,* 81.
90. *Language of the Gospel,* 82.
91. Jeremias, *Parables,* 12, meaning that the parables give the appearance of being free from "problematic elements."
92. Wilder, *Language of the Gospel,* 81.
93. Dodd, *Parables,* 22.
94. *Parables,* 26.
95. The quotation is found in Dodd, *Parables,* 80. Cf. 71ff.
96. Wilder, *Language of the Gospel,* 82.
97. Contrast the parables in the Gospel of Thomas, in which an earthy image looks not to the mundane but to an ethereal realm. This difference between the parables of Jesus and those in Thomas was called to my attention by James M. Robinson.
98. Barfield, "The Meaning of the Word 'Literal,'" 48f.
99. The illustration is drawn from P. G. Wodehouse, *Leave It to Psmith.*
100. I do not propose to explore the various ways in which concomitant meanings can be related to each other, as, e.g., in allegory and symbolism, but to confine myself to the concomitance of the poetic metaphor and the parable.
101. Barfield, "The Meaning of the Word 'Literal,'" 49.
102. Barfield, "Poetic Diction and Legal Fiction," 54.
103. Barfield, *Poetic Diction,* 173f. The metaphysical poets in particular use this device in a characteristic way. George Herbert, for example, is fond of importing a "plain, cold, manufactured" article into an alien context:

    When God at first made man,

    Having a glass of blessings standing by,

    "Let us," said He, "pour on him all we can. . . ."

    (cited by Barfield, *Poetic Diction,* 174). It is easy to see that *glass* in this context loses its manufactured character and takes on the incandescence of, let us say, the Holy Grail. On the other hand, the word *glass* lends immense concreteness to "standing by" and "pour" and the other, more ethereal language, to say nothing of the subject matter. This reciprocity is what Fraenkel, Riezler, and others have identified as characteristic of the Homeric metaphor (cf. Snell, *Discovery of Mind,* 200 f and n. 20). Homer, (*Iliad* 15.615) describes the Greek battle line enduring Hector's assaults as a rock in the sea endures, despite wind and waves. The inanimate object illuminates human behavior because it is viewed anthropomorphically, but that is possible only because the Greek battle line is viewed petromorphically at the same time (Snell, *Discovery of Mind,* 201). The interplay between the two is revealing, and it is difficult to estimate whether the Greeks or the rock have gained the more.

104. Barfield, *Poetic Diction*, 171 (italics his).
105. Dodd, *Parables*, 21.
106. Jeremias, *Parables*, 29ff. He borrows the phrase "shock tactics" from Vincent, "The Parables of Jesus as self-Revelation," 80.
107. Wilder, *Language of the Gospel*, 85.
108. Bultmann, *History of the Synoptic Tradition*, 166f.
109. *History of the Synoptic Tradition*, 167 n. 1, gives this definition.
110. Findlay, *Jesus and his Parables*, 10, regards the "element of surprise" as of the essence of the parable.

Chapter 2: Crossing Over

1. Politzer, *Franz Kafka*, 1.
2. Kafka, "My Destination."
3. Borges, *Other Inquisitions*, 180.

Chapter 3: Parable as Trope

1. Funk, *Poetics of Biblical Narrative*, 292–94.

Chapter 4: The Old Testament in Parable

1. Cf., e.g., Anderson, *The Old Testament and Christian Faith*; Westermann, *Essays on Old Testament Hermeneutics*.
2. According to Conzelmann, *The Theology of St. Luke*, 162, it is a special theme of Luke that scripture belongs to the church by virtue of the fact that it has the "correct" interpretation, a view that plays its role in Luke's argument that the church is the legitimate heir of Israel.

    It is instructive to notice that both Roman Catholicism and Judaism have understood this point in one way, Protestantism in another. For the former, what is revealed in scripture cannot be properly understood apart from tradition which correctly interprets scripture. Valid tradition and possession of scripture therefore go together. Tradition, moreover, is understood as the solution to the hermeneutical problem. Protestantism, on the other hand, so far as it remains under the influence of the Reformation, rejects this understanding of tradition, and thus this means of laying claim to scripture. It has to devise other means of validating its claim, with the consequence that hermeneutic remains a perennial problem in Protestantism. Cf. Ebeling's lucid discussion in *Word and Faith*, 305ff.
3. Cf. *Word and Faith*.
4. Editor's Note: Marcion was a teacher in Rome in the mid-second century whose system had two gods. The creator god, identified with the Jewish Scriptures, was evil, while the god of Jesus was a god of love. Marcion produced his own scriptures that used the Gospel of Luke and an edited version of Paul's Letters. Many scholars believe that the orthodox canon is a response to Marcion.
5. See below, note 32.
6. The tense is important: it is only the fact that the Old Testament *was* a Jewish book before the rise of the church that promotes this alliance. That the Old Testament is still a Jewish book is not relevant to historical criticism; it is now also, by the claim of the church, a Christian book, which is equally irrelevant.

7. Cf. Funk, *Language, Hemeneutic, and Word of God*, 129f.
8. In his survey of the influence of the Old Testament on the parables, Jeremias (*Parables*, 31f.) notes that there is a remarkably small number of references to scripture. Lk. 13:24–30 is a mosaic: the conclusion of one parable (Mt. 25:10--12) is merged with three related similes (Mt. 7:13f., 22f., 8:11f.), two of which involve scriptural references (Lk. 13:27/Mt. 7:23 = Ps. 6:8; Lk. 13:29/Mt. 8:11 = Ps. 107:3) (Jeremias, 95f.). Mt. 25:31, 46 may be editorial (Jeremias, 31 n. 27; 84 n. 83; 206). The allusions to Isa. 5:1ff. and Ps. 118:22f. in the parable of the Wicked Tenants (Mk. 12:1–12 and parallels) are seen to be secondary by a comparison of the three Synoptic versions and Thomas (Logion 65): Luke and Thomas lack the former, and Thomas reports the latter as an independent logion (66) (Jeremias, 31). Mark 4:32 and parallels (the Mustard Seed), Mt. 13:33 and parallel (the Leaven), and Mk. 4:29 (Seed Growing Secretly) may contain original scriptural allusions; in the first two instances, however, Jesus employs the Old Testament images in their opposite sense (Jeremias, 31f., 149)! In addition, Jeremias thinks the publican's prayer in Lk. 18:13 may reflect the opening words of Ps. 51 (Jeremias, 144). While there appears to have been a tendency in the tradition to elucidate the parables by means of scripture, the instances in which scripture was utilized by Jesus in the elaboration of the parable seem to have been few indeed (Jeremias, 32).
9. Riesenfeld, "The Parables in the Synoptic and the Johannine Traditions," 37–61, cited by Wilder (*Language of the Gospel*, 81); cf. Hoskyns and Davey, *The Riddle of the New Testament*, 182–88.
10. Gerhardsson, *The Good Samaritan*.
11. Dodd, *Parables*, 20f. (italics his). Cf. above chapter 1, 43–49.
12. Dodd, *Parables*, 21; cf. his remarks on the symbol of the heavenly banquet (p. 121), which Jesus alludes to merely as a banquet.
13. Wilder, *Language of the Gospel*, 81f.
14. *Language of the Gospel*, 81. Cf. his further remark on the same page: "In the parable of the Lost Sheep the shepherd is an actual shepherd and not a flash-back to God as the Shepherd of Israel or to the hoped-for Messiah who will shepherd Israel."
15. Dodd, *Parables*, 19f.
16. Mowry, "Parable," 650. The exceptions are: the Rich Fool, the Rich Man and Lazarus, the Publican and the Pharisee, and the Good Samaritan. It might be inquired whether the "religious" content of these four parables is really religious, or whether it is religion viewed as a secular phenomenon.
17. Wilder, *Language of the Gospel*, 82.
18. Fuchs, "The New Testament and the Hermeneutical Problem," 126 (italics his).
19. Fiebig, *Die Gleichnisreden Jesu*, 239f.; Mowry, "Parable," 652; Gerhardsson, *The Good Samaritan*, 25; Jüngel, *Paulus und Jesus*, 166. Wilder (*Language of the Gospel*, 81 n. 1) rightly warns against overemphasizing this point: the rabbinic parables are occasionally prophetic and noncasuistic in character; cf. Berakoth 28b, Pirke Aboth 3.17, Shabbath 153a.
20. Gerhardsson, *The Good Samaritan*, 25.
21. Bornkamm, *Jesus of Nazareth*, 69. Cf. Fiebig, *Die Gleichnisreden Jesu*, 239f., 260.

22. I.e., omitting Lk. 10:25–28, 37b (the imperative), but including vv. 29, 36–37a (Gerhardsson, *The Good Samaritan*, 9f.).
23. *The Good Samaritan*, 10.
24. Jeremias, *Parables*. 21f., 123, 145f., 166f., 169, *et passim*.
25. The priest and the Levite do not represent a Jewish party, but the religious leaders as a whole (Gerhardsson, *The Good Samaritan*, 11 n. 2); cf. above chapter 1, 36–38, 50f.; and *Language, Hemeneutic, and Word of God*, 176–82.
26. Gerhardsson, *The Good Samaritan*, 14. On pp. 11–14, he analyzes Jn. 10:1–16 and Ezek. 34 as a basis of these judgments; he concludes that Ezek. 34 lies behind Jn. 10.
27. *The Good Samaritan*, 14f.
28. *The Good Samaritan*, 15–18.
29. *The Good Samaritan*, 19–21, 25–29.
30. *The Good Samaritan*, 17.
31. *The Good Samaritan*, 15.
32. *The Good Samaritan*, 3–5. Gerhardsson summarizes, p. 5: "*The 20th century exegetes seem as united in their opposition to a christological interpretation as the early fathers in their support of it.*" Italics his.

    Twentieth century-exegetes are not quite as united as Gerhardsson seems to think. Cf. Fiebig's early attack upon Jülicher's strong opposition to allegory *(Die Gleichnisreden Jesu; also Altjüdische Gleichnisse und die Gleichnisse Jesus*; and Bultmann's remarks, *History of the Synoptic Tradition*, 197ff.). This was followed up by Kittel, *Jesus und die Rabbinen*, 7; Hauck, "παραβολή," 747, 750; and Vincent, "The Parables of Jesus as Self-Revelation," 79–99, esp. 81. Among the list of those either attacking Jülicher or attempting to re-establish an allegorical method of interpretation, in addition to Gerhardsson should be numbered Daniélou, "Le Bon Samaritain"; Brown, "Parable and Allegory Reconsidered," 36–45; Baird, "A Pragmatic Approach to Parable Exegesis," 201–7; Tinsley, "Parable, Allegory and Mysticism," 153–92.
33. Gerhardsson, *The Good Samaritan*, 18.
34. *The Good Samaritan*, 19f.
35. *The Good Samaritan*, 20.
36. *The Good Samaritan*, 27.
37. *The Good Samaritan*, 29.
38. *The Good Samaritan*, 26–28. Cf. Stendahl, *The School of St. Matthew*, 185ff.; Brownlee, "Biblical Interpretation Among the Sectaries of the Dead Sea Scrolls," 54–76.
39. Cf. Jeremias, *Parables*, 33–66.
40. Gerhardsson, *The Good Samaritan*, 21. Gerhardsson, however, thinks this injunction may not be wholly secondary (21, n. 4); it is a set phrase from the language of the Jewish schools (10 and n. 1), and is suitable to the Lucan context (23f.).
41. Gerhardsson, *The Good Samaritan*, 22–29.
42. It does not matter that a precise Hebrew equivalent for νομικός cannot be established; the lawyer in any case was a learned student of the law (Gerhardsson, *The Good Samaritan*, 23). Cf. Manson, *The Sayings of Jesus*, 260, who surmises that Luke uses "lawyer" rather than "scribe" because the latter would be misunderstood by Gentile readers. Cf. Gutbrod, "νομιχός," 1081.
43. The two are introduced with the same initial question, which is

answered out of the law.

44. Gerhardsson, *The Good Samaritan*, 29. One might have expected him to draw a parallel also between the Good Samaritan and the parable of the Lost Sheep (Lk. 15:4–7/Mt. 18:12–13), but he does not seem to notice this possibility.

45. Fuchs, *Hermeneutik*, 223ff.; *Zur Frage nach dem historischen Jesus*, 136–42; cf. Jüngel, *Paulus und Jesus*, 87, 87f. n. 3; Jeremias, *Parables*, 230.

46. Gerhardsson wants to distinguish his understanding of the parable as an *allegoric parable* from the patristic understanding of it as a *timeless allegory* (*The Good Samaritan*, 22). Here he parts company with Daniélou, "Le Bon Samaritain," 457ff., who wants to reinstate the patristic allegory (Gerhardsson, *The Good Samaritan*, 31 additional note). If the patristic view is that the parable is a timeless allegory of the history of the human race or soul, Gerhardsson's view is that it contains a timeless christological didache; in his own judgment it is a difference between two types of universality and timelessness.

47. Jülicher, *Die Gleichnisreden Jesu*, II, 596; Gerhardsson, *The Good Samaritan*, 6; Jeremias, *Parables*, 205.

48. E.g., Jülicher, *Die Gleichnisreden Jesu*; Bultmann, *History of the Synoptic Tradition*, 178; Jüngel, *Paulus und Jesus*, 169f., decides that vv. 25–28 are secondary, but leaves the question open whether vv. 29, 36f. are also.

49. E.g., by Manson, *The Teachings of Jesus*, 301; Jeremias, *Parables*, 205; Gerhardsson, *The Good Samaritan*, 28f.

50. Gerhardsson (*The Good Samaritan*, 19) correctly emphasizes this point. Manson (*Sayings of Jesus*, 261) does not follow the dominant view, but holds that the parable does not define neighbor at all.

51. Gerhardsson, *The Good Samaritan*, 9; cf. Jüngel, *Paulus und Jesus*, 170.

52. Michaelis, *Die Gleichnisse Jesu*, 205; Bultmann, *Jesus and the Word*, 96; Jüngel, *Paulus und Jesus*, 170.

53. Gerhardsson (*The Good Samaritan*, 8f.) notes that the situation with respect to the message of Jesus has changed materially since Jülicher formulated his views. It is strange that Jülicher's reading of the Good Samaritan as a *Beispielerzählung* has gone virtually unchallenged. The Lucan tradition has given support, however, to a moralistic reading, terminating as it does with the exhortation, "Go and do likewise."

54. Jeremias, *Parables*, 42–48 *et passim*.

55. Bultmann, *History of the Synoptic Tradition*, 178 n. 1; cf. 177f.; Jülicher, *Die Gleichnisreden Jesu*, I, 112; II, 585; Linnemann, *Gleichnisse Jesu*, 55; Jüngel, *Paulus und Jesus*, 170f.

56. Bultmann, *History of the Synoptic Tradition*, 198.

57. Gerhardsson, *The Good Samaritan*, 5 and n. 6; p. 9.

58. The other parables identified as exemplary stories are: the Rich Fool, the Pharisee and the Publican, the Rich Man and Lazarus, (the Wedding Guest [Lk. 14:7–11], the Proper Guests [Lk. 14:12–14]): Jülicher, *Die Gleichnisreden Jesu*, I, 112; II, 585–641; Bultmann, *History of the Synoptic Tradition*, 178f. Naturally we are not considering here whether the designation is appropriate in these other cases, but it is interesting to note that the exemplary stories are also those identified as having religious content (see n. 15), except for the two Lucan examples added by Bultmann.

59. Günther Bornkamm, *Jesus of Nazareth.*, 112f., thinks this point is crucial and I agree.

60. Bornkamm, *Jesus of Nazareth.*; Jeremias, *Parables*, 205.

61. Jeremias, *Parables*, 204.
62. Manson, *Sayings of Jesus*, 263: we may suppose that the man who fell among thieves was a Jew. According to rabbinic teaching, an Israelite was not to accept alms or a work of love from a non-Jew, since Israel's redemption is thereby delayed: Jüngel, *op. cit.*, 172, quoting Grundmann, *Die Geschichte Jesu Christi*, 90; cf. Strack and Billerbeck, *Kommentar zum Neuen Testament*, 538f., 543f.
63. Jeremias, *Parables*, 204.
64. The Pharisees excluded non-Pharisees from their definition of neighbor, the Essenes were to hate all sons of darkness, and a rabbinical saying ruled that heretics, informers, and renegades should be pushed (into the ditch) and not pulled out. Personal enemies were also excluded from the circle (Mt. 5:43): Jeremias, *Parables*, 202f. The victim in the ditch could also belong to one of these categories; every listener becomes victim. The parable would not have been offensive to listeners of this type.
65. Dodd, *Parables*, 24ff.
66. I am indebted to Hart ("Imagination and the Scale of Mental Acts," 3–21, esp. 19f.) for the elements of this formulation.
67. See above chapter 1, 31–43, and a recent article by Forstman, "Samuel Taylor Coleridge's Notes," especially 319ff.
68. It is for this reason that the parables should not be allegorized (allegory: reduction to a congeries of ideas or concepts, for which the narrative elements are ciphers), but it is also the reason why the parables cannot be reduced to a leading idea (Jeremias, *Parables*, 115) or understood to teach "spiritual truths." Rationalization in any form maims the parabolic image.
69. Cf. Käsemann, "God's Righteousness in Paul," 109f., who uses the phrase in a formulation from the Pauline perspective.
70. Gerhardsson, *The Good Samaritan*, 27.
71. *The Good Samaritan*, 31.
72. That is to say, one cannot allow the common tradition to dominate the question of Jesus' own mode of discourse. That the latter is to be determined in relation to the former is true enough, but the particularity of the historical relativizes the significance of correlative modes and structures. The crucial item is what Jesus does with the common tradition.
73. Cf. Wilder, "Eschatology and the Speech-Modes of the Gospel,", 27. Wilder's criticisms in this article and another ("Form-History and the Oldest Tradition," 3–13) of Gerhardsson's broader thesis with respect to tradition and interpretation in the early church, fully articulated in *Memory and Manuscript*, serve as background for my criticisms of Gerhardsson's treatment of the parable of the Good Samaritan in particular.
74. See above, n. 52.
75. Bultmann, *History of the Synoptic Tradition*, 178.
76. Jüngel, *Paulus and Jesus*, 171.
77. Jeremias (*Parables*, 203f.) carefully considers this point and finds it dubious on two grounds: (1) Did the priest and Levite consider the man to be dead (v. 30, ἡμιθανῆ, half-dead)? (2) Was the Levite governed by ritual considerations? It is perhaps the ambiguity of the situation that gives the parable its pinch: the priest and Levite wanted to debate the issue.

78. Bultmann, *Jesus and the Word,* 96; Bornkamm, "Das Doppelgebot der Liebe," 85; Jüngel, *Paulus und Jesus,* 172.
79. Bornkamm, "Das Doppelgebot . . .," 86. The rabbis of course occasionally gave brief synopses of the law, but would have been opposed to a reduction in principle.
80. Bornkamm, "Das Doppelgebot . . ." 92. Bornkamm thinks Matthew and Luke had variants of the Marcan text before them; Manson *(Sayings of Jesus,* 259) thinks the Lucan story is independent of Mark.
81. Bornkamm, "Das Doppelgebot . . .," 93.
82. Manson *(Sayings of Jesus,* 260) suggests that the Lucan account presupposes, so to speak, the Marcan account in that the lawyer gives what he knows to be Jesus' answer in order to raise the further question. The Lucan version begins in earnest where the Marcan account leaves off. One can reach this conclusion by inference from the parable itself rather than by attempting to establish first the authenticity of the Lucan context as Manson does.
83. Bornkamm, *Jesus of Nazareth,* 110; cf. the remarks of Ebeling, "Theology and the Evidentness of the Ethical," 112f. and n. 18), e.g., "The 'blessed of the Father' [Mt. 25:40] have as little idea of having done something to Jesus as those who are 'cursed' for their failure have any idea that they have been guilty of failing Jesus. Those who took the part of the hungry, homeless, sick, and lonely had done so simply because they saw the need as a plain opportunity to intervene remedially. They did what impressed itself on them in this case as reasonable, because necessary. The interpolation of the idea that it was to be done for Jesus' sake would threaten to ruin the whole." Ebeling also quotes some cutting remarks of Wilhelm Herrmann.
84. Bornkamm, *Jesus of Nazareth,* 113.
85. Ebeling, "Theology and the Evidentness of the Ethical," 119.
86. Jüngel, *Paulus und Jesus,* 173.
87. Jüngel, *Paulus und Jesus.*
88. Bornkamm, *Jesus of Nazareth,* 113.
89. *Contra* Jeremias, *Parables,* 205: "The alteration in the form of the question hardly conceals a deeper meaning."
90. Fuchs, *Zum hermeneutischen Problem,* 286f.,290.
91. Cf. Ebeling, "Theology and the Evidentness of the Ethical," 112f.
92. Fuchs, *Zum hermeneutischen Problem,* 287 (italics his).
93. The reader may wish to compare my earlier reading of the parable in "How Do You Read?," 56–61.

Chapter 5: The Good Samaritan as Metaphor

1. John Dominic Crossan, "Parable and Example in the Teaching of Jesus," and Dan Via, "Parable and Example Story."
2. Gleason, "Contrastive Analysis," 41.

Chapter 6: The Leaven

1. Steiner, *Language and Silence,* 8f.
2. Editor's Note: for a discussion of Q, see *The Five Gospels,* 10–13.
3. Jeremias, *Parables,* 148–49.
4. Dodd, *Parables* (1961 ed.), 154, 155f.
5. Dodd, *Parables* (1961 ed.), 23ff.; Jeremias, *Parables,* 18ff.

6. Jülicher, *Die Gleichnisreden Jesu, 576.*
7. Dodd, *Parables,* 192.
8. Bornkamm, *Jesus of Nazareth,* 71ff.
9. The tree as the locus of divine epiphany in these accounts is faintly suggestive of the juxtaposition of the mustard (tree) and leaven in the synoptic tradition, but the concatenation is, I think, merely fortuitous. The mustard is linked with the mighty cedar rather than the oak.
10. Even among the Greeks, to judge by Plutarch and Persius.
11. Smith, *Jesus of the Parables,* 71.
12. Kafka, "An Imperial Message"
13. Bornkamm, *Jesus of Nazareth,* 62.
14. Hart, "American Home-World."
15. "American Home-World."
16. Steiner, *Language and Silence,* 11.

Chapter 7: The Looking-glass Tree Is for the Birds

1. Dodd, *Parables,* 191.
2. Q is a sayings gospel embedded in Matthew and Luke. It has been extracted from Matthew and Luke and reconstructed in Kloppenborg et al, *The Q-Thomas Reader,* and in R. J. Miller, *The Complete Gospels.*
3. Jeremias, *Parables,* 149.
4. Dylan, *Like a Rolling Stone.*

Chapter 8: The Narrative Parables

1. Gaston, *Horae Synopticae Electronicae,* 43.
2. Taber, *The Structure of Sango Narrative,* 87.
3. Denniston, *Greek Prose Style,* 124.
4. Black, *Aramaic Approach,* 160–85.
5. Denniston, *Greek Prose Style,* 135; Blass-Debrunner, *Greek Grammar,* §488[3].
6. Blass-Debrunner, *Greek Grammar,* §4.
7. Toelken, "Pretty Language," 222f.
8. Dundes, "Texture, Text, and Context," 254; Toelken, "Pretty Language," 223.
9. Spitzer, *Linguistics and Literary History,* 18.

Chapter 9: Parable, Paradox, and Power

1. See Patte, "An Analysis of Narrative Structure and the Good Samaritan."
2. I first advanced the reading of the Samaritan as metaphor in "How Do You Read," *Interpretation* (1964), developed the reading in "The Old Testament in Parable," *Encounter* (1965) and in *Language, Hermeneutic, and Word of God* (1966, 199–22 [see chapter 4 above]), then consummated it in "The Good Samaritan as Metaphor," *Semeia* (1974 [see chapter 5 above]). The case was taken up by J. Dominic Crossan (*In Parables* [1973, 57–66] and "The Good Samaritan" [1974]) and approved by Norman Perrin ("The Modern Interpretation of the Parables" [1971] and *Jesus and the Language of the Kingdom* [1976,138–41]). It goes without saying that this reading has not been universally accepted.

Chapter 10: From Parable to Gospel

1. Jeremias, *Parables* (1955 ed.), 103.
2. *Parables* (1955 ed.), 103, n. 70.
3. *Parables* (1955 ed.), 105–6.
4. *Parables* (1955 ed.), 106.
5. Tannehill, *Sword of His Mouth,* 165–71.
6. *Sword of His Mouth,* 198, n. 116.
7. Editor's Note: "actants" are the functions in a narrative, see "Parable, Paradox, and Power" (see chapter 9) above.
8. *Sword of His Mouth.* 52, 88–101.
9. *Sword of His Mouth,* 90.
10. *Sword of His Mouth,* 92.
11. *Sword of His Mouth,* 71.
12. Schutz and Luckman, *The Structures of the Life-World,* 3.
13. *The Structures of the Life-World,* 5.
14. *The Structures of the Life-World,* S.
15. *The Structures of the Life-World,* 7.
16. *The Structures of the Life-World,* 6.
17. *The Structures of the Life-World,* 19.
18. *The Structures of the Life-World,* 18.
19. Kee, *Community of the New Age,* 180, n. 58.
20. *Community of the New Age,* 180–81, n. 58.
21. *Community of the New Age,* 181, n. 58.
22. Bultmann, *Theology of the New Testament,* vol. 1, 22–26.
23. *Theology of the New Testament,* vol. 1, 26–32.
24. Hart, *Unfinished Man and the Imagination,* 282.
25. *Unfinished Man and the Imagination,* 304.

Chapter 13: The Mythical Matrix and God as Metaphor

1. Cupitt, *Taking Leave of God,* 105.

Works Consulted

Achtemeier, Paul. J. *An Introduction to the New Hermeneutic.* Philadelphia, Westminster Press, 1969.

Altizer, Thomas J. J. *The Gospel of Christian Atheism.* Philadelphia: Westminster Press, 1966.

———. and Wm. Hamilton. *Radical Theology and the Death of God.* Indianapolis: Bobbs-Merrill, 1966.

Anderson, B. W., ed. *The Old Testament and Christian Faith.* New York: Harper & Row, 1963.

Armstrong, Karen. *The Battle for God.* New York: Ballantine, 2000.

———. *A History of God: The 4000–Year Quest of Judaism, Christianity and Islam.* New York: A. A. Knopf, 1993.

Baird, J. Arthur. "A Pragmatic Approach to Parable Exegesis: Some New Evidence on Mark 4:11, 33–34." *Journal of Biblical Literature* 76 (1957), 201–7.

Barfield, Owen. "The Meaning of the Word 'Literal'." Pp. 48–62 in *Metaphor and Symbol,* edited by L. C. Knights and Basil Cottle. London: Butterworth Scientific Publications, 1960.

———. "Poetic Diction and Legal Fiction." Pp. 51–71 in *The Importance of Language,* edited by Max Black. Englewood Cliffs, NJ: Prentice-Hall, 1962.

———. *Poetic Diction: A Study in Meaning.* 2d ed. London: Faber & Faber, 1952.

———. *Saving the Appearances: A Study in Idolatry.* London: Faber & Faber, 1957.

Black, Matthew. *An Aramaic Approach to the Gospels and Acts.* 3d ed. Oxford: At the Clarendon Press, 1967.

Blass, F. and A. Debrunner. *A Greek Grammar of the New Testament and Other Early Christian Literature.* Translated and revised by Robert W. Funk. Chicago: University of Chicago, 1961.

Bonhoeffer, Dietrich. *Letters and Papers from Prison.* Translated by Reginald Fuller. New York: Macmillan, 1953.

Borges, Jorge Luis. *Labyrinths. Selected Stories and Other Writings,* edited by Donald A. Yates and James E. Irby. New York: New Directions Publishing Corporation, 1964.

———. *Other Inquisitions, 1937–1952.* Translated by Ruth L. C. Simms, with an introduction by James E. Irby. New York: Simon & Schuster, 1964.

Bornkamm, Günther. "Das Doppelgebot der Liebe." Pp. 85–93 in *Neutestamentliche Studien für Rudolf Bultmann.* Beihefte zur Zeitschrift für die neutestamentliche Wissenschaft 21. 2d ed. Berlin: Topelmann, 1957.

———. *Jesus of Nazareth.* Translated by Irene and Fraser McLuskey with J. M. Robinson. New York: Harper & Brothers, 1960.

Borg, Marcus. *The God We Never Knew: Beyond Dogmatic Religion to a More Authentic Contemporary Faith.* San Francisco: HarperSanFrancisco, 1997.

Bowen, Clayton R. "The Kingdom and the Mustard Seed." *American Journal of Theology* 22 (1918), 562–69.

Brooks, Cleanth. "Metaphor and the Function of Criticism." In *Spiritual Problems in Contemporary Literature*, edited by S. R. Hopper. New York: Harper Torchbook, 1957.

Brown, Raymond E. "Parable and Allegory Reconsidered." *Novum Testamentum* 5 (1962), 36–45.

Brownlee, W. H. "Biblical Interpretation Among the Sectaries of the Dead Sea Scrolls." *Biblical Archaeologist* 14 (1951), 54–76.

Bultmann, Rudolf. *The History of the Synoptic Tradition.* Translated by John Marsh. New York: Harper & Row, 1963.

———. *Jesus and the Word.* Translated by L. P. Smith and E. H. Lantero. New York: Charles Scribner's Sons, 1958 [1934].

———. *Jesus Christ and Mythology.* New York: Scribner, 1958.

———. "New Testament and Mythology." Pp. 1–44 in *Kerygma and Myth: A Theological Debate*, edited by Hans Werner Bartsch. Translated by Reginald Fuller. London: SPCK, 1957.

———. *Theology of the New Testament.* Vol. 1. Translated by Kendrick Grobel. New York: Charles Scribner's Sons, 1951.

Burrows, Millar. *An Outline of Biblical Theology.* Philadelphia: The Westminster Press, 1946.

Cadoux, A .T. *The Parables of Jesus: Their Art and Use.* London: James Clarke & Co., 1930.

Chatman, Seymour. *Story and Discourse. Narrative Structure in Fiction and Film.* Ithaca: Cornell University Press, 1978.

Conzelmann, H. *The Theology of St. Luke.* Translated by G. Buswell. New York: Harper & Brothers, 1960.

Crossan, John Dominic. *In Parables.* New York: Harper & Row, 1973. Reprint, Sonoma, CA: Polebridge Press, 1992.

———. "The Good Samaritan: Towards a Generic Definition of the Parable." *Semeia* 2 (1974), 82–112.

———. "Parable and Example in the Teaching of Jesus." *Semeia* 1 (1974), 63–104.

———. *Raid on the Articulate: Comic Eschatology in Jesus and Borges.* New York: Harper and Row, 1976.

———. "The Servant Parables of Jesus." *Semeia* 1 (1974), 17–62.

———. "Structuralist Analysis and the Parables of Jesus." *Semeia* 1 (1974), 192–221.

Cupitt, Don. *After All: Religion Without Alienation.* London: SCM Press, 1994.

———. *After God: The Future of Religion.* New York: Basic Books, 1997.

———. *The Last Philosophy.* London: SCM Press, 1995.

———. *Taking Leave of God.* London: SCM Press, 1980.

Dahl, N. A. "Gleichnis und Parabel. II. In der Bibel. 3. Im NT." Cols. 1617–19 in vol. 2 of *Die Religion in Geschichte und Gegenwart*, edited by K. Galling. 7 vols. 3d ed. Tübingen: J. C. B. Mohr [Paul Siebeck], 1957–1965.

Daniélou, J. "Le Bon Samaritain." Pp. 457–65 in *Mélanges Bibliques rédigés en l'honneur d'André Robert.* Paris: Bloud & Gay, 1957.

Davies, Paul C. W. *The Mind of God: The Scientific Basis for a Rational World.* New York: Simon & Schuster, 1992.

———. *God and The New Physics.* London: Penguin, 1983.

Denniston, J. D. *Greek Prose Style.* Oxford: At the Clarendon Press, 1952.

Dibelius, Martin. *From Tradition to Gospel.* Translated by B. L. Woolf. New York: Charles Scribner's Sons, 1935.

Dodd, C. H. *The Authority of the Bible.* Rev. ed. Glasgow: William Collins Sons [Fontana Books], 1960, 1962.

———. *The Parables of the Kingdom.* 3d ed. London: Nisbet & Co., 1936, 1952.

Dundes, Alan. "Texture, Text, and Context." *Southern Folklore Quarterly* 28, 4 (December 1964), 251–65.

Ebeling, Gerhard. "Theology and the Evidentness of the Ethical." *Journal for Theology and the Church* 2 (1965), 95–129.

———. *Word and Faith.* Translated by James W. Leitch. Philadelphia: Fortress Press, 1963.

Edwards, David L. *The "Honest to God" Debate.* Philadelphia: Westminster Press, 1963.

Farrar, Austin. *A Study in St. Mark.* London: Dacre Press, 1951.

Fiebig, P. *Altjüdische Gleichnisse und die Gleichnisse Jesus.* Tübingen und Leipzig: J. C. B. Mohr [Paul Siebeck] 1904.

———. *Die Gleichnisreden Jesu im Lichte der rabbinischen Gleichnisse.* Tübingen: J. C. B. Mohr, 1912.

Findlay, J. A. *Jesus and His Parables.* London: Epworth Press, 1950.

Forstman, H. Jack. "Samuel Taylor Coleridge's Notes Toward the Understanding of Doctrine." *Journal of Religion* 44 (1964), 310–27

Fuchs, Ernst. *Hermeneutik.* Bad Cannstatt: R. Müllerschön Verlag, 1954. 2d ed. with Ergänzungsheft, 1958.

———. "The New Testament and the Hermeneutical Problem." Pp. 111–45 in *The New Hermeneutic.* Vol 2 of *New Frontiers in Theology,* edited by J. M. Robinson and J. B. Cobb, Jr. New York: Harper & Row, 1964.

———. *Zur Frage nach dem historischen Jesus.* Vol. 2 of *Gesammelte Aufsätze.* Tübingen: J. C. B. Mohr [Paul Siebeck], 1959 = *Studies of the Historical Jesus.* Translated by A. Scobie. Studies in Biblical Theology 42. London: SCM Press, 1965. References to the English version are given in square brackets.

———. *Zum hermeneutischen Problem in der Theologie: Die Existentials Interpretation.* Vol. 1 of *Gesammelte Aufätze.* Tubingen: J. C. B Mohr [Paul Siebeck}, 1959.

Funk, Robert W.

———. *A Beginning-Intermediate Grammar of Hellenistic Greek.* 3 vols. Missoula: Scholars Press, 1973.

———. *A Credible Jesus: Fragments of a Vision.* Santa Rosa, CA: Polebridge Press, 2002.

———. *Honest to Jesus: Jesus for a New Millennium.* San Francisco: HarperSanFrancisco, 1996.

———. "How Do You Read?' (Luke 10:25–37)." *Interpretation* 18 (1964), 56–61.

———. "The Good Samaritan as Metaphor." *Semeia* 2 (1974), 74–81.

———. *Jesus as Precursor. Semeia* Supplements 2. Philadelphia: Fortress Press and Missoula, MT: Scholars Press, 1975; Rev. ed. 1994.

———. *Language, Hermeutic, and Word of God.* New York: Harper & Row, 1966.

———. *Parables and Presence: Forms of the New Testament Tradition.* Philadelphia: Fortress Press, 1976.

———. "The Old Testament in Parable: A Study of Luke 10:25–37." *Encounter* 26,2 (1965), 251–67.

———. *Poetics of Biblical Narrative.* Sonoma, CA: Polebridge Press, 1988.

Funk, Robert W. et al. *The Five Gospels: The Search for the Authentic Words of Jesus.* New York: Macmillan, 1993.

Gaston, Lloyd. *Horae Synopticae Electronicae: Word Statistics of the Synoptic Gospels.* Sources for Biblical Study 3. Missoula, MT: Society of Biblical Literature, 1973.

Geering, Lloyd. *Faith's New Age: A Perspective on Contemporary Religious Change*. London: Collins, 1980. Reprint, *Christian Faith at the Crossroads: A Map of Modern Religious History*. Santa Rosa, CA: Polebridge Press, 2001.

———. *God in the New World*. London: Hodder & Stoughton, 1968.

———. *Tomorrow's God: How We Create Our Worlds*. Wellington: Bridget Williams Books, 1994. Reprint, Santa Rosa, CA: Polebridge Press, 2000.

———. *The World to Come: From Christian Past to Global Future*. Santa Rosa, CA: Polebridge Press, 1999.

Gerhardsson, Birger. *The Good Samaritan—The Good Shepherd?* Coniectanea neotestamentica 16. Lund: C. W. K. Gleerup, 1958.

———. *Memory and Manuscript: Oral Tradition and Written Transmission in Rabbinic Judaism and Early Christianity*. Translated by Eric J. Sharpe. Acta seminarii neotestamentici upsaliensis 22. Lund: C. W. K. Gleerup; Copenhagen: Ejnar Munksgaard, 1961.

Gleason, H. A., Jr. "Contrastive Analysis in Discourse Structure." Georgetown Monograph Series on Languages and Linguistics 21 (1968), 39–63.

Gowler, David. *What Are They Saying About Parables?* Mahwah: Paulist Press, 2000.

Grundmann, W. *Die Geschichte Jesu Christi*. 2d ed. Berlin: Evangelische Verlagsanstalt, 1959.

Gutbrod, W. "νομιχός." Pp. 1080–81 in vol. 4 of *Theologisches Wörterbuch zum Neuen Testament*, edited by G. Kittel and G. Friedrich. Stuttgart: W. Kohlhammer Verlag, 1932–1979.

Harnack, Adolf von. *What is Christianity?* Translated by T. B. Saunders. New York: Harper Tourchbooks, 1957.

Hart, Ray L. "The American Home-World: Reality and Imagination." Lecture delivered in a series "Imagination and Contemporary Sensibility." University of Montana, inaugurating the Department of Religious Studies, 1970 (unpublished).

———. "Imagination and the Scale of Mental Acts." *Continuum* 3 (1965), 3–21.

———. *Unfinished Man and the Imagination: Toward an Ontology and a Rhetoric of Revelation*. New York: Herder and Herder, 1968.

Hauck, F. "παραβολή." Pp. 741–59 in vol. 5 of *Theologisches Wörterbuch zum Neuen Testament*, edited by G. Kittel and G. Friedrich. Stuttgart: W. Kohlhammer Verlag, 1932–1979.

Hawking, Stephen. *A Brief History of Time: From the Big Bang to Black Holes*. New York: Bantam Books, 1989.

Hedrick, Charles W. *Many Things in Parables. Jesus and His Modern Critics*. Louisville, KY: Westminster/John Knox, 2004.

Heidegger, Martin. *Being and Time*. Translated by J. Macquarrie and E. Robinson. London: SCM Press, 1962.

Herzog, William R. *Parables as Subversive Speech: Jesus as Pedagogue of the Oppressed*. Louisville: Westminster/John Knox, 1994.

Hick, John. *The Metaphor of God Incarnate: Christology in a Pluralistic Age*. Louisville: Westminster/John Knox Press, 1993.

———. *The Existence of God*, New York: Macmillan, 1964.

———. *Death & Eternal Life*. New York: Harper & Row, 1994.

Hoskyns, E. and N. Davey. *The Riddle of the New Testament*. London: Faber & Faber, 1931.

Jeremias, Joachim. *The Parables of Jesus*. Translated by S. H. Hooke. New York: Charles Scribner's Sons, 1963.

Jones, Roger S. *Physics for the Rest of Us*. Chicago: Contemporary Books, 1992.

Jülicher, Adolf. *Die Gleichnisreden Jesu*. 2 vols. Tübingen: J. C. B. Mohr, 1888–1899. Reprint (2 vols. in 1), Darmstadt: Wissenschaftliche Buchgesellschaft, 1963.

Jüngel, Eberhard. *Paulus und Jesus. Eine Untersuchung zur Präzisierung der Frage nach dem Ursprung der Christologie*. Hermeneutische Untersuchungen zur Theologie 2. Tübingen: J. C. B. Mohr [Paul Siebeck], 1962.

Kafka, Franz. *Parables and Paradoxes*. New York: Schocken Books, 1961.

Käsemann, Ernst. "God's Righteousness in Paul." *Journal for Theology and the Church* 1 (1965), 100–110.

Kee, Howard Clark. *Community of the New Age: Studies in Mark's Gospel*. Philadelphia: Westminster Press, 1977.

Kittel, Gerhard. *Jesus und die Rabbinen*. Berlin: E. Runge, 1914.

Kloppenborg, John S. et al. *The Q-Thomas Reader*. Sonoma, CA: Polebridge Press, 1990.

Lewis, C. S. "Bluspels and Flalansferes." Pp. 36–50 in *The Importance of Language*, edited by Max Black. Englewood Cliffs, N.J.: Prentice-Hall, 1962.

Linnemann, E. *Gleichnisse Jesu. Einführung und Auslegung*. 2d ed. Göttingen: Vandenhoeck & Ruprecht, 1962.

Lovelock, James. *Gaia. A New Look at Life on Earth*. New York: Oxford University Press, 1979.

Lüdemann, Gerd. *Heretics: The Other Side of Early Christianity*. Translated by John Bowden. Louisville, Westminster/John Knox Press, 1995.

Manson, T. W. *The Sayings of Jesus*. London: SCM Press, 1949 [1961].

———. *The Teachings of Jesus*. Cambridge: The University Press, 1951.

Michaelis, W. *Die Gleichnisse Jesu. Eine Einführung*. 3d ed. Hamburg: Furche, 1956.

Miles, Jack. *God: A Biography*. London: Touchstone, 1995.

Miller, Robert, ed. *The Apocalyptic Jesus, A Debate*. Santa Rosa, CA: Polebridge Press, 2001.

———. ed. *The Complete Gospels: Annotated Scholars Version*. Sonoma, CA: Polebridge Press, 1991.

Mowry, Lucetta. "Parable." Pp. 649–53 in vol. 3 of *The Interpreter's Dictionary of the Bible*, edited by G. A. Buttrick. 4 vols. Nashville, TN: Abingdon Press, 1962.

Patte, Daniel. "An Analysis of Narrative Structure and the Good Samaritan." *Semeia* 1 (1974), 1–26.

Patterson, Stephen J. *The God of Jesus: The Historical Jesus and the Search for Meaning*. Harrisburg, PA: Trinity Press International, 1998.

Perrin, Norman. "The Modern Interpretation of the Parables of Jesus and the Problem of Hermeneutics." *Interpretation* 25 (1971), 131–48.

———. *Jesus and the Language of the Kingdom*. Philadelphia: Fortress, 1976.

Politzer, Heinz. *Franz Kafka: Parable and Paradox*. Ithaca: Cornell University Press, 1966.

Primavesi, Anne. *From Apocalypse to Genesis: Ecology, Feminism and Christianity*. Minneapolis: Fortress Press, 1991.

———. *Sacred Gaia: Holistic Theology and Early System Science*. London: Routledge, 2000.

Propp, Vladimir. *Morphology of the Folktale*. 2d ed. Austin: University of Texas, 1968.

Ramsey, Ian. *Models and Mystery*. London and New York: Oxford University Press, 1964.

Riesenfeld, Harald. "The Parables in the Synoptic and the Johannine Traditions." *Svensk exegetisk årsbok* 25 (1960), 37–61.

Robinson, James M. "Jesus' Understanding of History." *Journal of Bible and Religion* 23 (1955), 17–24.

Robinson, John A. T. *Honest to God*. Philadelphia: Westminster Press, 1963.

Rohrbaugh, Richard L. 1993. "A Peasant Reading of the Parable of the Talents/Pounds: A Text of Terror?" *Biblical Theology Bulletin* 23 (1993), 32–40.

Sagan, Carl. *The Demon-Haunted World: Science as a Candle in the Dark*. New York: Random House, 1995.

Schmidt, Daryl. "It All Began with Grammar." *The Fourth R* 19,2 (2006), 8.

Scott, Bernard Brandon. *Hear Then the Parable, A Commentary on the Parables of Jesus*. Minneapolis: Fortress Press, 1989.

Schutz, Alfred and Thomas Luckmann. *The Structures of the Life-World*. Translated by Richard M. Zaner and Tristram Englehardt, Jr. Evanston: Northwestern University Press, 1973.

Sheehan, Thomas. *The First Coming: How the Kingdom of God Became Christianity*. New York: Vintage Books, 1988.

Smith, B. T. D. *The Parables of the Synoptic Gospels: A Critical Study*. Cambridge: At the University Press, 1937.

Smith, C. W. F. *The Jesus of the Parables*. Philadelphia: Westminster Press, 1948.

Snell, Bruno. *The Discovery of Mind*. Translated by T. G. Rosenmeyer. New York: Harper Torchbook, 1960.

Spitzer, Leo. *Linguistics and Literary History: Essays in Stylistics*. Princeton, NJ: Princeton University Press, 1967.

Spong, John S. *Why Christianity Must Change or Die: A Bishop Speaks to Believers in Exile*. San Francisco: HarperSanFrancisco, 1998.

Stanford, W. B. *The Sound of Greek. Studies in the Greek Theory and Practice of Euphony*. Berkeley: University of California Press, 1967.

Steiner, George. *Language and Silence: Essays on Language, Literature, and the Inhuman*. New York: Atheneum, 1967.

Stendahl, K. *The School of St. Matthew and Its Use of the Old Testament*. Acta seminarii neotestamentici upsaliensis 20. Uppsala: C. W. K. Gleerup, Lund, 1954.

Strack, H. L. and P. Billerbeck. *Kommentar zum Neuen Testament aus Talmud und Midrash*. Vol. 4. 2d ed. Munich: C. H. Beck'sche Verlagsbuchhandlung, 1956.

Strauss, David Friedrich. *The Old Faith and the New*. Translated by Mathilde Blind. New York: H. Holt, 1872. Reprint, Amherst, NY: Prometheus Books, 1997.

Taber, Charles Russell. *The Structure of Sango Narrative*. 2 vols. Hartford Studies in Linguistics 17. Hartford, CT: Hartford Seminary Foundation, 1966.

Tannehill, Robert C.. *The Sword of His Mouth*. Semeia Supplements 1. Philadelphia: Fortress Press; Missoula, MT: Scholars Press, 1975.

Tillich, Paul. *The Protestant Era*. Translated by J. L. Adams. Chicago: University of Chicago Press, 1948.

———. *Systematic Theology*. Vol. 1. Chicago: University of Chicago Press, 1951.

Tillich, Paul. *The Shaking of the Foundations*. New York: Charles Scribner's Sons, 1948.

Tinsley, E. J. "Parable, Allegory and Mysticism," Pp. 153–92 in *Vindications: Essays on the Historical Basis of Christianity*, edited by Anthony Hanson. London: SCM Press, 1966.

Toelken, J. Barre. "The 'Pretty Language' of Yellowman: Genre, Mode, and Texture in Navaho Coyote Narratives." *Genre* II, 3 (1969), 211–35.

Tolkien, J. R. R.. "On Fairy-Stories." Pp. 3–84 in *The Tolkien Reader: Stories, Poems and Commentary by the Author of* The Hobbit *and* The Lord of the Rings. New York: Ballantine Books, 1966.

Via, Dan O. "Parable and Example Story: A Literary-Structuralist Approach." *Semeia* 1 (1974), 105–33.

———. *The Parables: Their Literary and Existential Dimension*. Philadelphia: Fortress Press, 1967.

Vincent, J. J. "The Parables of Jesus as Self-Revelation." Pp. 79–99 in *Studia evangelica*, edited by K. Aland et al. Berlin: Akademie-Verlag, 1959.

Westermann, C., ed. *Essays on Old Testament Hermeneutics*. Richmond, VA: John Knox Press, 1963.

Wheelwright, Philip. *The Burning Fountain*. Bloomington, IN: Indiana University Press, 1954.

———. *Metaphor and Reality*. Bloomington, IN: Indiana University Press, 1962.

Wilder, Amos. "Eschatology and the Speech-Modes of the Gospel." In *Zeit und Geschichte. Dankesgabe an Rudolf Bultmann zum 80. Gebunstag*, edited by E. Dinkler. Tübingen: J. C. B. Mohr, 1964.

———. *Early Christian Rhetoric: The Language of the Gospel*. London: SCM Press, 1964.

———. "Form-History and the Oldest Tradition." Pp. 3–13 in *Neotestamentica et Patristica*, edited by W. C. van Unnik. Leiden: E. J. Brill, 1962.

———. *The Language of the Gospel: Early Christian Rhetoric*. New York: Harper & Row, 1964.

Wilson, E. O. *The Creation: An Appeal to Save Life on Earth*. New York: W. W. Norton, 2006

Parable Index

Assassin, 166

Corrupt Judge, 173

Dinner Party, 16, 43, 46, 121, 123, 124, 132, 134, 135, 137, 138, 148, 166, 172, 173, 193

Empty Jar, 166, 174

Fishnet, 43
Friend at Midnight, 49, 173

Leased Vineyard, 70, 166, 202
Leaven, 8, 10, 12, 13, 15, 20, 23, **95–108**, 116, 148, 166, 173, 193, 202
Lost Coin, 45, 49, 136, 147, 166, 172, 173, 174, 193
Lost Sheep, 45, 46, 49, 136, 147, 166, 174, 204

Money in Trust, 16, 121, 122, 123, 124, 132, 133, 134, 135, 138, 166
Mustard Seed, 10, 13, 20, 46, 95, 96, 101, 104, 108, **114–120**, 148, 158, 166, 173, 174, 193, 202

Pearl, 39, 43, 166
Pharisee and Toll Collector, 48, 166, 172, 193, 195, 202
Prodigal Son, 14, 16, 17, 18, 20, 22, 45, 49, 63, 102, 121, 122, 123, 124, 132, 134, **136–138**, 146, 147, 148, 152, 154, 155, 166, 172, 173, 174, 193

Rich Man and Lazarus, 195, 204
Rich Farmer, 195, 204

Sabotage of Weeds, 45, 48
Samaritan, 3, 7, 8, 9, 10, 11, 14, 15, 16, 17, 18, 20, 22, 23, 48, **67–84**, **85–90**, 121, 123, 129, 132, 134, 135, 136, 137, 138, 139, 143, 144, 145, 146, 148, 151, 152, 154, 155, 166, 172, 173, 194, 195, 204
Seed and Harvest, 202
Shrewd Manager, 45, 137, 148, 166, 173, 196
Sower, 3, 7, 8, 48, 49, 166, 173, 193, 200

Ten Maidens, 16, 121, 123, 132, 133, 134, 135, 138, 202
Treasure, 101, 166

Unforgiving Slave, 102, 124, 148, 173

Vineyard Laborers, 16, 39, 45, 50, 102, 121, 123, 124, 125, 126, 127, 12, 132, 134, 135, 137, 138, 146, 148, 152, 166, 173, 174, 193, 198

Scripture Index

Genesis
18   102

Exodus
12:17–20   102
23:18   102
34:25   102

Leviticus
2:11   102
6:17   102

Judges
6:19   102

1 Samuel
1:24   102
17:20   73

Psalms
6:8   202
107:3   202
118:22   202

Isaiah
5:1   202

Ezekiel
17   101, 116, 117
17:22–24   113
31   101, 116, 117
34   73

Daniel
4   101, 114, 116

Hosea
12:12   73

Matthew
5:39   152
6:3   153, 169
7:7–11   167
7:13   202
7:16   169
7:22   202

10:25–28   203
10:34–36   150
10:37b   202
11:25   100
12:46–50   148
13:31–33   114
13:32   115
13:33   95
13:36–43   48
13:44   101
13:45–46   39
17:20   118
18:27   124
18:32–34   124
20:1–16   39
20:1–2   124
20:1   123
20:3–5   125
20:7–8   123
20:16   169
21:31   103
22:34–40   81
23:12   117
25:6   123
25:11   123
25:16   122
25:19   123
25:26   124
25:31   202
25:46   202

Mark
2:1–28   149
2:17   168
2:19   168
2:27–28   168
3:1–6   149
3:11   149
3:20–21   150
3:35   151
3:21–35   149
3:23–26   169
3:31–35   18, 148, 149
3:33–34   169
4:11   101
4:12   104

4:21   168
4:30–32   114
4:32   115
7:15   153
7:8–23   153
9:50   168
10:17   74
12:17   168
12:28–31   81
12:28–34   84
13   106
13:32   169
15:2   168
15:4–5   167

Luke
8:19–21   148
10:18   167
10:21   100
10:25–37   72, 74
10:29   75, 80
10:30–35   85
10:33   123
10:36   73, 75, 80
10:37   82
11:2   167
11:20   167
12:6–7   20, 167
12:22–24   20, 167
12:27–28   20, 167

12:49–56   150
13:18–21   114
13:18–19   115
13:20   95
13:24–30   202
14:7–11   204
14:11   117
14:12–14   204
14:21   124
15:20   124
15:28   124
17:21   104
18:33   169

John
19:19   168

1 Corinthians
1:18–31   118
6:6–8   103
15:3–5   161

1 John
4:19   80

Thomas
20:1–4   114
20:3–4   115
96:1–2   95

Author Index

Achtemeier, Paul, 195
Anderson, R. W., 201
Armstrong, Karen, 189

Baird, Arthur, 203
Barfield, Owen, 4, 10, 31, 32, 33, 46,
   47, 49, 59, 196, 197, 198, 199, 200,
   201
Beckett, Samuel, 129
Black, Matthew, 127, 207
Blass, F., 14, 207
Borges, Jorge Luis, 21, 58, 59, 201
Bornkamm, Gunther, 72, 81, 101,
   105, 202, 204, 206, 207
Bonhoeffer, Dietrich, 179, 181
Bowen, Clayton, 196
Briggs, C. A., 184
Brooks, Cleanth, 197
Brown, Raymond, 203
Brownlee, W.H., 203
Bruno, Giordano, 177
Bultmann, Rudolf, 3, 18, 29, 37, 50,
   80, 160, 161, 162, 163, 179, 180,
   181, 182, 195, 197, 196, 201, 203,
   204, 205, 206, 207
Burrows, Millar, 163

Cadoux, A. T., 37, 38, 40, 97, 195,
   197, 198
Chatman, Seymour, 22
Coleridge, 47
Conzelmann, Hans, 201
Copernicus, 177, 184
Crossan, John Dominic, 85, 195, 206,
   207
Cupitt, Don, 21, 180, 181, 182, 186,
   208

Dahl, N. A., 196
Daniélou, J., 203, 204
Darwin, Charles, 184, 185, 190
Debrunner, A., 14
Denniston, J. D., 127, 207
Dibelius, Martin, 198
Dodd, C. II., 3, 4, 6, 9, 11, 12, 18, 29,
   30, 31, 34, 37, 38, 40, 41, 42, 43,
   44, 45, 50, 70, 71, 85, 96, 97, 100,

115, 116, 117, 195, 196, 198, 199,
   200, 201, 202, 205, 206, 207
Dundes, Alan, 129, 207
Dylan, Bob, 119, 207

Ebeling, Gerhard, 82, 201, 206

Falwell, Jerry, 184
Farrar, Austin, 198
Fiebig, P., 202, 203
Findlay, J. A., 201
Forstmann, Jack, 205
Freud, Sigmund, 187
Fuchs, Ernst, 6, 42, 43, 71, 75, 109,
   199, 202, 204. 206

Galileo, 177, 184, 190
Gaston, Lloyd, 207
Geering, Lloyd, 21, 179, 181, 182
Gerhardsson, Birger, 70, 72, 73, 74,
   75, 76, 77, 78, 79, 80, 202, 203,
   204, 205
Gleason, H. A., 14, 15, 206
Gowler, David, 195
Greimas, A. J., 131, 132
Grundmann, W., 205
Gutbrod, W., 203

Han Yu, 58
Harnack, Adolf, 4, 195
Hart, Ray, 33, 106, 163, 197, 205, 207,
   208
Hauck, F., 203
Hedrick, Charles, 22
Heidegger, Martin, 4, 10, 32, 38, 197
Hermann, Wilhelm, 206
Herzog, William, 23
Hick, John, 183
Housman, A. E. 197
Husserl, Edmund, 106, 156, 157

Ionesco, 129

Jefferson, Thomas, 179
Jeremias, Joachim, 3, 6, 9, 12, 18, 30,
   37, 38, 39, 40, 41, 42, 44, 50, 70,
   73, 76, 85, 96, 97, 101, 102, 108,

116, 117, 146, 147, 196, 197, 198, 199, 200, 201, 202, 203, 204, 205, 206, 207, 208
John Paul II, 177
Jülicher, Adolf, 3, 5, 6, 8, 9, 10, 12, 21, 38, 40, 41, 43, 80, 83, 85, 96, 97, 98, 100, 198, 203, 204
Jung, Carl, 187
Jüngel, Eberhard, 83, 2020, 204, 205

Kafka, Franz, 1, 10, 11, 12, 13, 15, 20, 21, 53, 54, 55, 56, 57, 58, 59, 105, 111, 129, 154,
Käsemann, Ernst, 205
Kee, Howard, 162, 207
Kennedy, D. J., 190
Kierkegaard, Soren, 58
Kittel, Gerhard, 203

Lewis, C. S., 31, 196
Lohmeyer, Ernst, 103
Linnemann, E., 204
Luccock, Halford, 172

Manson, T.W., 203, 205, 206
Miles, Jack, 189
Miller, Robert, 195, 207
Mowry, Lucetta, 71, 202

O'Connor, Flannery, 171
Origen, 73

Patte, Daniel, 207
Perrin, Norman, 207
Politzer, Heinz, 201
Propp, Vladimir, 131

Ramsey, Ian, 32, 196
Riesenfeld, Harald, 70, 202
Robertson, Pat, 184
Rohrbaugh, Richard, 16, 195
Robinson, James, 199, 200
Robinson, John A. T., 179, 181
Rosetti, Christina, 47

St. Vincent Millay, Edna, 111
Schmidt, Daryl, 3, 195
Schutz, Alfred, 156, 207
Scott, Bernard, 195
Smith, C. W. F., 101, 103, 108, 207
Snell, Bruno, 200
Spitzer, Leo, 129
Spong, John S., 21, 180, 182
Stanford, W. B., 127
Steiner, George, 93, 110,111, 206, 207
Stendahl, K., 203
Strauss, David Friedrich, 21, 179, 180, 182

Tabor, Charles, 124, 207
Tannehill, Robert, 148, 152, 153, 154, 195, 207
Tillich, Paul, 179, 181, 187, 197
Tinsley, E. J., 203
Toelken, J. Barre, 129, 207
Tolkien, J. R. R., 157
Twain, Mark, 189

Usher, James, 184

Van Impe, Jack, 184
Via, Dan, 9, 10, 85
Vincent, J.J., 198, 203

Westermann, C., 201
Wheelwright, Philip, 32, 196, 197
Whitehead, Alfred North, 162
Wilde, Oscar, 171
Wilder, Amos, 7, 10, 38, 39, 44, 45, 46, 50, 62, 71, 196, 197, 198, 199, 200, 201, 202, 205
Wilson, E.O., 195
Wodehouse, P.G. 200

Zeno, 58

Robert W. Funk (Ph.D. Vanderbilt University) served on the faculties of Texas Christian University, Harvard Divinity School, Emory University, Drew University, Vanderbilt Divinity School, and the University of Montana. In 1986 he retired from teaching to found the Westar Institute, a non-profit research and educational institute dedicated to the advancement of religious literacy. A Guggenheim Fellow and Senior Fulbright Scholar, Funk also served as Annual Professor of the American School of Oriental Research in Jerusalem and as Executive Secretary of the Society of Biblical Literature, the learned society of bible scholars. His many books include *Language, Hermeneutic, and Word of God* (1966), *Jesus as Precursor* (1975), *Parables and Presence* (1982), *The Poetics of Biblical Narrative* (1988), *The Five Gospels: The Search for the Authentic Words of Jesus* (1993, with Roy W. Hoover) and *The Acts of Jesus: The Search for the Authentic Deeds* (1998) (both with the Jesus Seminar), *Honest to Jesus: Jesus for a New Millennium* (1996), and *A Credible Jesus* (2002), as well as two Greek grammars.

Bernard Brandon Scott is Darbeth Distinguished Professor of New Testament at Phillips Theological Seminary in Tulsa, Oklahoma. A Charter Member of the Jesus Seminar, he is the author of *Hear Then the Parable* and *Re-Imagine the World: An Introduction to the Parables of Jesus*. Scott earned his Ph.D. at Vanderbilt University where he was a student of Robert Funk.